# *Real* World Project Management

## BEYOND CONVENTIONAL WISDOM, BEST PRACTICES, AND PROJECT METHODOLOGIES

Richard Perrin, PMP, CSM

**WILEY**

John Wiley & Sons, Inc.

Published by John Wiley & Sons, Inc., Hoboken, New Jersey.
Published simultaneously in Canada.

For general information on our other products and services or for technical support, please contact our
Customer Care Department within the United States at (800) 762-2974, outside the United States at
(317) 572-3993, or fax (317) 572-4002.

Wiley also publishes its books in a variety of electronic formats. Some content that appears in print may
not be available in electronic formats. For more information about Wiley products, visit our Web site at
www.wiley.com.

ISBN 978-0-470-17079-3

Printed in the United States of America.

10  9  8  7  6  5  4  3  2  1

# Contents

# Introduction

The concept for this book originally grew out of feedback received over several years while I served as a director of development, a senior program/project manager, and corporate trainer teaching Project Management and PMP (Project Management Professional) preparation. Many aspiring and experienced project managers have noticed that there can be a substantial disconnect between how *A Guide to the Project Management Body of Knowledge (PMBOK),* published by the Project Management Institute, describes the framework of project management (PM) and how projects actually unfold in the real world. Given that project management is not for the faint of heart, one imagines that over the years some science of project management has evolved to help keep projects on track, on time, and on budget, and with a minimum of confusion. True, the theory is neat and tidy, but real life is very messy.

In addition to the mess most PMs must address, the story being spin-doctored by the senior executive suite of most businesses paints a picture of project discipline and process that bears little resemblance to the daily realities PMs face in managing projects. The PM is left with the somewhat schizophrenic task of attempting to reconcile what the business tells the world it is doing versus what it is actually doing. Most of the examples and cases are delivered from the point of view of the PM practitioner looking up from the trenches at what executive management claims is happening but dealing with what is actually happening. Thus, the entire first section of the book is addressed from the point of the practitioner looking up at the belly of the beast and dealing with it as best he or she can.

Finally, previous versions of the *Guide* (1996 and 2000 editions) contain a bewildering array of tools and techniques mentioned in passing, only a few of which are described even at the 50,000-foot level. Many PMs have experienced frustration in having to locate a wide variety of sources from which to obtain some information about each tool and technique, which has proved very time consuming and frustrating for most.

Therefore, this book is designed to help project managers, or anyone else faced with having to make a decision about anything, understand and utilize some of the most useful tools and techniques cited in the *PMBOK*, and to provide some depth and background in the use of these tools with some practical hints and tips in their execution. In addition, some specific recommendations are given that can be utilized to implement the decision tools without spending a fortune on software or requiring a PhD to understand. Most of the tools can be easily implemented utilizing Microsoft Excel or any other commercial spreadsheet package that contains a good library of statistical functions. In addition, there is a recommended reading list at the end of various chapters for those who are interested in pursuing any of the areas in greater depth.

Although we are merely scratching the surface of some areas that have significant depth and require significant study to know inside-out, this guide will at least get you to the point of understanding what they are and enable you to hold an intelligent conversation with anyone about the tools and techniques contained herein. As the saying goes, "Project managers are a mile wide and an inch deep," meaning that they know something about everything but without requiring in-depth detail knowledge. The goal of this guide is to continue to be a mile wide but increase knowledge to about a *foot* deep.

Remember, the title of the *PMBOK* starts out with the words, "A Guide. . . . " It is not the "Definitive Be-All-End-All Reference for Every Project Management Concept and Practice in the Entire Known Universe." Don't worry about trying to learn *everything*—take the hitchhiker's approach: Learn key tools and skills you can master and they will take care of you 99% of the time. (That's better odds than you will get in the stock market.)

So, whether you are a novice PM, an experienced PM, or someone just looking for some help trying to decide what thinking or decision process to use to select the best new car, keep track of costs, schedule a home-improvement project, pick the best investment, analyze a business plan, or accomplish any other endeavor that involves complex decision making—try *Real World Project Management* on for size.

And when all else fails, developing a keen sense of humor will get you through the issues with fewer headaches, ulcers, and nightmares.

Richard J. Perrin, PMP SSBB QFDGB CSM

*November 2007*

# Section
# 1

# In the Project Trenches

# Chapter
# 1

# So . . . Where Are We with Project Management and What's with All These *Tools* Anyway?

"There is a theory which states that if ever anybody discovers exactly what the Universe is for and why it is here, it will instantly disappear and be replaced by something even more bizarre and inexplicable. There is another theory which states that this has already happened."
—Douglas Adams

So MUCH HAS BEEN written about project management (PM) in the last 15 to 20 years that it's difficult to find the few books that actually contain the information you need to be effective in project management. A lot of strange things have also been written about project management and project managers (PMs)—some of them insightful, some of them outright loony, and some completely inaccurate. However, all of these sources generally say that effective project management is a necessary thing to do if you want your projects to succeed.

So the first thing we will do is dispel some myths and inaccuracies about project management:

**Myth #1:** Project management fundamentally deals with soft skills.

This leaves the reader with the impression that mastering project management simply means quoting pop-psychology gurus and sitting around a campfire eating granola. "I'm okay—you're okay"—*group hug* everyone!

Nope. Sorry folks, that's not it. Even the so-called *soft skills* of negotiation and team building require study, understanding, and practice.

**Myth # 2:** Project managers spend most of their time in bean-counting microdetails that would only make a Vogon[1] happy.

This is not exactly true. Project managers need to be detail oriented, but in reality, they spend most of their time communicating with the project team members and the project stakeholders to make sure everyone is on the same page. Many of the communication skills require the ability to take complex material and simplify it for senior management so that they get the big picture. Most C-levels don't have time for excruciating detail.

**Myth # 3:** Project management is really just fluff—a lot of process for the sake of process.

If you analyze what a business does, something should become obvious: The business is either *in production,* that is, in an operational mode in which the product of the company is being marketed, manufactured, and delivered to customers, or *undertaking projects* to create, improve, or enhance a product, service, or process. Since at least half of what a business does can be considered a project, that's a lot of business activity to be assigned to the "fluff" category. If you're still not convinced, see the rebuttal in the section below.

Before we dive into this dissertation we need to address an important year for project management—1969. Here are some significant facts:

- The Project Management Institute (PMI) was founded.
- The United States landed a human being on the surface of the moon and returned him safely to Earth without being too much the worse for wear.
- IBM was running its mainframe on punchcards.

In 1969, I worked for a small engineering company and was devoting my days and nights to the Apollo Program, designing and building launch critical hardware for the first stage of the Saturn booster. What you are about to read comes from first-hand experience.

In 1969, there was no IT industry to speak of—certainly the PC did not exist and mainframe computers were the stuff of science fiction. However, this was all about to change because of the U.S. manned moon landing. One of the problems NASA was facing was that they needed a mainframe-type computer on board the Apollo Command Module: Mainframes usually took up medium-sized rooms stuffed with vacuum tubes and machinery, and the Command Module only had room for a mainframe the size of a breadbox.

Enter Texas Instruments (TI). TI developed the CMOS chips that enabled the miniaturization of the cumbersome, multi-ton mainframes down to the size of a breadbox. What no one knew at the time, except for a few forward-thinking visionaries, is that this miniaturization would bring about the birth of products never before seen in the marketplace. The first of the products began to appear about eight years after the manned moon landing in the form of something called a personal computer (PC). In 1977, we had the Apple II, the Commodore PET, and Radio Shack's TRS-80 (affectionately dubbed the *Trash 80*). Even TI entered the fray with the first 16-bit microprocessor in the TI-99/4 in 1979, and later with the much-improved TI-99/4A in 1981; and with that the PC and the modern IT industry was born.

Twenty-seven years later, the ubiquity of the PC, workstation, and server models all connected via LAN/WAN technologies makes the IT component a requirement for any business. Nothing runs without computers, from the mainframe to your cell phone/PDA—IT is *everywhere*.

PMI woke up to this fact in the early to mid-1990s and realized that the *PMBOK* model increasingly needed to address the management of software and IT projects. Thus, various software deployment models were added to the *PMBOK* to accommodate software/IT project concerns. Most of the discussions that follow will focus on this aspect of project management.

# WHERE ARE WE WITH PROJECT MANAGEMENT?

Maybe a better question would be, "Where *aren't* we with project management?"

The Standish Group, the 800-pound gorilla in researching IT project failure in the U.S. Fortune 1000, has produced some eye-opening studies that bear mentioning here. The Standish Group produces something called the *CHAOS Report,* which assesses the failure and success rates of IT projects in the United States. In 1994, the *CHAOS Report* showed the following startling results:

- Total project expenditures: $250 billion
- Total project success rate: 17%
- Total project challenged rate: 52%
- Total project failure rate: 31%
- Cost of failed or challenged projects: *$140 billion*
- Average cost overrun (for failed/challenged projects): *180%*

The first time I read those statistics I had to find my jaw and reattach it to my head. Even more jaw-dislocating is the fact that, in terms of GDP, *the money wasted on failed IT projects in the United States in 1994 made the cost of U.S. IT project failure the 23rd largest economy in the world.* (GDP of all countries was taken from the 1994 *CIA Factbook.*) This represents the outcome of work done by people who possessed the necessary *hard skills* to do the job—that is, programming, networking, telecommunications, and so on.

Fast forward to 2004: After 10 more years of research, and 40,000 projects later, the January 2004 *CHAOS Report* showed the following startling results:

- Total project expenditures: $255 billion
- Total project success rate: *34%*
- Total project challenged rate: 51%
- Total project failure rate: *15%*

- Cost of failed or challenged projects: *$55 billion*
- Average cost overrun (for failed/challenged projects): *43%*

In other words, the project success rate *doubled*, the project failure rate *was more than cut in half*, $85 billion dollars were saved, and cost overruns were cut by more than 75%.

*Most of this change was attributable to implementing effective project management controls where none or inadequate controls existed before and the development of repeatable, predictable process in the form of quality improvement.*

This $85 billion reduction in waste and the elimination of failed projects is what occurred when the so-called *soft skills* that are described in Myth #1 were implemented. That's a lot of hard currency saved just from eating granola. There is measurable, documented, hard improvement from implementing effective project management processes in an organization. The improvements are substantive and real.

Yet, in spite of the improvements and the trending in the right direction, we are still a long way from numbers that most evaluations would deem a success. Consider the following:

- *A grade of 34% correct on any exam in the U.S. public school system would earn the student a failing grade.* This puts the 2004 *CHAOS Report* project success rate into a slightly different perspective, doesn't it? A grade of 34% on any test I took in high school would have gotten me grounded for a week. However, in this case, the score is more a reflection on the quality and effectiveness of the instruction than on the desire to learn or the natural ability of the student. We continue to fail at effectively educating our people. More interesting than that, the executive suite consistently ignores the data that points to the issues and consistently fails to do anything about it. We will address some of those issues in this book and prescribe some cures that are proven to work.

- *After 10 years, more than half the projects continue to be challenged.* A challenged project means, according to The Standish Group, that the project (1) was past the due date, (2) was over budget, (3) was lacking in critical features, or (4) was missing written requirements. The fact that this number has barely changed in 10 years is disturbing to say the least. It points to an ongoing failure of most U.S. companies to properly scope, define, or get the necessary buy-in for at least half the projects that are attempted.

Although PMI has put forth a usable framework for project implementation, there still remain gaps in the application of the framework that confuse many practitioners. Part of the issue lies in the *PMBOK* itself. Many students and colleagues have expressed dismay with the framework even after passing the PMP (Project Management Professional) examination and achieving the certification of *Project Management Professional*. There continues to be an ongoing disconnect between how the framework states a project should be managed and how projects are actually managed in the real world.

This is not as much of an issue in industries where the project process has existed in essentially the same form for years and is well understood, such as in the construction industry. A practitioner can utilize well-documented estimates for construction processes, such as are found in the publications offered at the R.S. Means web site. Here, the practitioner can obtain the construction cost estimation price guide used by professional construction estimators to obtain accurate pricing, by U.S. region, for almost every conceivable job that occurs at a construction site.

However, for the software industry, no such guide yet exists. While there are guides that discuss *best practices*, there exists no guide that offers price points or time estimates for well-defined software components or products. The practitioner is faced with the option to either go online to CDW or some similar distributor and perform a competitive price comparison for shrink-wrapped software applications, or create requests for proposals (RFPs) to obtain competitive bids for custom software development.

While the construction industry is considered an area consisting of well-established mature processes and technology (after all, the Pyramids are still standing after thousands of years), the software industry is, in contrast, more like a cantankerous, obstinate, argumentative teenager fraught with post-pubescent angst and the occasional suicidal depression who will fly into a rage whenever a "parent" (the business) requests that he clean his room or suggests that his behavior appears erratic or unfocused, or that his bad habits continue to be (defiantly) repeated despite numerous requests to conduct himself to the contrary. After all, the electronic data storage medium that finally replaced punchcards for the mainframe—the IBM 3380 disk pack—came into existence only in 1980, merely 27 short years ago. It took until 1990 for IBM to roll out the first PS/1 PC equipped with a 286 CPU. Sixteen years later, this machine is considered an *antique*. However, in spite of the geometric improvements in the quality and capability of hardware and software *tools* in the last 16 years, the parallel development of comparable business processes has been painfully slow. As a result, a project manager can effectively manage a construction project utilizing the PMI framework with little difficulty; but managing a software or IT project, especially a complex one, is a very different story.

Yet, in spite of this disconnect, many businesses look at project managers with the PMP certification as a magic bullet that will somehow make their troubled projects suddenly work. At many companies seeking skilled project managers to manage the ever-increasing number of IT projects—with fewer resources—a PMP certification is a prerequisite to being hired, even if you have an MBA or a PhD!

Part of the issue lies with the *PMBOK* framework itself. There is little guidance from PMI regarding the priority of the defined process areas, leaving readers at loose ends:

- Which of the inputs, outputs, and tools and techniques in each of the process areas are of the most value to the practitioner? These elements are not prioritized in any way.

- Some descriptions in the *PMBOK* are not clear and leave the reader confused.

- Some of the more important and relevant tools are only mentioned in passing or glossed over in the *PMBOK*.

Here is a list of tools that are referenced in some detail, simply mentioned in passing, or implied in passing by the 2000 or 2004 editions of the *PMBOK* in each process area. They are organized by the chapters in the *PMBOK* in which they are referenced in each "Tools and Techniques" section:

- *Project Integration Management:* Monte Carlo analysis, project management information system, earned value management, change control system

- *Project Scope Management:* Decision trees, forced choice, Analytic Hierarchy Process, logical framework analysis, cost/benefit analysis, work breakdown structure (WBS), functional decomposition

- *Time Management:* Precedence diagramming method, analogous estimating, critical path method, PERT, GERT, Monte Carlo analysis, variance analysis

- *Cost Management:* Parametric modeling, analogous estimating, bottom-up estimating, earned value management, discounted cash flow (implied processes: present value (PV), net present value (NPV), and internal rate of return (IRR) calculations)

- *Quality Management:* Cost/benefit analysis, design of experiments (DOE) (implied process: Taguchi designs), flowcharting, control charts, Pareto charts, cause-and-effect diagrams, statistical sampling, trend analysis, audits, histograms

- *Human Resource Management:* Team-building activities (implied process: conflict resolution), reward/recognition systems, collocation, training, organizational theory (implied processes: Theory X/Y, Maslow's Hierarchy of Needs, Herzberg's Hygiene Theory, expectancy theory, achievement theory, contingency theory)

- *Communications Management:* Variance analysis, trend analysis, earned value analysis, sender/receiver models (implied process: lines of communication calculation)

- *Risk Management:* Brainstorming, Delphi technique, checklists, cause-and-effect diagrams, influence diagrams, SWOT analysis, Monte Carlo analysis, risk analysis matrix, sensitivity analysis, decision tree analysis, earned value analysis

- *Procurement Management:* Make-or-buy analysis, contract type selection, weighting system, screening system

The *PMBOK* does a reasonable job of describing the *precedence diagramming method* and the computation of *earned value*—we will not rehash them in detail here. The focus we will take in this book is first on some of the critical tools that the current millennium PM must master, because the tools usually provide a measurable, quantifiable output that enables the project manager, management, and stakeholders to deal with issues based on data and fact.

Because the *PMBOK* is an overview, most of these critical tools are mentioned only in passing, leaving the user with the daunting task of performing extensive web searches to find whitepapers, books, and tutorials on the subjects mentioned. It is these tools and their implementation that will be the focus of this book, specifically *Monte Carlo analysis, decision tree analysis, design of experiments, Ishikawa tools, analytical hierarchy process,* and *lean process tools.*

All these tools provide critical data and fact in the following *PMBOK* areas: *human resource conflict management, schedule and timeline management, communication planning, stakeholder analysis, risk management, risk identification prioritization,* and *procurement management selection criteria.* The quality tools such as the Pareto chart, cause-and-effect diagrams, and SPC charts are similarly glossed over in the *PMBOK.* We will devote considerable time to these processes so that they are demystified and made useful to the novice or experienced PM.

The remaining tools will be detailed to the extent that the PM will be able to add them to his/her PM toolbox and be knowledgeable in their use as well as when to use them for the best result.

You might be a novice PM, an experienced PM, doing PM tasks without having the formal title of PM, or making a decision about:

- Which job offer you should take
- What neighborhood to move into

- Where to send the kids to school
- What family car to buy
- Evaluating the best IRA investments
- Finding the most enjoyable vacation you and your family can go on
- Which project provides the strongest financial benefit to the company
- What tools are best for collecting project metrics
- Designing and building your dream house
- The best contractor to rebuild your kitchen
- Deciding the critical features of your company's new ERP system
- Deciding on the best construction company for your new corporate headquarters
- How to solve the city's bussing issues
- How to mange new product/project development given that the PMI framework doesn't seem to fit your company's needs
- What would be the best process to make crops grow—in the desert
- How to determine the real probability that your project will complete within the given timeline and budget, and how to manage the risk

The effectiveness of your decision tools, decision processes, and your ability to execute will make the difference between success and potential disaster.

Finally, from the perspective of organizational project management, it is always better to plan how the organization will implement the project lifecycle in an organization; how the Project Management Office will be organized, with its strategic and tactical purpose; how PMs will be trained; what standards, tools, and techniques will be implemented, and so on. It is best to do this kind of planning with a clear head and an eye for what the organization hopes to accomplish 5 or 10 years down the road.

Yet, most organizations do their organizational project planning in crisis, aka "Monsoon" mode (i.e., trying to fix the hole in your roof that is gushing water while in the middle of a monsoon). At best, the process is haphazard and produces minimally useful PM disciplines and processes. At worst, the processes gradually fall into disuse, leaving the organization as bad as or worse off than it had been because management never fully supported the effort from the start. Do yourself a favor and do your planning in an unstressed state—you'll make better decisions.

## NOTE

1. *The Hitchhikers Guide to the Galaxy*, by Douglas Adams, Del Ray 1995. If you don't know what a Vogon is, read the book or see the movie.

# Chapter 2

# The Quality Lesson— Can We Get It Right This Time?

"Politicians use statistics like a drunken man uses a lamp-post: for support rather than illumination."

—Attributed to Andrew Lang

T HE ABOVE QUOTE APPLIES equally to the CEO, CIO, CFO, or CTO of your organization. If it did not, Sarbanes-Oxley would not be necessary and the incredible financial malfeasance at Enron, WorldCom, and Global Crossing would have never occurred at the disastrous levels that brought these companies and their CEOs down.

Nonetheless, it did happen and there were huge losses—not only to the companies in question, but to their employees and society at large. We are all worse off because of the almost incomprehensible fraud perpetrated by the leaders of these organizations. The loss to society is a key concept that keeps coming back in the writings of all the quality gurus of the last 50 years. From Deming, Juran, and Crosby, to Ishikawa, Akao, and Taguchi, the message is the same: When quality suffers, everyone suffers.

Probably one of the most problematic chapters in the *PMBOK* is the chapter on *quality*. The most recent version of the *PMBOK* (2004) has made some minor improvements, but fundamental issues remain. A case in point follows that describes the "Cost of Quality (COQ)"— paragraph 8.1.2.4:

> *Quality costs are the total costs incurred by the investment in preventing non-conformance to requirements, appraising the product or service for conformance to requirements and failing to meet requirements (rework). . . . Failure costs are also called cost of poor quality.*

This paragraph implies that the costs for preventing nonconformance constitute the greatest costs for quality, followed in descending order by appraisal costs and failure costs. It also implies that there is an additional cost to implement quality above and beyond the normal cost of doing business that has to be accounted for separately in the project budget.

This statement is curious given that in 1999, the *PMBOK* framework was certified as ISO 9000 compliant. ISO elaborates, if nothing else, a set of specifications that define minimum quality standards across a wide variety of industries. In essence, the entire *PMBOK* is a *quality process*.

In reality, PMI's definition of "quality costs" misses the point: *When is it not cheaper to do the work right the first time?* That's what implementing quality does for your project.

Phil Crosby, the VP for Quality at ITT under the legendary CEO Hal Geneen, in his 1979 book, *Quality Is Free*, said it best:

> *The cost of quality is the expense of doing things wrong. It is the scrap, rework, service after service, warranty, inspection, tests, and similar activities made necessary by non-conformance problems.*[1]

Reading through the chapter on quality, it appears PMI's message is that quality is not something that is inherent in the project, but something that is tacked onto project processes that has to be managed and controlled, just like the budget, the timeline, and scope.

This promotes the idea that quality is something you obtain from a vending machine or can install like a laser-jet printer or a desktop PC. To me, the concept of "Quality Control" is an oxymoron: Why would anyone attempt to "control" quality?

Instead of looking at a project as a series of vending-machine handles that the user pulls to obtain a "cost bucket," a "timeline bucket," a "scope/requirements bucket," a "risk bucket," a "human resources bucket," a "procurement bucket," a "communications bucket," and, yes, even a "quality bucket," let's turn the paradigm on its head and approach the project from the only perspective that makes sense from the *customer's* point of view: Deliver a product or process that guarantees predictable quality, predictable costs, and a predictable timeline and that meets or exceeds my expectations.

In other words, *if we wrap the entire project in an envelope of quality and ensure that we are delivering customer value at every step in the process, every process in the project framework becomes a quality process*: from the elaboration of scope, to the development of the project timeline, costs, risk assessment, human resource allocation, vendor management, and so on.

In order to see how we implement the project from a quality perspective, some history from the quality leaders of the past 70 years is in order. The first step we shall take is to answer a fundamental and obvious question: What exactly do we mean by *quality*?

The International Organization for Standardization (ISO) defines quality as:

> *The totality of characteristics of an entity that bear on its ability to satisfy stated or implied needs. (ISO 8402, 1994).*

That's a fairly succinct and straightforward definition, albeit terse and vaguely clinical. It encompasses the basics but leaves most of us with a nebulous, unsatisfied feeling. Most people ask me, "What do they mean by 'stated or implied needs?'" You have to extrapolate that statement a bit to divine what is meant here. *Stated needs* are what the user or stakeholder tells you. *Implied needs* are what the stakeholder or user doesn't tell you. If you didn't take that college course—Requirements Clairvoyance 101—you might have real trouble deducing the implied needs. (We will address the implied needs concept in a later chapter).

There may be any number of reasons for the presence of implied needs: from an assumption that you completely understand the user's business, and therefore no explanation is necessary, to deliberate obfuscation on the part of the user. (The latter happens more than anyone cares to admit.) In any case, determining implied needs takes experience, skill, finesse, tenacity, and the ability to build *trust* with the stakeholders so that they will share what is really on their minds.

A better, more understandable definition for quality was put forth by Peter Drucker:

> *Quality in a product or service is not what the supplier puts in. It is what the customer gets out and is willing to pay for. A product is not quality because it is hard to make and costs a lot of money, as manufacturers typically believe. This is incompetence. Customers pay only for what is of use to them and gives them value. Nothing else constitutes quality.*[2]

The reason Drucker's definition is much more satisfying is that he implies that the idea of quality is fundamentally relational in nature. Other than wanting to implement predictable, repeatable processes that save the business time and money, why bother to implement quality processes at all? Why do we go through all the effort? The payoff is that when the product exceeds expectation or delights your customer (because it works so well), you have done something that helps insure the survivability of your business: You have built an ongoing relationship with your customer. So essentially, quality has a relational characteristic. Why do we go through this quality effort? *We do it to build and sustain relationships with our customers.* On projects, this becomes critical because frequently, the same general group of people will be working on subsequent projects together within the same company. Building a positive ongoing relationship with your internal customers is a key element in ongoing project success.

There has been *so* much written and discussed about quality processes that it all seems to be a jumbled mess of quality overkill. (For

**Figure 2.1**

| Processes (short list) | Organizations (short list) | Pioneers (short list) |
|---|---|---|
| TQM | ANSI | Walter Shewhart |
| TQC | APQC | W. Edwards Deming |
| CMMI | ASQ | Joseph Juran |
| Six Sigma | ISO | Kaoru Ishikawa |
| QFD | ISACA | Genichi Taguchi |
| DOE | ITGI | Yoji Akao/Shigeru Mizuno |
| Seven Quality Tools | ITIL | Shigeo Shingo/Taiichi Ono |
| *Poka-Yoke* (Quality Control = Zero) | PMI | Philip B. Crosby |
| JIT (Just in Time) (*Kanban*) | SEI | Armand Feigenbaum |
| *Kaizen* (continuous improvement) | | Noriaki Kano |
| Hoshin Kanri | | |
| Loss Function | | |
| RUP | | |

more on this subject, see Chapter 7, "Negotiating the Quality Quagmire.") See Figure 2.1 for a partial listing of a few of the processes, organizations, and pioneers associated with quality.

## THE QUALITY TIMELINE

Over the last 15 years or so, much has been made of attempts at implementing quality in corporate America. TQM (total quality management), TQC (total quality control), and other quality methodologies have been utilized, written about, and reported on in trade magazines—and in many instances, the documented failures abounded as businesses attempted to make quality processes work.

Much has been written about how these quality processes did not help the company; rather, they created more processes than the actual work, culminating in a tsunami of red tape and bureaucracy equaled only by the most wasteful of government projects. Most of these writings ultimately conceded the "fact" that the same quality processes that worked in Japan could not possibly work here because of the cultural differences.

This is nonsense. When a quality process doesn't work, one or a combination of the following has transpired to sabotage it:

- *The organization did not seek out the external expertise to help them with their internal quality problems.* Attempting to solve the company's internal quality problems internally is like a mental patient trying to be his/her own therapist. The help has to come from outside. Most companies in trouble don't know how to solve their internal problems because they are too close to them. It requires external expertise to help the ailing company solve its quality issues.

- *Senior management—that is, the CEO or president—did not buy into the quality improvement.* Quality starts at the top—if the person running the show doesn't get it, the quality processes will never become company policy. If senior management at the company is not trained in quality processes so as to enable him or her to lead the charge throughout the rest of the organization, the quality transformation will never take place.

- *Quality was simply "installed" rather than made a part of the culture.* Once again we are dealing with the vending-machine approach to implementing quality processes. This is another recipe for failure and does not recognize what needs to take place: a transformation in the way the company does its business. Without getting everyone in the organization involved in implementing quality processes, it will be business as usual.

- *There was failure to execute.* A good idea that didn't work doesn't mean the idea was bad; it means you implemented it incorrectly. This can happen because:

- ☐ Employees are protecting their turf from a perceived threat—"these newfangled 'quality' ideas will 'reinvent' me out of a job!"
- ☐ Employees have misinterpreted or misunderstood how to use the quality tools.
- ☐ Employees feel quality is just another management "flavor of the week," and next week they'll be pushing a different flavor.
- ☐ Employees are resistant to change.
- ☐ Corporate leadership doesn't understand the quality processes and undermines them whenever it is not convenient to follow them.
- ☐ Senior management read every book on quality they could get their hands on but failed to enlist the help of qualified resources to help them implement any of the processes correctly.

- ■ *The improvement model was incorrectly applied to the improvement process.* Bob Galvin, the former CEO of Motorola, stated, "The lack of initial Six Sigma emphasis in the non-manufacturing areas was a mistake that cost Motorola at least $5 billion over a four year period."[3] Remember Iridium? It was probably the most publicized product introduction disaster of the second half of the twentieth century, costing the company billions and nearly putting them out of business. It appeared that the company that invented Six Sigma could not eat its own dog food, but in reality the core issue was that the company failed to extend the approach to their business processes as well. Had they done so and applied the concepts of *lean* (or at least a well-defined QFD—Quality Function Deployment) to the business process, things may have turned out differently.

This does not constitute an exhaustive list of the problems, but it addresses the most prevalent issues encountered in businesses that have failed at implementing quality processes for their organizations.

In fact, for more than 70 years, a number of national and international organizations have developed frameworks and standards to help businesses understand and implement the *what* of quality practices. The *why* should be obvious at this point. Businesses that don't understand that product and process quality are the keystones to maintaining ongoing business relationships with their customers are doomed to extinction. As W. Edwards Deming, the American quality expert, was quoted as saying: "Learning is not mandatory—neither is survival."

Figure 2.2 provides an approximate *quality timeline*—it outlines the major quality developments, processes, and organizations of the last century, and, at a high level, shows how many of the developed quality processes interact.

## THE QUALITY PIONEERS

### Dr. Walter Shewhart

Dr. Shewhart was a Bell Labs scientist who invented Statistical Process Control (SPC)—so in a roundabout way you could say that SPC was a Bell Labs invention. The question many people ask is, why was SPC invented or needed at all?

Dr. Shewhart was working on some quality issues in the telco network that had a large financial impact on the organization. It seems that the Bell engineers of the first two decades of the twentieth century had difficulty figuring out what to fix and what not to fix on the network—or put in another way—figuring out what was broken and what was not broken. The financial aspects of the problem became alarming to Bell executives because there were elements being fixed on the network that were not broken, while elements that were broken were being ignored, causing an even larger failure down the road. In each case, this was costing the company a lot of money.

In essence, Dr. Shewhart developed SPC, primarily a financial stop-loss process, so the telco could get its costs under control. The following describes Dr. Shewhart's experience.

In 1918, Bell Telephone's engineers had been working to improve the reliability of their transmission systems. Because amplifiers and other equipment had to be buried underground, there was a business need to reduce the frequency of failures and repairs. Bell management had already realized the importance of reducing variation in

**Figure 2.2**

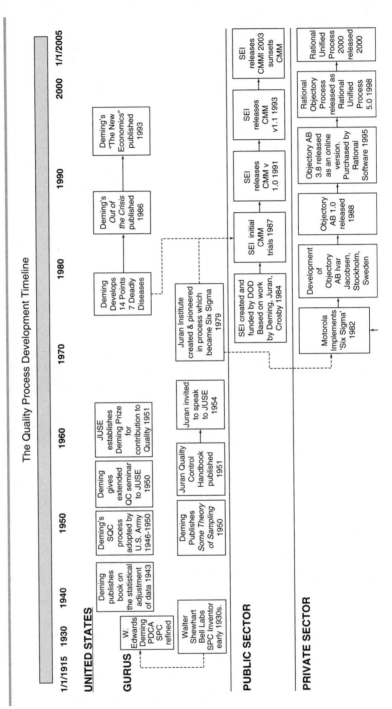

The Quality Process Development Timeline

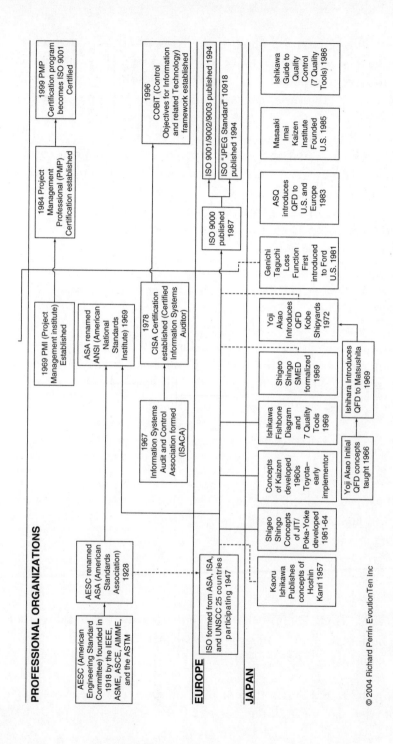

**PROFESSIONAL ORGANIZATIONS**

AESC (American Engineering Standard Committee) founded in 1918 by the IEEE, ASME, ASCE, AIMME, and the ASTM

AESC renamed ASA (American Standards Association) 1928

1969 PMI (Project Management institute) Established

1984 Project Management Professional (PMP) Certification established

1999 PMP Certification program becomes ISO 9001 Certified

ASA renamed ANSI (American National Standards Institute) 1969

1967 Information Systems Audit and Control Association formed (ISACA)

1978 CISA Certification established (Certified Information Systems Auditor)

1996 COBIT (Control Objectives for Information and related Technology) framework established

**EUROPE**

ISO formed from ASA, ISA, and UNSCC 25 countries participating 1947

ISO 9000 published 1987

ISO 9001/9002/9003 published 1994

ISO "JPEG Standard" 10918 published 1994

**JAPAN**

Kaoru Ishikawa Publishes concepts of Hoshin Kanri 1957

Shigeo Shingo Concepts of JIT/ Poka-Yoke developed 1961-64

Concepts of Kaizen developed 1960s Toyota– early implementor

Ishikawa Fishbone Diagram and 7 Quality Tools 1969

Shigeo Shingo SMED formalized 1969

Yoji Akao Introduces QFD Kobe Shipyards 1972

Genichi Taguchi Loss Function First introduced to Ford U.S. 1981

Yoji Akao Initial QFD concepts taught 1966

Ishihara Introduces QFD to Matsushita 1969

ASQ introduces QFD to U.S. and Europe 1983

Masaaki Imai Kaizen Institute Founded U.S. 1985

Ishikawa Guide to Quality Control (7 Quality Tools) 1986

© 2004 Richard Perrin EvoutionTen Inc

a manufacturing process, which is the basis of all *lean* production. Moreover, they had realized that continual process-adjustment in reaction to nonconformance (i.e., tampering with the system without understanding if the variation was a normal occurrence or constituted an error) actually increased variation and degraded quality. In 1924, Walter Shewhart described the problem in terms of "assignable-cause"—an error that the worker can fix—and "common-cause" variation—a problem only management can fix. As a result, he introduced the *control chart* as a tool for distinguishing between the two. Shewhart stressed that bringing a production process into a state of "statistical control," is necessary to predict future output and to manage a process economically.

Dr. Shewhart took the normal distribution and applied some statistical controls to the chart. He noticed that if he took a set of measurements, found the average, computed the standard deviation, and then set limits of three standard deviations above or below the average, he would get a data chart that included 99.73% of all the possibilities measured. For all intents and purposes, that measurement would tell you that the data points that fell inside the chart were "in control" and the points that fell outside the chart were "special causes" that needed attention (i.e., needed to be fixed). The results of applying Dr. Shewhart's new process to issues on the Bell network represented a huge step forward in the implementation of quality processes and controls.

A business is looking for equipment that will help order fillers in their warehouse handle heavy packages with minimum effort. They need to find out:

- What is the average weight of packages handled on a daily basis?
- How much does this weight fluctuate?
- What kind of equipment is needed that will assist the order pullers to easily handle heavy packages at a cost that is economical for the business?

The chart in Figure 2.3 not only shows the average package weight each day for a 29-day period, it also shows the upper (UCL)

**Figure 2.3**

### SPC—Shipping Weights Chart

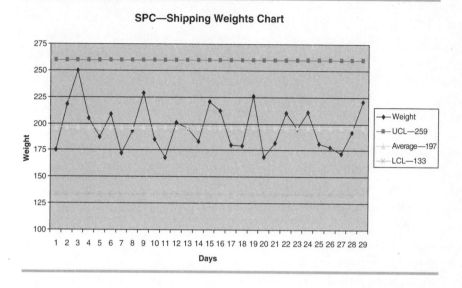

and lower (LCL) control limits—the maximum and minimum levels of weight that will be processed. The chart shows, with a 99.7% probability level, that the packages handled tend to fall within the ranges shown below. Anything falling above that level, in this case, would require different equipment to handle the weight. With a ceiling weight of 260 lb., the company can divide its shipping process in the warehouse into two categories:

1. Packages that weigh 260 lb. or less, which require equipment to provide only lift-assist capability (e.g., a "hydraulic harness" that can be worn by the order puller that enables packages weighing up to 260 lb. to be lifted with only 30 lb. of effort from the order puller). This constitutes 99.7% of all packages.

2. Packages that weigh over 260 lb. each, which require heavy forklift capacity. This constitutes less than 0.3% of all packages.

In his efforts to improve process quality all the way around, Dr. Shewhart also developed the *Plan-Do-Study-Act (PDSA) Cycle*

**Figure 2.4**

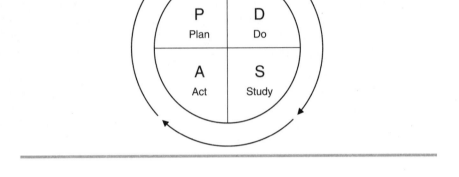

shown in Figure 2.4 and described the concept in his 1939 publication, *Statistical Method from the Viewpoint of Quality Control:*

- **Plan**—Develop a plan for improving a process or quality of a manufactured item.
- **Do**—Execute the plan, preferably on a small scale at first (i.e., a pilot program).
- **Study**—Study the results and use the feedback to either improve, modify, or abandon the current approach and try something different.
- **Act**—Act on the changes, pursue a new direction, or make the plan permanent.

## Dr. W. Edwards Deming

It is not possible to do justice to the lifework of Dr. W. Edwards Deming in the few pages here other than to say he was probably the most influential of the American quality experts to emerge in the last 60 years. Deming studied with Dr. Shewhart and further refined the PDSA cycle, which he reframed as the *PDCA* cycle: *Plan-Do-Check-Act.* Dr. Deming published two groundbreaking works that should be required reading at the executive levels of every Fortune 1000 company: *Out of the Crisis* (MIT Press, 1986), and *The New Economics for Industry, Government and Education* (MIT Press, 1994).

Deming is primarily known for developing his "14 Points," the basis of transformation for American industry (these are listed below). As of the first printing of *Out of the Crisis* in 1986, the United States was facing overwhelming international competition in manufacturing and service industries.

From *Out of the Crisis*, Dr. Deming writes:

*This book teaches the transformation that is required for survival . . . A company cannot buy its way into quality—it must be led into quality by top management. A theory of management now exists. Never again may anyone say that there is nothing new in management to teach.*

*When the management of any company is asked "How do you go about improving quality and productivity?" the usual answer that comes forth is "By everyone doing his best." Everyone doing his best is not the answer. It is necessary for people to know what to do. Drastic changes are required. Long term commitment to new learning and new philosophy is required of any management that seeks transformation. The timid and the fainthearted and people that expect quick results are doomed to disappointment.*

*Management in time will not be judged by the quarterly dividend, but by plans and innovation with the aim to stay in business, to protect investment, to ensure future dividends, and to provide jobs and more jobs through improvement of product and service for the future.*

A key point in the differences in approach to quality in the United States and in Japan can be summarized from the following passage in the first chapter of *Out of the Crisis* (in 1980, Dr. Yoshikasu Tsuda of Rikkyo University in Tokyo wrote a letter to Dr. Deming after completing a tour of industrial facilities of 23 countries in the northern hemisphere):

*"In Europe and America, people are now more interested in cost of quality and in systems of quality audit. But in Japan we are keeping very strong*

*interest to improve quality by use of methods which you started . . . when we improve quality we also improve productivity, just as you told us in 1950 would happen."*

*Dr. Tsuda is saying that Western Industry is satisfied to improve quality to a level where visible figures may shed doubt about the economic benefit of further improvement. As someone inquired, "How low may we go in quality without losing customers?" (that is, how far can the quality drop before the customer notices the difference . . . ). This question packs a mountain of misunderstanding into a few choice words. It is typical of management's misunderstanding in America. In contrast, the Japanese go right ahead and improve the process without regard to figures. They thus improve productivity, decrease costs and capture the market.*

## Deming's Fourteen Points

1. Create constancy of purpose toward improvement of product and service, with the aim to become competitive and to stay in business, and to provide jobs.

2. Adopt the new philosophy. We are in a new economic age. Western management must awaken to the challenge, must learn their responsibilities, and take on leadership for change.

3. Cease dependence on inspection to achieve quality. Eliminate the need for inspection on a mass basis by building quality into the product in the first place.

4. End the practice of awarding business on the basis of price tag. Instead, minimize total cost. Move toward a single supplier for any one item, based on a long-term relationship of loyalty and trust.

5. Improve constantly and forever the system of production and service, to improve quality and productivity, and thus constantly decrease costs.

6. Institute training on the job.

7. Institute leadership. The aim of supervision should be to help people and machines and gadgets to do a better job. Supervision of management is in need of overhaul, as well as supervision of production workers.

8. Drive out fear, so that everyone may work effectively for the company.

9. Break down barriers between departments. People in research, design, sales, and production must work as a team, to foresee problems of production and in use that may be encountered with the product or service.

10. Eliminate slogans, exhortations, and targets for the work-force asking for zero defects and new levels of productivity. Such exhortations only create adversarial relationships, as the bulk of the causes of low quality and low productivity belong to the system and thus lie beyond the power of the workforce.
    □ Eliminate work standards (quotas) on the factory floor. Substitute leadership.
    □ Eliminate management by objectives. Eliminate management by numbers or numerical goals. Substitute leadership.

11. Remove barriers that rob the hourly worker of his or her right to pride of workmanship. The responsibility of supervisors must be changed from sheer numbers to quality.

12. Remove barriers that rob people in management and in engineering of their right to pride of workmanship. This means abolishment of the annual or merit rating and of management by objectives.

13. Institute a vigorous program of education and self-improvement.

14. Put everybody in the company to work to accomplish the transformation. The transformation is everybody's job.

These 14 points are not slogans or management exhortations, as some reviewers of Deming's work have attempted to assert. Rather, they are ideas that require discussion and in-depth understanding. Discuss them with those who have gone through the points and have valuable experience to share with you.

In addition, Dr. Deming also pointed out that there are hurdles to achieving the goals stated in the 14 points, which he called the "Seven Deadly Diseases."

## Deming's Seven Deadly Diseases

1. Lack of constancy of purpose to plan product and service that will have a market and keep the company in business and provide jobs.

2. Emphasis on short-term profits: short-term thinking, fed by fear of unfriendly takeover and by push from bankers and owners for dividends.

3. Personal review system, or evaluation of performance, merit rating, annual review, or annual appraisal, by whatever name, for people in management, the effects of which are devastating. Management by fear would be better than management by objectives without a method for accomplishment.

4. Mobility of management; job hopping.

5. Use of visible figures only for management, with little or no consideration of figures that are unknown or unknowable.

6. Excessive medical costs.

7. Excessive costs of warranty, fueled by lawyers that work on contingency fees.

Another key point in Dr. Deming's teachings was what he called the "System of Profound Knowledge." The system consists of four parts:

1. Appreciation for a system

2. Knowledge about variation

3. Theory of knowledge

4. Psychology

## What Is a System?

A system can be defined as a series of interdependent components that work together to accomplish the aim of the system. If there is no aim (i.e., "what you are trying to accomplish"), then there is no system. The idea for any component of the system is to contribute its best to the system, not to maximize its own production, profit sales, or any other competitive measure. Sometime a component may operate at a loss to optimize the entire system. This is a very different concept from how most organizations are run in the United States—have the components in the organization compete with each other for the biggest bonus and the best perks; suboptimize the system, and so on. Deming elaborated the concept of seeing the system end-to-end as shown in Figure 2.5.

## Knowledge about Variation

Life as we have come to understand it is about variation—it exists in products, in people, in the weather, in services. How do businesses, managers, teachers, or anyone understand how to interpret variation—what it means and what to do about it?

The mistakes that are made concerning the understanding of variation occur when people attempt to fix problems without understanding what is really broken. There are two mistakes that most frequently occur:

1. Reacting to an outcome as if it was the result of a special cause, when actually the system is functioning within its limits (i.e., saying that something happened when it really didn't, otherwise known as an *alpha risk*).

2. Reacting to an outcome thinking the system is functioning within its limits, when actually there is a special cause for the outcome (i.e., not discovering that something happened when it really did, otherwise known as a *beta risk*).

The SPC chart that Shewhart created helps to identify when the system is suffering from a special cause or whether it is functioning within its designed limits—functioning in an unstable state or in a stable state.

## A Theory of Knowledge

Management in any form is prediction—the theory of knowledge helps us to understand that. Any kind of rational prediction is built on theory and requires systematic revision when impacted by reality. This is how knowledge is built—on a combination of prediction, observation, and adjustment of the prediction based on what has been observed. To quote Deming:

> *It is extension of application that discloses inadequacy of a theory, and need for revision, or even new theory. Again, without theory, experience has no meaning. Without theory, one has no questions to ask. Hence without theory there is no learning.*
>
> *Theory is a window into the world. Theory leads to prediction. Without prediction, experience and examples teach nothing. To copy an example of success, without understanding it may lead to disaster.*
>
> *Any rational plan, however simple, is prediction concerning conditions, behavior, performance of people, procedures, equipment or materials.*

## Psychology

From Deming, again, we learn: "Psychology helps us to understand people, interaction between people and circumstances, interaction between customer and supplier, interaction between teacher and pupil, interaction between a manager and his people and any system of management."

A manager of people must be aware of differences in how people learn, the speed at which they learn, and what motivates them, as well as how to use these differences for optimization of everyone's abilities.

## Dr. Joseph Juran

Dr. Juran is credited with bringing the concepts of quality management to Japan. Juran was Quality Manager at Western Electric and developed the *Western Electric Statistical Quality Control Handbook*. He started out as an engineer in 1924.

In 1951, his first book, *Quality Control Handbook,* was published and led him to international eminence. Juran was invited to Japan in the early 1950s by JUSE. And, like Deming, conducted seminars for top and middle-level executives.

His lectures had a strong managerial flavor and focused on planning, organizational issues, management's responsibility for quality, and the need to set goals and targets for improvement. In Japan, courses for foreman were offered on national radio and booklets were available at newspaper kiosks.

Juran stated four key points in identifying customer needs:

1. Be a customer.
2. Study customer behavior.
3. Communicate with customers.
4. Simulate customer use.

The Juran "quality trilogy," as it is known, includes *quality planning, quality control*, and *quality improvement*.

A key point from Juran is that there are no shortcuts to quality:

- Quality circles may not work in the West.
- The majority of quality problems are the result of poor management rather than poor workmanship on the shop floor.
- "Zero defects" as a slogan does not help.
- Training should start at the top.

Juran was a proponent of the *poka-yoke* process, or literally, the *mistake-proofing concept* (see the section on Shigeo Shingo later in this chapter). The basic idea is to stop the process whenever a defect occurs, define the cause, and prevent the recurring source of the defect. He argued that zero defects can be achieved in this way by using source inspection and the poka-yoke system. Together they constitute *zero defect quality control*.

Juran's concept of zero defects is different from the concept usually attributed to ITT's VP of Quality, Philip Crosby. The concept emphasizes the achievement of zero defects by engineering and process investigation, rather than an exhortation/slogan emphasis that has been associated with the quality campaigns of many American and western companies.

Juran defined quality as consisting of two different though related concepts. One form is income oriented—higher quality costs more: The customer is willing to pay more for it. The other form is cost oriented—higher quality costs less: The cost of doing business is reduced.

Throughout any organization there are three different languages spoken:

1. Upper management speaks in *dollars*.
2. Middle management speaks in *things and dollars*.
3. Lower management/workers speak in *things*.

Juran's approach concentrated on pursuing quality on two levels: (1) Firms must achieve high-quality products, and (2) each individual must individually achieve high quality.

In addition he identified four "Fitness of Quality" concepts that are central to the implementation of quality processes:

1. Quality of design: market research, product, and concept
2. Quality of conformance: management, staffpower, and technology
3. Availability, reliability, maintainability, and logical support
4. Full service: promptness, competency, and integrity

In the late 1970s, a Juran consulting engagement at Motorola led to the development of Six Sigma. In 1979, the Juran Institute was founded and to this day continues to provide high-level quality consulting services and training to industry and government.

On May 6, 2004, in Stamford, Connecticut, Dr. Juran delivered a lecture at a luncheon held in his honor for his 100th birthday. His observations are a sobering commentary on the state of quality in American business:

*The man whose ideas led to corporations adopting Six Sigma and other quality management strategies warns that U.S. companies are moving too slowly in improving the quality of business procedures, products and services. The nation's position in the world economy is at risk, according to Dr. Joseph M. Juran.*

*Juran, dean of quality professionals worldwide, told an audience which had come to Stamford, Connecticut (USA) to mark his 100th year and the Juran Institute's 25th anniversary: "The U.S. improvement of quality has been evolutionary, not revolutionary. We have exported jobs and lost entire industries. If these standards continue, there will be a severe risk that the U.S. will lose its status as an economic superpower."*[4]

## Kaoru Ishikawa

Kaoru Ishikawa (1915–1989) was the founder of the Union of Japanese Scientists and Engineers (JUSE) and the President of the Musashi Institute of Technology. Ishikawa had a vision for changing the way people thought about work. Improving product quality was only one part of the picture—he maintained that companywide quality control should not be limited to the factory but called for continuing customer service after the product left the factory.

He developed what are known as the "Seven Tools of Quality," one of which was the *cause-and-effect* or *fishbone diagram* (see Chapter 12, "The Seven Ishikawa Quality Tools"). W. Edwards Deming, a colleague of Ishikawa's, adopted the diagram and used it to teach quality principles in Japan in the early 1950s. Ishikawa, like Deming, also believed that quality implementation would be successful only with support from the highest levels in the organization and continually urged business leaders and top executive to take courses on quality management and control.

Ishikawa further advanced the Shewhart-Deming Plan-Do-Check-Act cycle by elaborating on the Plan and Do sections to create six cycles, as shown in Figure 2.6.

Ishikawa was the first to create the concept of *quality control circles,* which were first initiated at Nippon Telegraph and Cable in 1962, and was one of the first recipients of the Deming Prize in 1950.

**Figure 2.5**

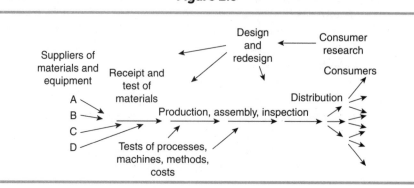

From *Out of the Crisis, Cambridge,* MA: MIT Press, 1986.

**Figure 2.6**

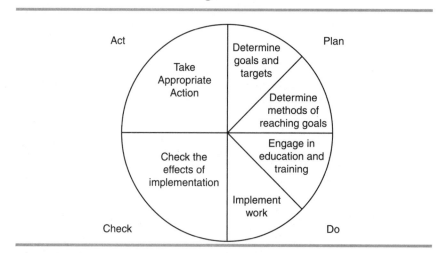

*Source:* Ishikawa. K. (Lu, D.J., trans.), 1985, *What Is Total Quality Control?,* Prentice-Hall, Englewood Cliffs, NJ.

## Genichi Taguchi

A four-time winner of the Deming prize, Taguchi revolutionized the manufacturing process in Japan through cost savings. He understood, like many other engineers, that all manufacturing processes are affected by outside influences (i.e., noise). However,

Taguchi realized methods of identifying those noise sources that have the greatest effects on product variability. His ideas have been adopted by successful manufacturers around the globe because of their results in creating superior production processes at much lower costs.

Here are some of the major contributions that Taguchi has made to the quality improvement world:

- *The loss function*: Taguchi devised an equation to quantify the decline of a customer's perceived value of a product as its quality declines. Essentially, it tells managers how much revenue they are losing because of variability in their production process. It is a powerful tool for projecting the benefits of a quality improvement program. Taguchi was the first person to equate quality with cost.

- *Orthogonal arrays and linear graphs*: When evaluating a production process, analysis will undoubtedly identify outside factors or noise that cause deviations from the mean. Isolating these factors to determine their individual effects can be a very costly and time-consuming process. Taguchi devised a way to use orthogonal arrays to isolate these noise factors from all others in a cost-effective manner.

- *Robustness*: Some noise factors can be identified, isolated, and even eliminated but others cannot. For instance, it is too difficult to predict and prepare for any possible weather condition. Taguchi therefore referred to the ability of a process or product to work as intended regardless of uncontrollable outside influences as robustness. Taguchi methods emphasize *quality through robust design, not quality through inspection.* Taguchi breaks the design process into three stages:
  1. *System design*—involves creating a working prototype.
  2. *Parameter design*—involves experimenting to find which factors influence product performance most.
  3. *Tolerance design*—involves setting tight tolerance limits for the critical factors and looser tolerance limits for less important factors.

## The Loss Function

To put it simply, Taguchi defined *quality* as the loss generated by the product to society. The key to loss reduction is not simply to meet the specifications, but to reduce variance from the target value. Taguchi believed that the customer becomes *increasingly* dissatisfied as performance departs from the target value. By reducing variance to the target a greater level of product consistency can be achieved and a higher level of customer satisfaction can be attained.

Currently, Dr. Taguchi is Executive Director of the American Supplier Institute and is widely acknowledged as a leader in the U.S. industrial quality movement. He is credited for starting the Robust Design movement in Japan more than 30 years ago. The use of "Taguchi methods," a system of cost-driven quality engineering that emphasizes the application of engineering strategies rather than advanced statistical techniques, has been widely and successfully implemented in U.S. manufacturing companies.

### Shigeo Shingo—Taiichi Ohno

Dr. Shigeo Shingo has had an enormous impact on the development of what has been recently identified as *lean manufacturing*. His contributions include:

- *Kaizen* or Just-in-Time—the Toyota Production System
- SMED—Single Minute Exchange of Dies
- *Poka-yoke* or mistake-proofing—zero quality control = zero defects

## Just-In-Time

The just-in-time concept was co-created by Dr. Shingo and Taiichi Ohno of Toyota Motor Company. The objective of implementing JIT in a production facility is to build competitive advantage into the process and increase productivity by eliminating the following seven types of waste:

- Waste from overproduction
- Excess transportation
- Excess inventory
- Waiting time
- Processing waste
- Wasted motion
- Waste from production defects

In applying these concepts, the company not only can realize monetary savings, but can improve the quality of the delivered product. The use of statistical process control helps assure that the outcome of production produces consistent and desired results.

The American Production and Inventory Control Society (APICS) has defined JIT as:

*A philosophy of manufacturing based on planned elimination of all waste and continuous improvement of productivity. It encompasses the successful execution of all manufacturing activities required to produce a final product, from design engineering to delivery and including all stages of conversion from raw material onward. The primary elements include having only the required inventory when needed; to improve quality to zero defects; to reduce lead time by reducing setup times, queue lengths and lot sizes; to incrementally revise the operations themselves; and to accomplish these things at minimum cost.*

## SMED

SMED (Single Minute Exchange of Dies) is a method for drastically reducing setup time on an assembly line. SMED was developed to reduce the high fixed cost associated with the setup and changeover of dies. As a result, the manufacturer is not hampered by expensive setup times and the necessity to run large production numbers to justify the expense of setup. Since the batch sizes can be much smaller without incurring additional cost, the reduced batch size also translates as lower costs associated with inventory storage. It allows the manufacturing system to rapidly adjust to engineering design changes and customer needs, incurring very little cost. In addition, SMED allows for higher machine utilization and in turn results in higher productivity.

SMED has literally enabled Toyota to build cars to order instead of the traditional approach of manufacturing models by the thousands in a single production run because retooling the assembly line is time consuming and expensive.

## Poka-Yoke

A poka-yoke (pronounced *po*-ka *yo*-kay) device is any mechanism that either prevents a mistake from being made or makes the mistake obvious at a glance. The ability to find mistakes at a glance is essential because, as Shingo writes, "The causes of defects lie in worker errors, and defects are the results of neglecting those errors. It follows that mistakes will not turn into defects if worker errors are discovered and eliminated beforehand" (Shingo, 1986, p. 50). He later continues, "Defects arise because errors are made; the two have a cause-and-effect relationship. . . .Yet errors will not turn into defects if feedback and action take place at the error stage" (Shingo, 1986, p. 82).

An example cited by Shingo early in the development of poka-yoke shows how finding mistakes at a glance helps to avoid defects. Suppose a worker must assemble a device that has two pushbuttons. A spring must be put under each button. Sometimes a worker will forget to put the spring under the button and a defect occurs. A simple poka-yoke device to eliminate this problem was developed. The worker counts out two springs from a bin and places them in a small dish. After assembly is complete, if a spring remains in the dish, an error has occurred. The operator knows a spring has been omitted and can correct the omission immediately. The cost of this inspection (looking at the dish) is minimal, yet it effectively functions as a form of inspection. The cost of rework at this point is also minimal, although the preferred outcome is still to find the dish empty at the end of assembly and to avoid rework even when its cost is small. This example also demonstrates that poka-yoke performs well when corrective action involves trying to eliminate oversights and omissions. In such cases, poka-yoke devices are often an effective alternative to demands for greater worker diligence and exhortations to "be more careful."[5]

The core of the poka-yoke process is the ZDQ (zero defects quality) system. The system is based on the discipline that the best way to stop defects from occurring is to prevent them from happening in the first place, that is, control the process to the point where defects are an impossibility.

The process understands that people make mistakes—the idea is not to engage in finger pointing when an error occurs but initiate a process to keep the errors from becoming defects by helping the worker. Instead of exhortations to "do a better job the next time," focus on how to fix the process so that the error becomes impossible.

The four major components of ZDQ are: (1) point-of-origin inspection, (2) 100% audit checks, (3) immediate feedback, and (4) poka-yoke.

The *point-of-origin inspection* is the only type of inspection process that eliminates defects because it focuses on prevention instead of detection. As a result, errors are caught and feedback is given *before* processing takes place.

The *100% audit checks* are unique in quality processing because they depart from the *statistical quality control* approach. With a point-of-origin inspection, every piece is inspected prior to being moved on in the production process. Since there is no sampling of produced parts that occurs, there is no assumption that defects will statistically occur.

*Immediate feedback* occurs when an error is detected—a signal or an alarm is activated so that the error can be immediately addressed. In some cases the production line is stopped so that the error can be corrected before it turns into a defect.

The *poka-yoke* part of the process is what is known as *mistake-proofing*. Poka-yoke devices do not have to depend on an operator catching a mistake but use a sensor or other device to catch errors. With poka-yoke:

- The error is caught immediately (point-of-origin inspection).
- Feedback for corrective action is given instantly.

Properly implemented, the poka-yoke process can catch errors before a defective part is manufactured 100% of the time.

## Philip B. Crosby

Phil Crosby was Corporate Vice-President for Quality under CEO Hal Geneen at ITT from 1965 to 1979. It was in 1980 that his book, *Quality Is Free*, was published, in which he outlined the process that was to become the basis for the stairstep model used to create the Capability Maturity Model (CMM).

Crosby focused on the idea that quality processes were not hard to do—they were hard to sell to management. He devoted the bulk of his effort to convincing management that the consequences of taking no action will lead to problems down the line. What he developed helped to sell the idea of quality to senior management. He called it the *Quality Maturity Grid*, and its components consisted of five stages:

**Stage 1:** *Uncertainty.* In this state, management has no understanding of quality, quality processes, or quality management as a tool to drive profitability for the business.

**Stage 2:** *Awakening.* In this state, management is beginning to realize that quality management can help, but it is not ready to commit dollars and resources to make it happen. It is here that the cost of quality is first calculated. It is usually assumed by management that this will be a large number, but when it really boils down to about 3% of sales, this is usually a pleasant and unexpected surprise for management.

**Stage 3:** *Enlightenment.* At this stage, management has decided to move forward with a funded, formal quality improvement program. At this stage the focus becomes more on fixing the process than blaming individuals for defects. The cost of quality will now get its first in-depth analysis.

**Stage 4:** *Wisdom.* At this stage, the company has the opportunity to make the changes initiated in Stage 3 permanent. Appraisals of the cost of quality are done more accurately than in any of the other phases and it is discovered that the money saved by paying attention to the cost of quality is far greater than anyone imagined it would be. Quality control is now a *real* thing to management.

**Stage 5:** *Certainty.* At this point, the company sees quality management as an indispensable component in overall company management.

## THE REAL COST OF QUALITY

Here is a quote from Philip Crosby:

> *Between 1967 and 1977, the manufacturing cost of quality at ITT has been reduced by an amount equivalent to 5 percent of sales. That is a great deal of money. The savings projected by the comptroller were 30 million in 1968; 157 million in 1971, $328 million in 1973; and in 1976, $530 million! We had eliminated through defect prevention—costs amounting to those dollar figures. [In 2007 dollars, that amounts to about $2 billion in savings.]*
>
> *. . . The facts of life today are that each year your cost of sales rises faster than your prices. That means you have to eliminate or reduce costs in order to make a profit. The best single way to do that is defect prevention. Results like these are why I say quality is free. And not only free but a substantial contributor to profit.*[6]

## NOTES

1. *Quality Is Free*, Philip B. Crosby, Mentor, 1979.
2. *Innovation and Entrepreneurship*, Peter S. Drucker, HarperCollins, 1985.
3. *Lean Six Sigma for Service*, Michael L. George, McGraw-Hill, 2003.
4. "In His 100th Year Juran Still an Advocate for Quality," Richard Lee, iSixSigma Special Correspondent, May 6, 2004.

5. "A Brief Tutorial on Mistake Proofing, Poka-Yoke and ZQC," John Grout and Brian T. Downs, http://csob.berry.edu/faculty/jgrout/tutorial .html.
6. *Quality Is Free*, Philip B. Crosby, Mentor, 1980.

# REFERENCES

Deming, W.E., *Out of the Crisis*, MIT Press, 1986.

Crosby, Philip B., *Quality Is Free*, Mentor, 1980.

Shingo, Shigeo, *Zero Quality Control: Source Inspection and the Poka-yoke System*, Productivity Press, 1986.

Juran, Joseph, *Juran on Quality by Design*, Juran Institute, 1992.

Walton, Mary, *The Deming Management Method*, Perigee, 1986.

# Chapter
# 3

# The 31.5-Minute Project Manager

T HERE ARE MANY INPUTS, outputs, and tools and techniques described in the *PMBOK* that offer an extensive list of elements that
need to be considered when implementing anything—for example,
the section on Risk Monitoring and Control offers the grid of gozintas
(inputs), gozoutas (outputs), and the tools and techniques shown in
Figure 3.1.

Certainly all these elements in some ways are needed, but the
reader must remember that there is a rather remarkable disclaimer
on page 39 of the 2004 *PMBOK* that states:

> However, just as not all the processes will be needed on all projects, not all
> of the interactions will apply to all projects or phases.[1]

No attention is really drawn to this statement, but it carries a lot of
weight. The subtext here is that this framework is still a thinking
process that requires evaluation for your particular situation. Blindly
following every input, output, and tool and technique in the *Guide*
will invariably get you into trouble. An engineer will not take everything learned in four years of engineering school and apply it blindly to every engineering problem or design. It's a toolbox, *not* a

**Figure 3.1**

| Inputs | Tools & Techniques | Outputs |
|---|---|---|
| Risk management plan | Risk reassessment | Risk register updates |
| Risk register | Risk audits | Requested changes |
| Approved change requests | Variance and trend analysis | Recommended corrective actions |
| Work performance information | Technical performance measurement | Recommended preventive actions |
| Performance reports | Reserve analysis | Organizational process assets updates |
| | Status meetings | Project management plan updates |

*Source: A Guide to the Project Management Body of Knowledge,* 3rd ed. Project Management Institute, 2004.

methodology. Learn how to use the tools and when to apply them correctly and you will keep your project and your sanity intact.

We will take a look at the PMI process areas and take the Pareto approach: About 20% of the processes will give you approximately 80% bang-for-the-buck. The questions is—*which 20% will do that for you?*

We will review the PMI processes for the major process groups and identify the key elements in each that will help you deliver results in each process area. It would also help to follow along with a soft or hard copy of the 2004 *PMBOK* to see the entire landscape and compare it to the areas that are being highlighted within this chapter.

The nine process areas in the *PMBOK* consist of the following:

1. Project integration management
2. Project scope management
3. Project time management
4. Project cost management

5. Project quality management

6. Project human resource management

7. Project communications management

8. Project risk management

9. Project procurement management

The chart in Figure 3.2 shows the subprocess areas—44 in all—inside of the primary process distinctions.

Instead of tackling the process areas in strict order, we will begin with the Scope, Time, and Cost Management areas. We will then scramble the order slightly for reasons that will become clear as we progress.

**Figure 3.2**

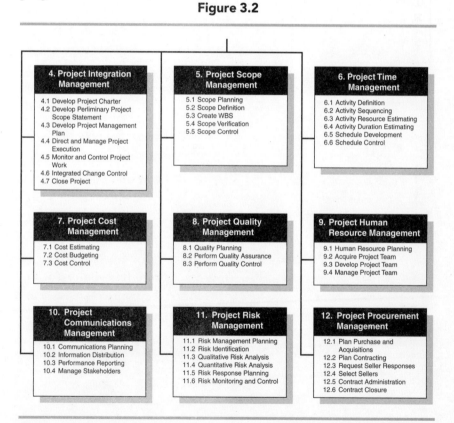

*Source: A Guide to the Project Management Body of Knowledge*, 3rd ed. Project Management Institute, 2004.

## Figure 3.3

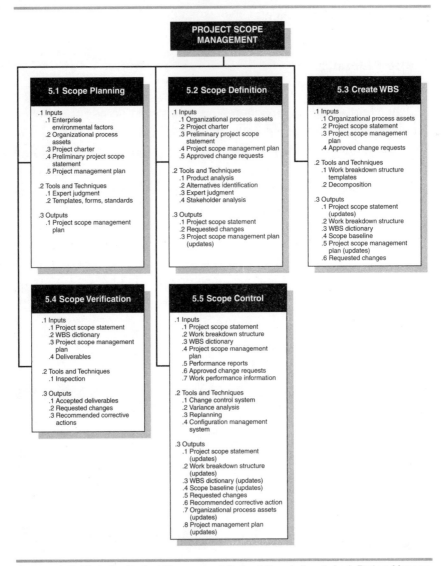

*Source: A Guide to the Project Management Body of Knowledge*, 3rd ed. Project Management Institute, 2004.

# SCOPE MANAGEMENT

Figure 3.3 is a diagram of the scope process areas.

## Scope Planning

The really important elements in the Scope Planning section are the Project Charter and the Scope Statement (inputs). You want to make sure your project is funded and supported (Charter) and you want to have some idea of what you are doing (Scope Statement). A formal Scope Management Plan (output) may or may not be needed depending on the size and complexity of the project. You may need only a brief one- or two-page document stating how scope changes in the project will be managed (i.e., how you will manage and control scope creep) and how you will verify the product of the project (i.e., how you will know you are done). Notice that the tools and techniques (T&T) section is general and vague compared to other T&T sections in the *PMBOK*. That is because the tool/technique most utilized in the Scope Planning section is your brain.

## Scope Definition

This is where the rubber meets the road. The product scope is defined in detail in this section. Your key input is the Preliminary Scope Statement and your key output is the Project Scope Statement (detailed)—this is essentially what happens in the Scope Definition section. When PMI talks about the detailed scope statement they mean it to include:

- Project objectives
- Requirements
- Deliverables
- Acceptance criteria
- Constraints
- Assumptions

- Risks
- Milestones
- Funding limitations
- Cost estimate
- Configuration management requirements
- Specifications
- Approval requirements

In other words, the Scope Definition is the proverbial kitchen sink and contains detailed information on all aspects of the project that involve any of the planning elements.

In the T&T section, there are two key elements: Alternatives Identification and Stakeholder Analysis. You need some alternative solutions in case the one you had hoped to implement cannot be executed for any number of reasons. It is also important to keep the project team from getting stuck on one approach to the project solution only to discover at a later time that the solution is not feasible or could have been implemented faster/cheaper/better. It is an area that is sometimes missed on a project and something that should *always* be considered.

Stakeholder Analysis is a polite way of introducing the idea that key stakeholders can sink your project if you do not accurately assess stakeholder wants, needs (stated or implied), expectations, issues, fears, or any other consideration, positive or negative, that may impact your stakeholders. The key to keeping your stakeholders in the loop is communicate, communicate, communicate. While this element is addressed specifically in the Communications section, it is mentioned here (as it will be mentioned again in other sections) because it is critical to insuring project success.

Product Analysis is not exactly what I'd call a tool or technique— it is something that is done by qualified professionals such as systems analysts or design engineers. They need to do their jobs to help define and refine the scope.

## Create WBS

Create the Work Breakdown Structure (WBS) for the project. The WBS resembles an affinity diagram in that it breaks down the work into elements that reflect how the organization thinks about the work being performed. The high-level WBS is taken from the highest level, where the major project components are grouped, to the lowest level, where actual tasks (work packages) may be defined. This drill down is called a *decomposition* or *functional decomposition*, but it means nothing more than a detailing of the work that needs to be performed.

The key elements in this section are the WBS itself and a WBS dictionary or glossary that defines a common language for WBS elements—this is so that we all know what we are talking about when we reference things like "Technical Requirements Document" or "Burn Down Chart."

## Scope Verification

What do you mean when you say your project is done? That's what Scope Verification is—it enables the stakeholders to verify the stated deliverables against what was actually delivered and outlines the process for the stakeholders to formally accept the deliverables.

The key element here is usually a document that resembles a checklist in which the stakeholders can go through the list and check off items, one-by-one, as the result is verified against the original scope. The client always has the option to accept all deliverables, accept some percentage of the deliverables, or reject the entire lot.

## Scope Control

Using a monolithic or *waterfall* approach to elaborating a project will force you to implement scope control, and with good reason. Sometimes change is inevitable on a project: A missed requirement, a misunderstood requirement, a discovery, or any number of elements can require a change to scope. Changes to scope cost time and money and therefore have to be managed.

You need to manage change so that:

- Stakeholders understand the impact of the change.
- There is common and peer-reviewed agreement on what changes need to be made.
- The customer has the option to accept or reject the change, but in any case does so in writing so that there is a permanent historical record of the decision. In the case of the acceptance of the change, the customer of the project agrees to the time and budget adjustments necessary to implement the change.
- The change is formally tracked in a programmatic or manual change control system. This becomes critical for the configuration management aspects of the project.

Thus, the key input in Scope Control is an Approved Change Request—this shows you where your baseline begins to move from the original project scope and baseline.

The key outputs from Scope Control are Requested Changes and Recommended Corrective Action. You want to keep track of requested changes and whether they are accepted or rejected. You also want to track any corrective action that is recommended and implemented or not implemented—not fixing a recommended issue can also have negative impacts to the project (i.e., we always have the option to do *nothing*!).

Three of the four T&Ts are valuable here: Change Control System, Configuration Management System, and Variance Analysis are key tools in helping to manage scope change.

- The Change Control system keeps track of all changes as they impact timeline and budget.
- The Configuration Management System tracks changes to key components and keeps everything current so when you finally ship the product, you don't ship an older version of a component that might cause an overall system failure or degradation.

- Variance Analysis enables you to collect metrics via the use of statistical process control tools to analyze variances in your project to determine where corrective action can be taken.

This section may give you the idea that the basic scope framework based on the waterfall approach is *change averse*, and you would be right in that perception. There is a *lot* of overhead in tracking and implementing changes from the original baseline of the project. Using the waterfall approach in high-risk product or process development is usually a recipe for project failure. We will discuss the cure for the high-risk, waterfall approach project when we address *agility* later in the book.

# TIME MANAGEMENT

See Figure 3.4 for a chart depicting project time management.

## Activity Definition

The key inputs in the Activity Definition section are the WBS and the WBS dictionary. These elements help you map out the tasks in the project down to the work package/detail level.

The key outputs are the Activity List and the Milestone List. The Activity List is the detail task breakdown of the all the elements in the WBS—the Milestone List specifically shows the key deliverables in the Activity List. Some project plans focus more on the milestone deliverables than on the detail tasks because senior management manages its own deliverables based on the completion of specific milestones.

The key T&T in the Activity Definition section is the decomposition technique. This enables you to break down the WBS components into detail tasks. While Rolling Wave Planning is a technique of progressive elaboration, it is not the only progressive elaboration approach. The idea is that you perform detail elaboration on tasks that are to be executed immediately while leaving the WBS at a higher

## Figure 3.4

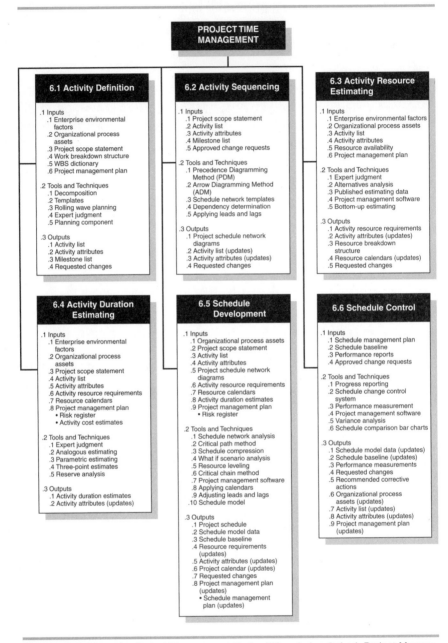

Source: A Guide to the Project Management Body of Knowledge, 3rd ed. Project Management Institute, 2004.

level for tasks the farther out they occur in the plan. While it is worth mentioning here, it is not a key T&T in all situations.

## Activity Sequencing

Activity Sequencing concerns itself with ordering the tasks in the project plan logically. The important idea to remember here is that some tasks must occur in a specific order, one after the other. Other tasks can occur simultaneously or can overlap to a high degree. Your activity sequencing diagram will graphically show which tasks:

- *Must occur in a specific sequence:* This is called a Finish-to-Start relationship; task A must complete before the start of task B.
- *Can occur simultaneously*: This is called either a Finish-to-Finish or a Start-to-Start relationship. For multiple tasks that truly start and finish simultaneously—three or more— performing accurate time estimates can be very risky and is almost always incorrect. We will discuss issues of what is called *merge bias* later in the book. (See Chapter 10 on Monte Carlo analysis.)
- *Can overlap:* Task A begins and, at some point in the execution of task A, task B can begin.

The key input here is the Activity List.

The key output is a completed detailed Network Diagram showing the project *critical path* and tasks where float/slack is applied.

The primary tools and techniques applied are the Precedence Diagramming method and identification of the dependencies between the tasks defined as follows:

- *Mandatory dependencies*—that is, task A *must* precede task B. For example, we must (A) clear the driveway of snow before (B) we can salt the driveway.
- *Discretionary dependencies*—that is, based on experience or some precedent, the project team may decide that the test team begin its planning activities (B) immediately after the business

requirements have been reviewed and accepted by stake-holders (A) instead of waiting until the detail design has been completed.

- *External dependencies*—that is, some activity that occurs out-side your project over which you have no control. For example, you are depending on the availability of storage on a large server farm installation that is following its own schedule. If there is a delay in the implementation and setup of the server farm, your project timeline could be impacted.

## Activity Resource Estimating

This section concerns itself with the resources needed for your project (people, hardware/software, machinery, material, etc.), how much of their time is needed, and when these elements are needed for the project.

The key inputs are the Activity List and Resource Availability. With a complete activity list the correct resource assignment can be made at the appropriate times, based on the resources' availability.

This will result in defining the key output—the Activity Resource Requirements. Here we essentially quantify the resource needs, for example:

- How many hours does a DBA need to create the database for the project?
- How long does the application team need "root" access to the UNIX server for application setup?
- How many hours does the requirements lead need to create and baseline the technical requirements, and what is the dead-line for completion?

The principal T&Ts used in this area are utilization of an industrial-strength project management software tool such as Microsoft Project Professional (for a single user) or Primavera's Team Play (for the en-tire enterprise) and implementation of a solid *bottom-up estimating process.* The software is useful for managing resource availability and scheduling on your project and can also help you drive the correct level of detail for an accurate bottom-up estimate.

However, this brings us to an area of unusual difficulty in the project management discipline and one that causes considerable angst, especially as it relates to IT/software projects.

## Activity Duration Estimating

Activity duration estimating remains, to this day, the most problematic and highest-risk area in IT project management. (See Chapter 5, "The Hitchhiker's Guide to Project Management," Principle #9, for a detailed look at schedule estimates for software projects.) Nonetheless, we will attempt to discuss the essentials from the unique perspective of the waterfall approach in implementing a project plan, with the assumption that the parts and pieces are well understood.

The key inputs are the Resource Requirements and the Project Management Plan's Risk Register and Cost Estimates.

The key output is the Activity Duration Estimates.

There are three primary tools and techniques in this area that PMI promotes: the Analogous estimate, the Parametric estimate, and the Three-Point estimate.

- The Analogous estimate can be used if you have historical data on previous projects that are similar to the current project. It is generally the least accurate of the estimating methods.

- The Parametric estimate considers the amount of time needed to perform the work and the actual resource performing the work. This estimate can be very accurate, within plus or minus 5%, if the capability of the resource is well understood and the effort required for the task is well understood. For IT resources, the difference in productivity between an inexperienced resource and a highly experienced resource can vary by a factor of 10!

- The Three-Point Estimate is similar to the PERT estimate as defined in the 2000 edition of the *PMBOK*. This estimate is based on taking an average between an Optimistic estimate, a Most Likely estimate, and a Pessimistic estimate. The PERT (Program Evaluation and Review Technique) uses a formula to compute the average:

$$\frac{O + 4(ML) + P}{6}$$

where:

- O is the Optimistic estimate
- ML is the Most Likely estimate
- P is the Pessimistic estimate

Unless this estimate is tempered with a probability distribution, the estimate will in all likelihood be highly inaccurate—potentially plus or minus 50%.

## Schedule Development

This section is where the actual schedule is laid out with start and finish dates for each task.

The key inputs are the Activity List, Activity Resource Requirements, and the Activity Duration Estimates.

The key outputs are the Project Schedule and, eventually, the Schedule Baseline. This can be implemented in the form of a complex Gantt chart (MS Project, Primavera's SureTrak, or some other graphic Gantt tool can be used) or as basic as an Excel spreadsheet. The Gantt software tools give you the option to set up various types of charts in their environments:

- Network diagram
- Bar or Gantt chart
- Milestone chart
- Precedence task list

In examining schedule development T&Ts, it is important to understand what each of the key tools offers:

- *Critical path method.* The critical path stacks up all the Finish-to-Start tasks in your timeline and produces an overall time estimate as a result. Unless you use one or two of the techniques mentioned below, you cannot possibly shorten or compress this timeline—it is what it is. Sometimes there are a few tasks that occur in parallel with critical path tasks, but that are shorter than the task on the critical path. These parallel tasks are said to have some wiggle room as to when they have to start. This wiggle room is called *float* or *slack*.

- *Schedule compression* through the use of Crashing or Fast Tracking:
  - *Crashing.* Forget a standard 40-hour workweek. When you crash the schedule, people work 10- to 16-hour days and sometimes Saturday and Sunday as well. It is the best method yet devised by management for burning out a team. Sometimes it is necessary because of an unforeseen event, but it usually occurs because of poor planning. Understand that we are not talking about the extraordinary project where the participants are on a do-or-die mission, such as the development of a breakthrough product like Toyota's Prius. In that case, the project stakeholders and engineers lived at the facility day and night and in two years produced what became the most significant change in the automobile industry in almost 100 years. What we are talking about in this case is what is commonly referred to as the *student syndrome*: Instead of steadily pacing work over the semester, the typical student will execute 70% of the work (completing papers, cramming for exams, etc.) in the last 20% of the semester.
  - *Fast Tracking.* This looks very good on paper but has a counterintuitive aspect that can produce unexpected and calamitous results. The idea here is that you have determined that several important high-level tasks can be run in parallel:
    - The network infrastructure buildout will take 10 weeks.
    - Application development will take 10 weeks.

- □ Server purchase, installation, certification, and operational readiness testing will take 10 weeks.

  Since there are three separate and distinct teams doing the work, these tasks do not have to be performed sequentially, taking 30 weeks, but can be performed in parallel, taking only 10 weeks! Management thinks you're a genius for knocking 20 weeks off the schedule. In reality, you will be facing a nasty gotcha called "merge bias." See Chapter 10 for a detailed look at a merge bias scenario and how it can clobber your schedule. This is a particularly effective area in which the Monte Carlo analysis can be applied.

- □ *"What if . . . " analysis.* The use of statistical modeling exampled by the Monte Carlo analysis enables the user to model other scenarios to see what might happen.

- □ *Resource leveling.* After you have already developed the critical path in your timeline, resource leveling is used to help allocate critical resources at the right time in your project. It is also applied with the idea that human resources should not be burned out having to expend 60 to 80 hours a week (the typical *Big 5* scenario) to get the job done. Resource leveling equalizes the time to a 40-hour week, or whatever a normal week is to your organization. I have seen project managers shy away from using this aspect in MS Project or similar tools because resource leveling a 9-month project can send your project end-date somewhere west of the dark side of the moon—effectively turning your 9-month project into a multiyear project! If you are in an organization dealing with unions or with resources that might get paid time-and-a-half or double-time for burning over 40 hours a week— resource leveling might save you some money, even if it extends the timeline.

- □ *Critical chain method.* The description as entered in the *PMBOK* may leave the reader a bit confused. Critical Chain Project Management is a technique developed by Dr. Eliyahu Goldratt of the Goldratt Institute. To date, it is the best method yet developed for shortening a project timeline; however, it is somewhat counterintuitive (read: "heresy" to most C-Levels) and requires executive support for the approach to work. However, the companies that have implemented Critical Chain Project Management (CCPM) have seen their project timelines decreased by 25–50% as a result of implementing this approach. There are a few organizations in the Chicago area using the approach that refuse to allow disclosure of what they are doing because the approach is giving them a competitive marketplace advantage. See Chapter 8 for a description of Critical Chain Project Management.

## Schedule Control

The key input is the actual Schedule Baseline. This will show you the current project status and where changes need to be managed if they occur.

The key outputs are Performance Measurements and Requested Changes or Corrective Actions:

- Performance Measurements will show actual schedule variances and enable you to compute the outcome. In terms of performing an Earned Value measurement, it shows you the SPI or Schedule Performance Index of the timeline. More on Earned Value will be offered in the Cost Management section.

- Requested Changes or Corrective Actions may be needed as a result of a subnominal SPI rating. Anything less than a *1* means that the schedule is slipping and that action will need to be taken. A change request can cause the timeline to be extended due to the nature of some additional work that needs to be performed. In this case, the PM tries to adjust the overall schedule baseline so that there is minimum impact on the overall schedule. This is called a *corrective action*.

The primary tools and techniques in this area are Performance Measurement and Variance Analysis.

Execution of performance measurements in the form of an Earned Value Analysis will explicitly illuminate any schedule variances. The analysis of schedule variance relies on the comparison of targeted completion dates with actual completion dates so that you can compute deviations.

Note that in statistics the analysis of variance is called *ANOVA* and is used in Six Sigma to perform sophisticated variance analysis. In this case, the concept of *variance* is an actual statistical term that defines a measure of statistical dispersion, indicating how possible values are spread around an expected value, such as the mean of a dataset. For a population sample, it is expressed in the following formula:

$$S^2 = \frac{\Sigma(X - M)^2}{N}$$

where:

- $S^2$ is the variance
- X is a measurement that was taken in the sample
- M is the arithmetic mean of the entire sample
- N is the number of elements in the sample
- $\Sigma$ is a symbol meaning "the sum of"

So, if you wanted to compute the variance in the age of fans attending a concert:

- X would equal the age of an individual concertgoer.
- M would be the arithmetic average of the age of all the concertgoers.
- N would be the total number of people attending the concert.

The variance is the sum of the square of all the differences of X − M, divided by the number of concertgoers.

As you can see, the way PMI addresses analysis of variance and the actual statistical formulas are very different. Statistical ANOVA

(<u>AN</u>alysis <u>O</u>f <u>V</u>ariance) would be a useful measurement to take in comparing the same function performed over a series of projects to determine if there was a significant variance, project to project, in the execution of a particular function, like building a database. One could then determine if the organization was consistent in its approach to building databases and would have hard data on variance and standard deviation for this function. An overall organizational improvement could then be implemented based on the collection and analysis of this data.

## COST MANAGEMENT

Figure 3.5 presents the chart for project cost management.

### Figure 3.5

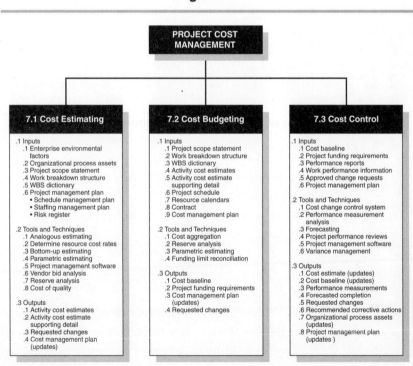

## Cost Estimating

The key inputs in Cost Estimating are Enterprise Environmental Factors, Organizational Process Assets, the Project Scope Statement, and the Project Management Plan. Here is what we derive from each:

- *Enterprise Environmental Factors.* You need to know what your human resources will cost. Consultants will be charged at an hourly rate or daily rate (the actual dollars) and employees on salary will be generally charged at an hourly generic "blended rate." This is because salary information is usually a closely guarded secret in an organization, so an average or blended rate is used to provide internal resource cost information. Don't forget that if you are dealing with salaried employees and they are being asked to work overtime (for no additional compensation), your real resource costs may never be captured unless you explicitly make the effort to do so. Other resources such as materials, hardware, or other products obtained externally are usually negotiated through the procurement area of the organization. I've rarely seen an IT area negotiate a contract for the procurement of high-end servers without the assistance of the procurement/contracts team. IT might know what they need technically, but they are generally not good at negotiating the best price for their organization. Even the PM might not know how to effectively negotiate a hardware deal unless she has experience in this area. There are some external databases that are kept by organizations like the Gartner Group that can provide research on a wide variety of topics such as market analysis, forecasts, hardware, consulting rates based on skill set, infrastructure, and a whole lot more.

- *Organizational Process Assets.* If your business keeps historical information on its projects, so much the better. This data can be used as a heuristic to help provide cost estimates. If your organization has templates and explicit procedures it uses for cost estimating, you need only plug in the numbers and, as they say, turn the crank.

- *Project Scope Statement.* This includes the detailed tasks and work packages from which you determine what resource at what experience level needs to be applied to the tasks so that the ground-up estimate can be created. You can also derive a list of deliverables and milestones for which you can create cost estimates for each deliverable or milestone.

The key output from Cost Estimating is the actual Activity Cost Estimates, with emphasis on the word *estimates.*

We derive these estimates through the use of the following key tools and techniques:

- *Bottom-up estimate.* This approach will usually give you an accurate estimate on actual costs provided you have some historical data on similar activities in other projects. Obviously, if you know what you are paying for resources it is easy to approximate the burn rate on the project based on the time you have allotted for each work package—it's a straight multiplication. Where you can get into trouble is if the time estimates are incorrect. If there is a danger of this happening, use instead the analogous estimate.

- *Parametric estimate.* The parametric estimate can be very accurate in that it analyzes historical data via the use of statistical tools and mathematical algorithms. Complete handbooks on the use and implementation of the parametric estimates have been written and used in industry and government. Check out NASA's Parametric Cost Estimating Handbook at http://cost.jsc.nasa.gov/PCEHHTML/pceh.htm and have a look at what they say in their Introduction to the handbook: "Defined, a parametric cost estimate is one that uses Cost Estimating Relationships (CERs) and associated mathematical algorithms (or logic) to establish cost estimates. For example, detailed cost estimates for manufacturing and test of an end item (for instance, a hardware assembly) can be developed using very precise Industrial Engineering standards and analysis. Performed in this manner, the cost estimating process is laborious and time consuming. However, if history has demonstrated that test (as the dependent variance) has normally been valued at about 25% of the manufacturing value (the independent variable), then a detailed test estimate need not be performed and can simply be computed at the 25% (CER) level. It is important, though, that any CERs used be carefully tested for validity using standard statistical approaches."[2]

## Cost Budgeting

The aggregated cost estimate of all activities and work packages constitutes the overall project budget. It is here you determine when your major material and hardware expenditures will occur. While resource burn rates may gradually increase or decrease over the course of the project, equipment expenditures may cause the outlay of a substantial chunk of dollars at one time (a SAN array or several filled racks of servers). Your budget should reflect when these outlays will occur and make sure the business is ready to fund the purchase. In addition, you may be able to create a "management reserve" of funds based on the probability that given risk events will occur. The ability to secure a management reserve depends on the risk tolerance of the organization—from a high tolerance for risk (e.g., "make my day") to a low tolerance for risk (the contract is fixed price and there is no room for risk reserve or anything else). I've experienced both kinds of organizations and there is no one right way to handle it, other than that you want to identify the risks and let leadership make the decision on how it wants to proceed.

The key inputs are the Activity Cost Estimates, the Project Schedule, and any contract that may exist with a third party or external organization.

The key outputs are the Cost Baseline and Project Funding requirements.

The T&Ts that are most useful include Cost Aggregation and Parametric Estimating. While management reserve (Reserve Analysis) may be included in the overall budget, it is not part of the cost baseline according to PMI, primarily because any expenditure tied to risk represents a possibility and not a certainty.

## Cost Control

Cost Control is an aspect of project management where your negotiation skills will be tested to their limits. Here you are on the lookout for any changes (or potential changes) to work effort or timeline that will impact your costs. This can include, but is not limited to:

- Formal change requests
- Scope creep
- Missed requirements
- A poor initial estimate ("This took longer than we thought it would")
- An enhancement that the user is calling a bug and wants you to fix for free
- Ad-hoc work that the project team thought would be okay but wound up impacting the budget
- Consultants who have been burning 60 hours a week to meet a deadline for the last month and you just found out about it

The principal Cost Control inputs are the Cost Baseline and Work Performance Information. The Cost Baseline, to reiterate, is your time-phased budget that represents your overall budget plan. The Work Performance Information is what is really happening in your plan:

- Completed and incomplete deliverables
- Authorized costs and costs you incurred (possibly without authorization)
- The actual burn rate on the project, which can be computed in the form of an Earned Value calculation
- How much budget will have been expended to complete all schedule activities by the end of the project (Estimate at Completion) and how much budget is needed to complete schedule activities until the end of the project (Estimate to Completion)

The key Cost Control outputs are the Performance Measurements (all the cost variance, schedule variance, CPI, and SPI values) and the Forecasted Completion estimates (EAC and ETC calculations).

The key T&T for this section is Performance Measurement Analysis, from which we derive the Earned Value Technique (EVT) and Forecasting, which enables us to deliver EAC/ETC estimates. The explanation of the EVT in the *PMBOK* is easy enough to follow, so I won't rehash it here. However, there has been some confusion about what is meant by Earned Value. PMI defines Earned Value as "the budgeted amount for the work actually completed on the schedule activity or WBS component during a given time period."[3] Most people come away still not understanding what this means, so here is a simplified way to think about Earned Value. You have three costs to think about:

1. *Planned Value (PV)*—that is, what you planned to spend for the completion of a specific task or component.
2. *Actual Cost (AC)*—that is, what you actually paid for the task or component.
3. *Earned Value (EV)*—that is, how much was *supposed* to be spent for the work that was completed. In other words, you know how much work will get done for a specific amount of money because you have an experienced crew and have collected historical data that tells you how long it takes to complete a specific task. Without this information, you may have no idea what anything is supposed to cost, in which case you might flip a coin and be just as accurate. *Without knowing EV, you have no idea what anything is supposed to cost.*

A specific example of EVT is given in Principle #9 in Chapter 5, "The Hitchhiker's Guide to Project Management."

ETC and EAC estimates are also based on Earned Value numbers in that EV is part of ETC and EAC estimates, so, once again, knowing something about your EV numbers is critical.

NOTE: I've spoken with a number of project managers about the benefits of EVT and have gotten a range of answers from: "It's very useful if you know how to use it," to "EVT is a complete waste of time," and everything in between. Some PMs compute Earned Value using only the Planned Value and Actual Costs, which is interesting (as in, I don't know how that works) but incorrect. Earned Value means that you understand the relationship between the level of effort and the dollars spent as it relates to the completion of the task or component. For example, if you planned to spend $1,000 on a task (PV) and you actually spent $1,200 (AC), what does that mean?

☐ It could mean that you miscalculated the actual cost of the work and that $1,200 is what you should have spent to get the task completed, in which case the PV is a fiction.

☐ It could mean that the people doing the work were inexperienced (or incompetent) and as a result you are overpaying for the task/component.

Without the Earned Value dollar figure to tell you what you *should* be spending for the task/component, how do you know which of the above is true?

In addition, if you are contracting for work performed by a third party, the only place that EVT really comes into play is with Cost Plus contracts. These contracts are of the greatest risk to the purchaser because you are buying expertise and the contract is for whatever the job costs plus a fixed percentage for the profit margin. With a Time and Materials contract, the situation is similar. However, if the contract is fixed price, the vendor is on the hook to deliver no matter what. In this case, you could make an argument that computing EV is a waste of time for you—it's the vendor's problem. In this instance you must insure that:

☐ Validation is received that the vendor's work was performed to your standards.

☐ You don't get change-ordered to death. This is where the vendor claims that some detail you have requested was not defined in the original requirements and specifications and that it will cost more to complete. Make sure the vendor builds to the stated requirements and no more.

# PROJECT QUALITY MANAGEMENT

Figure 3.6 depicts project quality management.

## Quality Planning

PMI says that Quality Planning focuses on identifying which quality standards in your organization apply to the project at hand and how to ensure these standards are satisfied. This is assuming, of course, that your organization *has* quality standards, which may be a moot point

## Figure 3.6

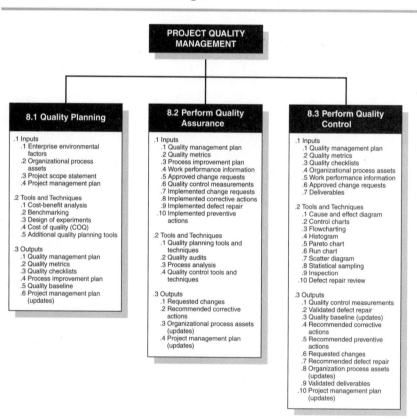

*Source: A Guide to the Project Management Body of Knowledge*, 3rd ed. Project Management Institute, 2004.

for many organizations. If you are in an organization that has documented quality standards, the next important question is: Are these standards followed and enforced by the organization, or is this just a story you tell your customers to keep their business when in reality you follow the processes only when they are convenient?

While you are thinking about that, ponder the key input needed for Quality Planning: the Scope Statement and all of its subsidiary parts.

The key Quality Planning outputs are the Quality Metrics and Quality Checklists. The metrics address what measurements you will take that let you know whether the product or process is meeting specification (read: the "voice of the customer"). This might involve the use of statistical process tools such as X bar R charts, X bar S charts, p, np, u, and c charts, scatter diagrams, Pareto charts, histograms, and the like.

A checklist is used to insure all the parts and pieces of a component or a task were completed and are used to verify the result.

In the tools and techniques for Quality Planning section, we have some tools with implications that go far beyond the basics, and there are some issues here as well that actually muddy the water:

- *Cost-benefit analysis.* This is usually used as a decision tool to determine whether you want to embark on the project. It is done in the early initial planning phases. To apply this idea to project quality implies that there is an economics to quality. Before you determine what quality cost benefit entails, you'd better ask your customer what constitutes quality to them. The problematic aspect of PMI's assessment here lies in the following statement in section 8.1.2.1: "The primary cost of meeting quality requirements is the expense associated with Project Quality Management activities."[4] It is problematic because every world-class quality expert from W. Edwards Deming, to Joseph Juran, Armand Feigenbaum, Philip B. Crosby, and others have stated repeatedly that this idea is 180° from reality. To quote Phil Crosby: *"The cost of quality is the expense of doing things wrong.* It is the scrap, rework, service after service, inspection, tests and similar activities made necessary by non-conformance problems."[5] First, find out what constitutes quality to your customer before making decisions on whether your cost-benefit tradeoffs are actually what the customer wants.

- *Benchmarking.* I've seen this approach abused more than it is properly used, so understand what you are doing when it comes to benchmarking. It is generally used to see if your internal project practices equal or exceed *best practices* in the industry. You can then measure your performance against the best practices to convince yourself that you are compliant with "standard industry practices," and deliver a self-congratulatory pat-on-the-back for doing a great job without ever asking your customer once if this is what they wanted (or needed). The only important benchmark is the one set by the customer. Satisfy that, and your benchmark will actually mean something. To me, "best practices" constitute one idea—mediocre. Most every company I encounter says they are compliant with best practices—if everyone is doing it, then it must constitute some kind of generic average. In an age where survival of a business depends on innovative thinking, flawless execution, and the ability to consistently exceed your customer's expectations, to their utter delight, "best practices" sounds like a spiel from a used-car salesman. So, if your company is *very* focused on best practices, it must mean it is "very mediocre." (Please send all hate mail to the publisher.)

- *Design of experiments (DOE).* I have asked participants in my seminars to read this paragraph in the *PMBOK* (8.1.2.3) and tell me, in plain English what it means. No one to date, except those who actually have used DOE, have any idea what this paragraph means. So, in plain English, DOE is a statistical tool used to help experimenters determine the optimal settings for a process or procedure in as few steps as possible. If DOE had been available as an experimental method in the late 1800s to Tom Edison, the 10,000 experiments needed to create the first successful light bulb might have been reduced to as few as 300 experiments using DOE. How this actually works is described in Chapter 15, "Design of Experiments." Understand that to undertake DOE effectively in your project or business is a non-trivial and complex activity requiring training and practice until you get good at it. DOE is the realm of the Six Sigma Black Belt and beyond. You'll also need a high-end statistical package like Minitab to perform the necessary crunching to simplify your efforts.

- *Cost of quality.* Once again, we are dealing with the same issue we encountered above, under "cost-benefit analysis." Please reread Phil Crosby's quote given there to understand the true cost of quality.

## Perform Quality Assurance

Quality Assurance (QA) is usually a documented and enforced activity that ensures that every project undertaken in the organization adheres to the company's quality policies, processes, and guidelines. Any tailoring of QA policy for a specific project can be implemented based on the scope of the work. If requirements documents require signoff by a team lead, the client/sponsor, and the requirements lead, QA will insure via an audit or some other process that the signoff occurs and is validated.

The key inputs for Quality Assurance are the Quality Metrics (what you will measure) and Quality Control Measurements (the actual measurements).

The key outputs are Requested Changes and Recommended Corrective Actions. Usually quality improvement occurs as a systematic and planned activity within an organization—it does not wait for a specific project unless the project uncovers an unseen weakness that requires immediate attention. The outputs above are designed to identify and implement quality improvement activities for the organization.

Key T&Ts of Quality Assurance are the Quality Audit and Process Analysis. The audit validates whether the project is complying with company policy, standards, and procedures, while process analysis is used to identify areas for improvement. PMI states in passing that process analysis includes *root cause analysis (RCA)*. This is potentially huge. We are not talking about a defect analysis on software or hardware to determine the cause of a specific failure. The RCA in its full-blown sense is a rather painful process that starts with the CEO and works its way down. If a full-blown RCA is being performed in your organization, it is usually because there has been a catastrophic event that requires serious investigation. For example:

- There was release of radioactive material into the atmosphere at Three Mile Island Nuclear Generating Station on March 28, 1979.

- A massive explosion at BP's Texas City refinery resulted in at least 15 deaths and more than 100 injuries (March 23, 2005).

- At Bourbonnais, Illinois, an Amtrak train crashed into a loaded semi-trailer. This disaster, which occurred 50 miles south of Chicago, claimed the lives of 11 people and injured 122 (March 15, 1999).

The U.S. Department of Energy produced a document in 1992 that details various RCA techniques and describes in depth what occurs in a formal root cause analysis—it is well worth the read not just for the process but for where you can go to obtain training in performing the RCA. Go to https://hss.doe.gov/NuclearSafety/techstds/standard/nst1004/nst1004.pdf to download the pdf. Kepner-Tregoe was mentioned as the most detailed and thorough of the RCA processes, requiring training in order to correctly implement an in-depth RCA.

## Perform Quality Control

Quality Control (QC) focuses on defect elimination and, in its best sense, defect prevention. QC should constantly monitor the state of the project processes to determine if the wheels are coming off the wagon and then determine what corrective action needs to be taken as a result.

The key input for Quality Control is the actual Work Performance Information: expected results, actual results, variances from established metrics, and so forth.

The key outputs for Quality Control are your Quality Control Measurements and Recommended Preventive Actions. Most people ask me why I don't include "Recommended Corrective Actions," "Recommended Defect Repair," and "Validated Defect Repair" as key outputs in this area. For one very important reason: Corrective action is like having your sprinkler system go off when there is a fire, instead of taking steps to prevent the fire in the first place. It's the same as shutting the barn door *after* the horses got out. Corrective actions and defect repair deal with the problem after the fact, and that is not where you want to deal with it. At that point, the rework and repair are costing you additional time and money. Phil Crosby was right: Defect Prevention is the best bang-for-the-buck cost-reduction strategy a business can employ.

The tools and techniques for Quality Control read like the *Who's Who* of the Six Sigma toolkit. Kaoru Ishikawa, one of the earliest winners of the Deming Prize in Japan, published in 1968 seven basic statistical tools in his book, *Guide to Quality Control*. Ishikawa stated that if these tools were taught and correctly used by line workers, 95% of defects occurring in the work environment could be eliminated. The seven basic statistical tools are:

1. Histograms
2. Cause-and-effect (Ishikawa) diagrams
3. Check sheets
4. Flowcharts
5. Pareto charts
6. Scatter diagrams
7. Statistical process charts

These tools are all included in the tools and techniques in the Quality Control section and they are all useful. Please refer to Chapter 12, "The Seven Ishikawa Quality Tools," for a detailed description and examples of each of the tools.

# PROJECT HUMAN RESOURCE MANAGEMENT

Figure 3.7 charts project human resource management.

**Figure 3.7**

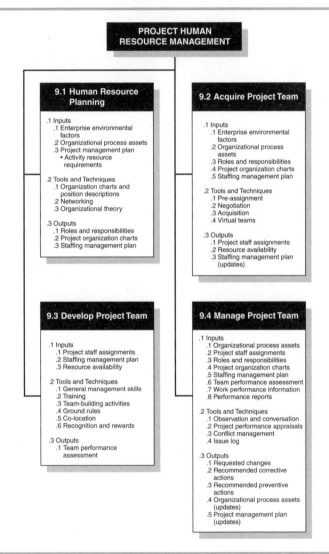

*Source: A Guide to the Project Management Body of Knowledge*, 3rd ed. Project Management Institute, 2004.

## Human Resource Planning

Here is where you define roles and responsibilities for your project and the project team. Depending on the size and duration of the project, you may need to create a Staffing Management Plan. A project running over a multiyear cycle and engaging many hundreds if not thousands of people will require some kind of plan to manage when resources roll on and off the project.

The key input in Human Resource Planning falls under the Enterprise Environmental Factors heading. Here you ascertain where resources will be supplied to the project, which departments are involved, what skill sets are required, whether the team is co-located or dispersed across continents, and what are the reporting relationships of the resources (i.e., do you as the PM have total control over resources or do they report to line managers in a matrixed reporting relationship?).

The key output is a documented Roles and Responsibilities grid. As one Executive Director at AT&T used to say, "Whose neck do I grab for this deliverable?" The Roles and Resps grid shows you just that. It tells you who they are, their skill set, their responsibility, and to whom they report, in case you need something escalated and the resource is nonresponsive. It is also the contact list for all the team members, containing office and (usually) cell phone numbers to be used in case of emergency. A project Org chart might be useful as well, but usually large companies will have an organizational hierarchy online so you can easily find a resource's manager, and his manager as well. These don't have to be created specifically for the project and exist on their own outside of the scope of the project.

The most useful T&Ts in this area are the matrix-based charts, such as a Responsibility Assignment Matrix, and some understanding of human psychology (Organizational Theory) to help bond the team and hit the ground running.

## Acquire Project Team

This element involves the actual acquisition of resources for the project.

The key input is, once again, the Enterprise Environmental Factors with the addition of Roles and Responsibilities.

The key output is the Project Staff Assignments.

The key tools and techniques in this area are Negotiation and Virtual Teams. Negotiation is always required for sought-after resources within an organization. PMs frequently refer to their negotiation tactics with line managers for key resources as "horse trading" (facetiously, of course). If the project is high visibility, this in turn can give key resources visibility to upper management, and the possibility of promotion or a generous bonus can play into the negotiations.

The Virtual Team is a relatively recent development in the project management arena, but it has great benefits in terms of the ability to marshal needed resources without having to co-locate them. Team members can work from home or in geographically dispersed locations. With the development of a cable infrastructure in the United States that supports 100 Mbps connectivity on the Web, and the ability to create secured VPNs (virtual private networks), the expense of having to co-locate teams may shortly become obsolete. After all, why burn gasoline and spend hours in traffic or on public transportation when you can access work as quickly and efficiently from home as you can from the worksite itself? Numerous empirical studies have been conducted in this area that consistently show that employees are more productive from home than they are at work.

## Develop Project Team

This involves improving the skills of the team members as well as coalescing the team into a highly productive, cohesive structure that consistently functions at a high level.

The key input here is the Project Staff Assignments.

The only output is the Team Performance Assessment.

The real deal in this section is the Tools and Techniques that are used to create processes that allow the team to bond and function as a high-performing team. This is the "organizational development" aspect of team building—what people generally refer to as the *soft skills*.

The key T&T will be your General Management Skills. You, as a project manager, need training in team dynamics, conflict resolution, motivation, needs assessment, and other aspects of psychology so that you can (1) understand what is going on in terms of how team members interact, (2) make the right decision when conflicts arise, (3) find out what motivates your team members (other than a paycheck, why do they get out of bed in the morning?), and (4) understand the difference between leadership and management so you know when to lead and when project elements need to be managed.

The other T&Ts (Training, Ground Rules, Co-location, Recognition and Rewards) are useful; however, be on the lookout for canned, management-imposed "team-building activities." In over 30 years of working for various Fortune 500 companies as well as public-sector organizations, one element has come through as crystal clear: Employees see through this ruse, roll their eyes, and laugh to themselves thinking, "Okay, management is trying to bond the team members by imposing a forced team-building activity—what fun. I'll just play along and waste half the day doing it." This is because most management treats employees like children, and if there is anything that absolutely riles an adult, it's being treated like a kid. An interviewer once asked Stephen Spielberg how it was that he worked so well with children and got such great performances out of them. His answer was simple—he doesn't treat children like children, he treats them like adults, and they respond in kind. Business managers should pay attention to that one.

If you want to conduct a real team-building activity, have some fun with the team away from the office: a golf outing, a baseball game, anything that has nothing to do with work. Find out who your team members really are instead of concocting some contrived event to help build team rapport, and you will have developed *real* team rapport.

## Manage Project Team

Over the course of the project, the PM manages all aspects of the project including the project team. PMI states that the role of the PM team is to track team performance, manage conflict, resolve issues, deliver input for performance appraisals, and coordinate changes.

Of the eight inputs described here, the *official* key inputs are Work Performance Information and Performance Reports. Work Performance Information will give you data about each individual team member and how he or she is performing in real time so that adjustments and corrections can be made. Performance Reports provide the team, as well as management, with a dashboard of information about the timeline, burn rate, and other elements that help the PM manage the project and determine future HR needs.

However, I would argue that the most important ability in managing a project team is your General Management Skills (outlined in the previous section). These skills are not only needed to develop the project team, they are needed throughout the entire project management process.

The key outputs are Recommended Preventive Actions, for the same reasons stated earlier in the Quality Management section, and Lessons Learned (a subset within Organizational Process Assets). Lessons Learned become part of the project documentation and are usually reviewed in some type of *project postmortem* to identify what worked, what didn't work, and what could be done differently the next time. Usually this data is never read or looked at again, unless it is part of the organization's project process that lessons learned from the previous project be reviewed before undertaking the next one. So learn this lesson: Implement lessons learned as they occur and integrate the lesson into your ongoing project instead of waiting until the end of the project, when everyone is looking to move on and forget the project ever happened. Making the lesson learned part of your immediate process is the real lesson learned.

The key T&T is the Issue Log—creating it, maintaining it, and continuously updating it. It is a historical compendium of *all* your project issues, who is responsible for resolving the issue (i.e., who owns it), the deadline for issue resolution, and what was done to resolve the issue. While the other elements are useful and occasionally needed (Observation and Conversation, Project Performance

Appraisals, and Conflict Management), these elements may not be required or continually performed throughout the project. The Issue Log is there from beginning to end, no excuses.

# PROJECT COMMUNICATIONS MANAGEMENT

PMI states that Communications Management involves processes that are "required to ensure timely and appropriate generation, collection, distribution, storage, retrieval, and ultimate disposition of project information"[6] Do you actually need a full-blown Communications Management Plan, described as the only output of Communications Planning? Depending on the size and length of the project and the number of resources on the project team, you might. In most instances, however, a straightforward contact list, the weekly/monthly/quarterly schedule of meetings, and the key stakeholders for each usually suffice. Figure 3.8 is the chart for project communications management.

## Communications Planning

If you ever took a course in journalism, think of the $5W + H$ list and you won't go wrong. In terms of project information and communications, you need to know:

- **Who**  needs information?
- **What**  information is needed?
- **Where**  is it needed?
- **When**  is it needed?
- **Why**  is it needed?
- **How**  (in what format) is it needed?

The key input is the Project Scope Statement and all of its subsidiary parts.

## Figure 3.8

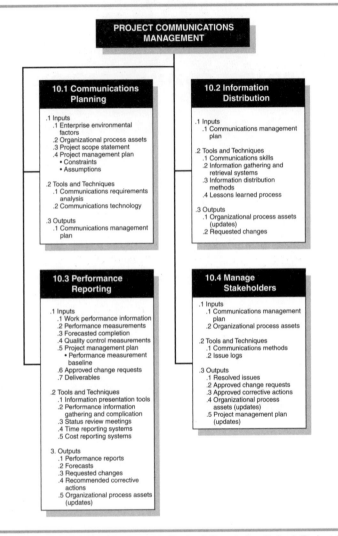

Source: A Guide to the Project Management Body of Knowledge, 3rd ed. Project Management Institute, 2004.

The only output is the Communications Management Plan. If all you need is an Excel spreadsheet containing the contact list and a page of bullet points indicating when meetings occur and who needs what, where, how, and why—so be it.

The key T&T here is the Communication Technology you will use to facilitate communications with the team. That can be face-to-face meetings, e-mails, video conferences, conference calls, progress/status reports, balanced-scorecard dashboard, or whatever combination of methods is standardized for your organization. More of this will be detailed in the Performance Reporting section.

## Information Distribution

The only input is the Communications Management Plan. If you are managing a project with 50 or more people, you would probably want to document which stakeholders need what kind of information and go through the 5 W's + H process. If it's only you and two or three others, a full-blown CM plan is a waste of time. Use a bullet list instead.

The key output is the Organizational Process Assets (Updates), specifically the Project Reports and the Feedback from Stakeholders. Project Reports give you a running history of what has transpired on the project and how issues and risks were addressed. Stakeholder feedback, especially from a key stakeholder like a sponsor or *the customer,* will give you a clear indication of how they think you are doing.

The key T&T is the Information Distribution Methods. This focuses on how you will actually implement the information sharing and dissemination process and what tools will be used to guarantee timely, accurate, and effective communications appropriately to all stakeholders. This can include tools that manage:

- Online documentation via shared network drives
- Intranet or extranet web sites
- Document/code configuration management and repository tools such as Clear Case or Documentum
- E-mail systems such as Outlook
- Audio or video conference systems
- Online meeting systems utilizing audio and graphics such as Webex

## Performance Reporting

This, as they say, is where the rubber meets the road. This is where all the hard-core data collection occurs and where it is summarized, interpreted, and acted upon.

The key inputs are Performance Measurements, Quality Control Measurements, Approved Change Requests, and Deliverables. We collect any performance measures that have an impact on the timeline, the budget, the quality of the deliverables, and the deliverables themselves. From these measurements we derive the outputs.

The key outputs are Performance Reports, Forecasts, and Corrective Actions. The actual reports of what was accomplished and where issues exist will drive future decisions for the project. Forecasts will help us make adjustments in effort, timeline, and budget before issues occur (a preventive action). The Corrective Action may be necessary due to an unforeseen event, a common occurrence on most projects. The better you become at forecasting, the less you will have to rely on corrective actions.

The key tools and techniques are Time and Cost Reporting Systems. These give you the data and facts necessary to manage the project and determine if there are any issues, real or imagined.

## Manage Stakeholders

This title is somewhat misleading. You don't actually manage stakeholders; you manage how information is fed to your stakeholders. This may be an important skill to master in that not all stakeholders are rational, process-focused individuals. Some stakeholders will fly into a panic at the drop of a hat depending on the information they receive.

The key input is not really mentioned in the *PMBOK*, so I will offer it here: Know whom you are dealing with. (If you need to give it a label, refer to the Communications Management Plan as a key input.) The real deal is to know and understand your stakeholders, determine their needs, respect and understand their hot buttons, and simply listen to what they are telling you. In this way you can address the key output.

The key output is Resolved Issues—resolving stakeholder issues is the most important aspect of any kind of stakeholder management. Take care of your stakeholders and you will get more of your changes and corrective actions approved than you might if you ignore or antagonize stakeholders.

As for the key tools and techniques, although PMI states that Communications Methods and Issues Logs are the tools, what is requested usually goes beyond these basics. In addition to the Issues Log, stakeholders will frequently want to see the Risk Log, any alterations to the requirements that potentially impact the project downstream, discovery elements (i.e., "we just found out that . . . "), formal jeopardies raised on a project (due to an impending missed deadline or some other showstopper), budget updates and burn rate, timeline, and whatever else your stakeholders think is important. To sum up: Determine what your stakeholders want and then use the appropriate tool to deliver it—whatever it is.

## PROJECT RISK MANAGEMENT

Figure 3.9 charts project risk management.

On all projects taking a monolithic, waterfall approach to development, Risk Management is probably the most talked about and one of the least well understood (next to, of course, accurately estimating the project timeline and level of effort). Understand that there are entire businesses and industry segments that have devoted themselves to the assessment, appraisal, and management of risk—for a price. I've experienced many projects where management had no idea what the real risks were, their impact on the project, or the likelihood of their occurrence, but forged ahead, spending inordinate amounts of time and dollars performing risk assessments on very-low-probability occurrences, usually because they got bitten once before and are now responding in knee-jerk fashion to the potential "risk."

Nonetheless, a well-thought-out, organized approach to Risk Management will save you time, dollars, and a lot of grief downstream on your project.

## Figure 3.9

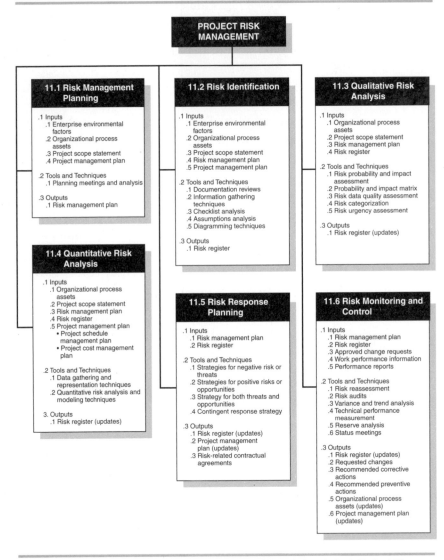

Source: *A Guide to the Project Management Body of Knowledge*, 3rd ed. Project Management Institute, 2004.

## Risk Management Planning

This is where you decide how to conduct risk management activities for a project. While you need all the Scope, Project Plan, and Organizational Process asset information, the key input here is the Enterprise Environmental Factors. What is the organization's tolerance for risk? The answer to this question will determine how you undertake your risk-planning activities. I've experienced many flavors of this question of risk tolerance in many business environments, but it generally falls into one of three fundamental categories:

1. **The Buckaroo-Bonzai approach (aka "Make My Day").** This is the "Damn the torpedoes, full speed ahead" type of risk tolerance attitude. This organization lives to embrace and wrestle risk to the ground. In this case, the risks are high but the rewards are potentially *gigantic*. Since you are taking it on the chin, companies usually have a Plan B and a Plan C if Plan A looks like it's not working.

2. **Dodging bullets 'R' Us.** Unlike the first group, this organization looks for ways to avoid impending risk by simply eliminating the possibility. For example, if there is a risk vendor A will deliver 25% of its goods two weeks late, avoid the problem by either (1) over-ordering the amount needed up front or (2) finding a reliable vendor that will deliver everything on time.

3. **If it moves—kill it.** This is the highly risk-averse organization. At one company where I functioned as a senior project manager, if any item on the risk assessment matrix for the project achieved a probability of over 20%, it got the notice of the group vice president. In this case, extraordinary pains were taken to address, mitigate, eliminate, and reduce exposure and otherwise squeeze the life out of any potential risk.

The only output from Risk Management Planning is the Risk Management Plan. Think of the $5W + H$ approach to define *what* approach you need to take, *who* are the responsible resources, *where* the actions are taken, *why* they are taken, *when* they are taken, and *how* they are implemented.

The only tools and techniques element is Planning Meetings and Analysis. The project team assembles and, in a series of meetings, develops the risk management plan.

## Risk Identification

Here you explicitly identify risk that may impact your project and document the characteristics of each risk. This is something you do throughout the duration of the project; some risks will evaporate while others may appear later in the project. Thus, a constant and continuous evaluation of risks must be performed.

The key input is the Risk Management plan.

The only output is the documented Risk Register (or Risk Log).

The essential tools and techniques in this area are Information Gathering Techniques and Diagramming Techniques. The most effective information-gathering techniques are usually some combination of *interviews* and *brainstorming*. Methods for identifying and addressing specific risks are the Wide Band Delphi and SWOT (Strengths, Weaknesses, Opportunities, and Threats) analysis.

Of the Diagramming approaches, once again, the Ishikawa (cause-and-effect) diagram demonstrates its flexibility for use in a wide variety of situations, including risk identification. One can focus on a specific risk and use the Ishikawa to graphically trace the contributing causes.

In spite of everything you may do to identify potential risks, the fundamental weakness faced by most organizations in this area is that the project participants *don't know what they don't know.* You can think you did a thorough job of risk identification only to get blind-sided by some *discovery* element later in the project that throws the proverbial monkey wrench in the works. David Apgar outlines four very practical rules to help teams manage what they don't know:

1. Identify which risks are learnable.
2. Identify risks you can learn about the fastest.
3. Sequence risky projects in a *learning pipeline*.
4. Keep networks of partners to manage all risks.[7]

Item number 4 is particularly useful in that getting some external help and a fresh set of eyes looking at your potential risks will help you uncover the unseen and the unknown.

## Qualitative Risk Analysis

This is the first place where you identify your potentially highest impact and highest-priority risks. There is some general probability assessment performed and assessment of potential project impacts if the risks are realized. The work done here provides grounding for the Quantitative Risk analysis (if needed) as well as Risk Response planning.

The key input is the Risk Register (Risk Log).

The only output is the Risk Register Updates that will contain the following key elements:

- Risk priority ranking
- Lists of risks requiring near-term or immediate response

The key tools and techniques used to create the prioritized risk listing are the Risk Probability and Impact Assessment and the Probability and Impact Matrix.

The risk probability is a value assigned indicating the likelihood that a specific risk will occur, while the risk impact assessment is a value that defines the potential effect of the risk on the project. For example, if there is a high risk that several key developers might go on vacation at the same time, the impact might not be significant if there are ample resources to cover for them.

On the other hand, if there are no resources to cover for them, your project could come to a dead stop.

The Probability and Impact Matrix (such as shown in Figure 3.10) will visually indicate general guidelines by which the organization prioritizes risks and their impacts by matching a probability scale against specific weighted impacts. Dark gray areas show the highest risk followed in turn by light gray and medium gray.

**Figure 3.10**

| Probability and Impact Matrix | | | | | | | | | |
|---|---|---|---|---|---|---|---|---|---|
| Probability | Threats | | | | | Opportunities | | | |
| 0.90 | 0.05 | 0.09 | 0.18 | 0.36 | 0.72 | 0.72 | 0.36 | 0.18 | 0.09 | 0.05 |
| 0.70 | 0.04 | 0.07 | 0.14 | 0.28 | 0.56 | 0.56 | 0.28 | 0.14 | 0.07 | 0.04 |
| 0.50 | 0.03 | 0.05 | 0.10 | 0.20 | 0.40 | 0.40 | 0.20 | 0.10 | 0.05 | 0.03 |
| 0.30 | 0.02 | 0.03 | 0.06 | 0.12 | 0.24 | 0.24 | 0.12 | 0.06 | 0.03 | 0.02 |
| 0.10 | 0.01 | 0.01 | 0.02 | 0.04 | 0.08 | 0.08 | 0.04 | 0.02 | 0.01 | 0.01 |
|  | 0.05 | 0.10 | 0.20 | 0.40 | 0.80 | 0.80 | 0.40 | 0.20 | 0.10 | 0.05 |

Impact (ratio scale) on an objective (e.g., cost, time, scope, or quality)

Each risk is rated on its probability of occurring and impact on an objective if it does occur. The organization's thresholds for low, moderate, or high risks are shown in the matrix and determine whether the risk is scored as high, moderate, or low for that objective.

*Source: A Guide to the Project Management Body of Knowledge*, 3rd ed. Project Management Institute, 2004.

## Quantitative Risk Analysis

The Quantitative risk analysis analyzes information gathered in the Qualitative analysis and assigns a numerical rating to the risks. Uncertainty models and probabilities can be calculated using tools to model risk potential, such as the Monte Carlo analysis and Decision Tree analysis.

The key input, once again, is the Risk Register.

The only output is Risk Register Updates. However, included with the prioritized risk listing is a new key element: the probability analysis. Here you will see a model of whether the cost and schedule estimates will achieve their desired outcomes along with a numeric confidence level associated with each. It is this kind of reality check that validates or invalidates your assumptions and gives more weight to your ability to manage with data and facts.

The key tools and techniques in this area are the Probability Distributions and Modeling techniques such as Sensitivity analysis,

Monte Carlo analysis, and Decision Tree analysis. For details on the Monte Carlo analysis, see Chapter 10; for the Decision Tree analysis, see Chapter 11.

## Risk Response Planning

After you have performed in-depth analysis, it is in the Risk Response Planning section that we develop the options and scenarios to mitigate or eliminate risks and threats to the project.

The key input is the Risk Register.

The key output is the Risk Register (Updates) that will additionally include the following new elements: risk owners and their responsibilities, risk response strategies, identification of risk triggers, defined impacts to budget and timeline if implementing a risk response, contingency plans, residual risks, secondary risks, and fallback plans (in the event of an ineffective risk response).

Three of the four tools and techniques in this area are loosely based on the SWOT grid:

1. Strategies for negative risks or threats
2. Strategies for positive risks or opportunities
3. Strategy for both threats and opportunities

Basically there are four ways to handle a risk:

1. Transfer—that is, buy insurance.
2. Avoid—do something else.
3. Mitigate—reduce the impact.
4. Accept it—usually done when the probabilities of being impacted by the risk are less than 5%.

Don't forget, if you definitely think the risk will happen and your confidence is very high, chances are it's no longer a risk—it is now an issue that must be addressed proactively.

RANT WARNING: While many recent articles and even some books talk about "positive risk" or "upside risk," these terms are considered by this author to be oxymorons and will not be referred to as such in this text. *Webster's Dictionary* offers the following definitions for the noun *risk:*

1. possibility of loss or injury: *peril*
2. someone or something that creates or suggests a hazard
3. **a:** the chance of loss or the perils to the subject matter of an insurance contract; *also:* the degree of probability of such loss **b:** a person or thing that is a specified hazard to an insurer (a poor *risk* for insurance) **c:** an insurance hazard from a specified cause or source (war *risk*)
4. the chance that an investment (as a stock or commodity) will lose value[8]

The terms *positive risk* and *upside risk* do not appear in the reference above. While I'm sure some marketing type decided it was a great idea to come up with a new way to define *risk*, the original English definition has far more impact and gets us away from redefining the meaning of words à la George Orwell's *1984*. Before we start changing the meaning of important words like *risk*, let's at least put it to a vote.

## Risk Monitoring and Control

Here is where project risks are tracked and appropriate responses to risk events are implemented.

The key inputs are the Risk Register and the Performance Reports.

The key outputs are Risk Register (Updates) and Recommended Preventive Actions.

The primary tools and techniques are Variance and Trend Analysis. While the other elements may need some attention (Risk

Reassessment, Risk Audits, Technical Performance measurement, and Reserve Analysis), it is the statistical tools used for plotting variance and trend analysis that will provide the data to assess current and future risks.

# PROJECT PROCUREMENT MANAGEMENT

If the project needs resources external to the organization in the form of products or services you will need to manage the procurement process. This will also involve contract management and administration of the third-party resource. Most organizations have areas or departments that specialize in contract administration because there are aspects of contract administration that must be reviewed and approved by qualified legal professionals. Figure 3.11 is the project procurement management chart.

## Plan Purchases and Acquisitions

When identifying where to make build-or-buy decisions, this is the area where you have decided that the project needs are best served by acquiring products or services from outside the organization.

The key input is the Project Scope Statement. This will help you identify what elements of the project cannot be satisfied internally and what technical issues or risks may be resolved by the acquisition of external resources or products.

The key outputs are the Procurement Management Plan and the Contract Statement of Work. The Procurement Management plan outlines how all the procurement processes will work, from what kind of contract is used to the metrics utilized to evaluate the  seller once the contract has been completed and everything in between. View it as a parallel project to your project with the same level of planning, scope definition (in this case it's called a Statement of Work or SOW), risks, schedule development, and so on that you would elaborate in your own project. The additional difference is the close coordination and identification of cross-functional dependencies needed between the

# Figure 3.11

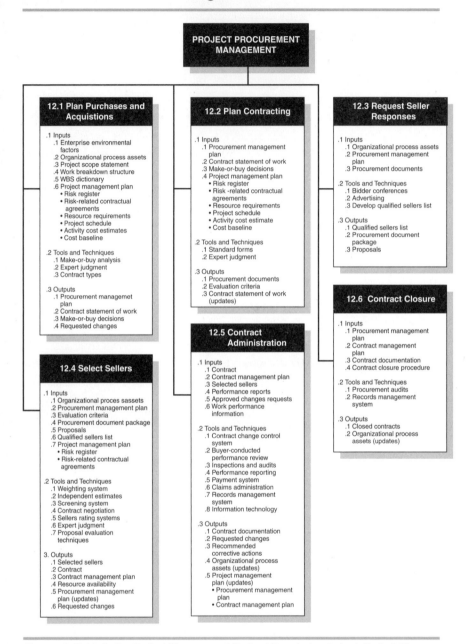

**PROJECT PROCUREMENT MANAGEMENT**

**12.1 Plan Purchases and Acquistions**

.1 Inputs
  .1 Enterprise environmental factors
  .2 Organizational process assets
  .3 Project scope statement
  .4 Work breakdown structure
  .5 WBS dictionary
  .6 Project management plan
    • Risk register
    • Risk-related contractual agreements
    • Resource requirements
    • Project schedule
    • Activity cost estimates
    • Cost baseline

.2 Tools and Techniques
  .1 Make-or-buy analysis
  .2 Expert judgment
  .3 Contract types

.3 Outputs
  .1 Procurement managemet plan
  .2 Contract statement of work
  .3 Make-or-buy decisions
  .4 Requested changes

**12.4 Select Sellers**

.1 Inputs
  .1 Organizational proces sassets
  .2 Procurement management plan
  .3 Evaluation criteria
  .4 Procurement document package
  .5 Proposals
  .6 Qualified sellers list
  .7 Project management plan
    • Risk register
    • Risk-related contractual agreements

.2 Tools and Techniques
  .1 Weighting system
  .2 Independent estimates
  .3 Screening system
  .4 Contract negotiation
  .5 Sellers rating systems
  .6 Expert judgment
  .7 Proposal evaluation techniques

3. Outputs
  .1 Selected sellers
  .2 Contract
  .3 Contract management plan
  .4 Resource availability
  .5 Procurement management plan (updates)
  .6 Requested changes

**12.2 Plan Contracting**

.1 Inputs
  .1 Procurement management plan
  .2 Contract statement of work
  .3 Make-or-buy decisions
  .4 Project management plan
    • Risk register
    • Risk -related contractual agreements
    • Resource requirements
    • Project schedule
    • Activity cost estimate
    • Cost baseline

.2 Tools and Techniques
  .1 Standard forms
  .2 Expert judgment

.3 Outputs
  .1 Procurement documents
  .2 Evaluation criteria
  .3 Contract statement of work (updates)

**12.5 Contract Administration**

.1 Inputs
  .1 Contract
  .2 Contract management plan
  .3 Selected sellers
  .4 Performance reports
  .5 Approved changes requests
  .6 Work performance information

.2 Tools and Techniques
  .1 Contract change control system
  .2 Buyer-conducted performance review
  .3 Inspections and audits
  .4 Performance reporting
  .5 Payment system
  .6 Claims administration
  .7 Records management system
  .8 Information technology

.3 Outputs
  .1 Contract documentation
  .2 Requested changes
  .3 Recommended corrective actions
  .4 Organizational process assets (updates)
  .5 Project management plan (updates)
    • Procurement management plan
    • Contract management plan

**12.3 Request Seller Responses**

.1 Inputs
  .1 Organizational process assets
  .2 Procurement management plan
  .3 Procurement documents

.2 Tools and Techniques
  .1 Bidder conferences
  .2 Advertising
  .3 Develop qualified sellers list

.3 Outputs
  .1 Qualified sellers list
  .2 Procurement document package
  .3 Proposals

**12.6 Contract Closure**

.1 Inputs
  .1 Procurement management plan
  .2 Contract management plan
  .3 Contract documentation
  .4 Contract closure procedure

.2 Tools and Techniques
  .1 Procurement audits
  .2 Records management system

.3 Outputs
  .1 Closed contracts
  .2 Organizational process assets (updates)

*Source: A Guide to the Project Management Body of Knowledge*, 3rd ed. Project Management Institute, 2004.

internal project work and the work performed by the vendor. That is something that needs to be watched and measured closely.

The primary tools and techniques are the Make-or-Buy Decisions and the various Contract Types. The make-or-buy decision can be tricky when it comes to software development, but a good heuristic to use is this: If you are not in the business of writing software, then you are better off buying what you need than attempting to build it in house. Not that it's not possible—it will simply cost you a lot more than you thought and will take a lot longer than you thought. Go with a company that has product out on the street for a number of years and that has a favorable track record of delivery, functionality, and quality that can be verified by its customers. If you have something proprietary, you need to develop in house, and don't have the technical skill sets in house to do the work, it will take time to acquire and develop those resources. If you have to go with a third party to develop your idea, make sure that appropriate *nondisclose* and *noncompete* elements are part of your contract with the vendor.

The various contract types from a high-level perspective are well enough defined in the *PMBOK*, so I won't rehash them here except to say that recently, almost all the contract types I've seen are Firm Fixed Price vehicles with the occasional T&M (Time and Materials) contract.

## Plan Contracting

This is the area where the actual needs from the external vendor are formalized in documentation culminating in the creation of an RFQ (Request for Quote) or an RFP (Request for Proposal).

The key input is the Contract Statement of Work.

The key outputs are the Procurement Documents (RFQ or RFP) and the Evaluation Criteria used to evaluate seller responses to the RFQ/RFP.

The primary tools and techniques are whatever standard forms the organization uses to help facilitate the RFQ/RFP process.

SELLER'S WARNING: This all sounds fairly cut-and-dried and it usually is. However, there is a caveat of which you should be aware: Know something about the motives and intentions of the buyer before you sink thousands of dollars, resources, and time into an elaborate RFP response. A former employee of a major U.S. oil company confided to me that the company would frequently issue an RFP but not to actually have the work done by an outside vendor. It was used to either (1) validate the buyer's software architectural approach by comparing it to solutions from third parties or (2) validate that the buyer had covered all the potential options for development by validating their approach against third-party solutions. It was a ploy designed to obtain some free consulting. The issuers of the RFP would then go back to management and say, "See—we had it figured right all along. Look at the RFP responses. We have validation that we are offering a cutting-edge solution and that we are on the right track from a technology standpoint."

One way you can tell if the buyer is playing games with you is simply to ask the following: What are the deadlines for RFP selection, development, and delivery of the product or service? If the buyer is vague about any of this, thank them for their time and offer a *no bid*. Unless you are in the business of offering free consulting at your own expense, pass on this opportunity.

## Request Seller Responses

Once the RFQ/RFP has been issued, the seller responses are returned by a specified deadline that has been spelled out in the originating RFQ/RFP document.

The key input is the Procurement Document itself—either the RFQ or the RFP.

The key output is the Proposals received from the vendors.

The key T&T is the Bidder Conferences.

Usually an organization will have a list of approved vendors that they have prescreened where there may be some type of Master Services Agreement already in place with the vendor. It greatly simplifies the assessment process by getting most of the administrivia out of the way up front so the team can focus on evaluating the key elements in the RFQ/RFP response.

Essentially, once the bidder responses are received, the buyer will then cull all the responses down to a short list of vendors that appear to have the best and most cost-effective proposals. At this point, the buyer will hold a bidders conference where the vendors are collected to ask questions and clarify elements in the RFQ/RFP prior to oral presentations. In the oral presentation, the vendor is one-on-one with the buyer and does a presentation of the solution, high-lighting the key elements in the solution to the buyer. The buyer can then ask direct questions of the vendor to clarify any points in the presentation and the solution.

In most RFQ/RFP responses it is usually stipulated by the buyer that any price structure offered in the RFQ/RFP shall remain in force for six months after the RFQ/RFP selection is made. This prevents any price gouging by the vendor in case the buyer needs additional time to evaluate and select the best proposal (or if the originally se-lected vendor's solution proves to be nonviable).

## Select Sellers

Here all the proposals submitted by qualified vendors are evaluated and a solution selected.

The key inputs are the Evaluation Criteria and the Proposals. These are the two key elements needed to select the vendor for the work being solicited.

The key outputs are the Selected Seller(s) and the Contract. If it is one RFP and one vendor you are seeking to retain, the seller will be selected and the contract will be drawn up.

Of the tools and techniques, several of the tools such as Weight-ing System, Screening System, and Seller Rating system can be usually combined into an evaluation matrix that considers all the ele-ments simultaneously. One of the most useful, effective, and tamper-proof tools in this area (unfortunately no longer referenced in the *PMBOK*) is the Analytic Hierarchy Process (AHP). For details on how to implement an AHP, see Chapter 9. The other key tool and technique is Contract Negotiation. This in itself is a specialized area that you would be wise to learn at the hand of an expert.

## Contract Administration

This area primarily focuses on ensuring that the vendor and the buyer meet their contractual obligations. Usually there is a specific area of the business that manages the legalities of the contract and will do so separately from the team managing the project.

The key input is the Contract—it outlines what the vendor is required to deliver and when it is to be delivered.

The key outputs include Contract Documentation and Requested Changes, which can also include Corrective Actions to bring the vendor back in compliance with contract terms.

The primary tools and techniques are the Contract Change Control System and Performance Reporting. The change control system will keep track of any contract modifications needed along with the associated costs and timeline changes that result. The Performance Reporting tells you how your vendor is doing and the information collected here ties into Buyer-Conducted Performance Review and Inspections and Audits Tools.

## Contract Closure

Contract Closure verifies the work that was done (or not done) and formally closes out the contract prior to project closeout. Understand there are generally two ways to close out a contract ahead of its stated completion:

- *Cancellation for Convenience*—usually occurs if the original condition of the business need changes or the buyer changes its mind. Here the contract can be closed out, the vendor gets paid for what it completed—no harm, no foul—and all parties go their separate ways.

- *Cancellation for Cause*—generally engages the buyer's legal department and a legal action is taken against the vendor, usually for a cardinal breach in the contract. I have seen general contractors get thrown off projects due to cardinal contract breaches—sometimes there are damage claims filed against the vendor depending on the gravity of the breach.

Otherwise, the contract closes out with all deliverables agreed on and there is a formal acceptance of the work product.

The key input is the Contract Documentation.

The key output is the Closed Contract.

The primary T&T is the Procurement Audit.

# PROJECT INTEGRATION MANAGEMENT

We saved this section for the end so that after reviewing all the individual project components you can see how they are tied together in the Integration section. Figure 3.12 charts project integration management.

## Develop Project Charter

This is the document that formally authorizes the project—it funds the project and identifies the project manager.

The key input is the Project Statement of Work. While the other elements such as Enterprise Environmental Factors and the Organizational Process Assets support this function—the specifics of the project are outlined in the Project Statement of Work.

The only output is the completed Project Charter.

The key tool and technique in this area is utilizing some organized approach to implementing project management processes. That can be your Project Management Methodology, a Project Framework, or whatever process the organization has created to put discipline and rigor around its internal project processes.

**Figure 3.12**

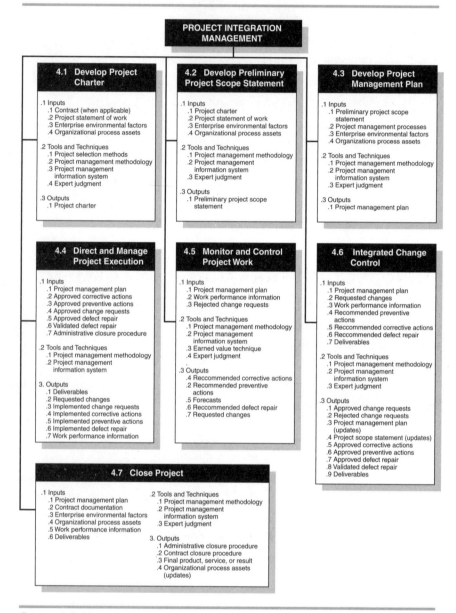

Source: *A Guide to the Project Management Body of Knowledge*, 3rd ed. Project Management Institute, 2004.

## Develop Preliminary Scope Statement

This is the area that defines the project, the aim and goals of the project—in short, why we are gathered here at all.

The key inputs are the Project Charter and the Project Statement of Work.

The only output is the Preliminary Scope Statement.

The critical tool and technique is once again having a disciplined Project Methodology or Project Framework.

## Develop Project Management Plan

The project management plan is your roadmap for how you are going to manage the project and either contains the other management plans or has embedded links to these plans that have been created as separate documents.

The key input is the Preliminary Scope Statement.

The only output is the completed Project Management Plan. In most organizations, this is a peer-reviewed document that requires signoff by the key project stakeholders. It is critical that your stakeholders agree on the project approach.

The primary T&T is, for the third time, your Project Management Methodology or Project Framework. However, to support this framework, we need a system that allows you to track all the documentation, code, system configuration, and any potential changes to the system. Thus, on the hard-core tools side, you need a Configuration Management System and a Change Management System, preferably at a level that gives you end-to-end control over the entire process. Clear Case, CVS, PVCS, and other tools are well-known Configuration Management and Change Management tools. Documentum is used in situations where all documents require configuration and change control across an entire enterprise. While this *can* be done manually, the recommendation is to let a system handle the administrivia programmatically—it will save you big headaches in the long run.

## Direct and Manage Project Execution

Once the project plan and your systems are prepared and in place, you can now manage the execution of the project across its various phases.

The key input is an *approved* Project Management Plan.

The key outputs are your Deliverables and Work Performance Information. You want to know as you execute the project what is being delivered, when it is being delivered, who owns the deliverable (i.e., the responsible party), what issues arise and their impacts, risk triggers, budget burn rate, and so forth. In other words, you want the key measurements from each of the management plans: Scope, Budget, Timeline, Quality, Human Resources, Communications, and Risk and Procurement.

The key tool and technique that helps you collect, analyze, summarize, and interpret all this data is your Project Management Information System.

## Monitor and Control Project Work

Monitor and Control activities are performed simultaneously with managing the project execution.

The key input is the Work Performance information.

The key output is similar to the Quality output: Recommended Preventive Activities and Forecasts. Keeping defects from occurring is always less expensive in the long run than applying corrective action or repairing defects (rework). Forecasting is the best tool you can use, if it's done well, for helping you to formulate the best preventive actions to take. That's why it's a good idea to use these two approaches hand-in-hand.

The T&Ts are, once again, the Project Management Information System and in some cases use of the EVT. When using EVT it is important to recall the description in the Cost Management section and determine whether you have sufficient historical information to determine Earned Value numbers.

## Integrated Change Control

It's called *integrated* change control rather than simply change control for the following reason: All changes in any aspect of the project must be coordinated centrally to determine whether there are any cross-functional dependencies or impacts that result if a change is implemented. Changes impact the product configuration and can impose additional risks or issues that must be addressed by the project team.

The key inputs are the Requested Changes, Recommended Preventive Actions, and the Deliverables.

The key outputs are primarily the Approved or Rejected Change Requests. Any defect repair, corrective, or preventive action will be referenced in a Change Request (CR) and that CR can be either approved or rejected.

The key T&T is, once again, the Project Management Information System—the repository where all CR information is collected and reviewed.

## Close Project

Closure activities can occur at various points in the project. Most think that *closure* refers only to the end of the project; but in reality there are phases of a project that need to be completed and closed off before other phases can begin:

- The project initiation phase needs to be closed out before the essential planning activities begin.
- Planning needs to be completed; design and requirements documents need to be baselined and approved before coding can begin.
- Coding must be completed before overall system testing can start.

The reason for this separation is that a business will usually have charge codes associated with various aspects of the work; once an area of work is closed out, reopening closed charge codes is a nightmare—not to mention outright impossible in some organizations. If a design or requirement needs to be revisited later in the project, it is documented as a CR and logged under the CR charge code so that the organization has some idea how good a job it did at creating the initial estimates and following through with them.

The key inputs are Contract Documentation and Deliverables. The Contract specifies the external deliverables while the Deliverables specify the internal deliverables. At the close of the project, you need to know if what was scoped was actually delivered.

The key outputs are in order: (1) Contract Closure, (2) Final Product, Service, or result, and (3) Administrative Closure Procedure.

The key tool and technique is (you guessed it) the Project Management Information System.

Once the project is closed, take the whole project team to your favorite restaurant or watering hole and celebrate! You've earned it.

---

NOTE: Please understand that the short list presented in this chapter doesn't cover every situation, but it will keep you focused on the key elements that generally need the most attention. Also be mindful that the framework as shown here is used fundamentally in a *waterfall* project implementation. See the next chapter for a general summary on the various Development Lifecycle Models (DLMs), of which the waterfall implementation is one.

---

## NOTES

1. *A Guide to the Project Management Body of Knowledge*, 3rd ed., Project Management Institute, 2004.
2. "Parametric Cost Estimating Handbook," http://cost.jsc.nasa.gov/PCEHHTML/pceh.htm.
3. *PMBOK*, 173.
4. Ibid., 185.
5. *Quality Is Free*, Philip B. Crosby, Mentor, 1980.
6. *PMBOK*, 221
7. *Risk Intelligence*, David Apgar, Harvard Business School Press, 2006.
8. Merriam-Webster's Online Dictionary, 2007.

# Chapter
# 4

# The Dog Ate My Project Plan

# And Other Management Fables

"Our business world has accepted errors as a way of life. We live with them, we plan for them, and we make excuses for them. They have become part of the personality of our business. Our employees quickly recognize our standards and create errors so that they will not disappoint us."

—H. James Harrington

MANY PROJECT TEAMS and project managers attempt to execute all of their projects based on the waterfall approach to project management, which approximately follows the steps as shown in Figure 4.1. Notice an attempt has been made in the figure to show how the process areas shown in the 2004 *PMBOK* map against or are included in the Software Development Life Cycle (SDLC) steps.

I've heard the diagram in Figure 4.1 frequently referenced as an *intelligent waterfall* design. It is intelligent because it recognizes that the budget numbers are pretty much a SWAG (Scientific Wild-Ass

Figure 4.1

## Figure 4.1

### Waterfall Project Implementation

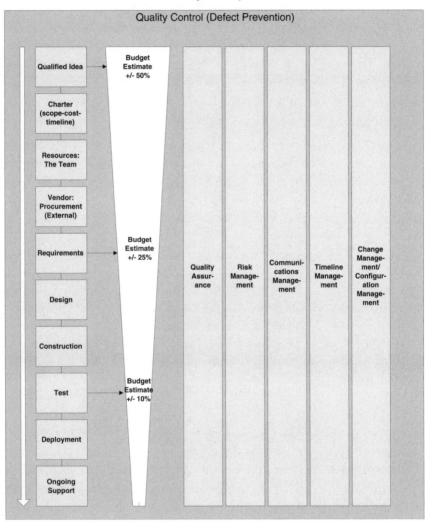

Guess) at the beginning of the SDLC and then tighten up as the true progressive elaboration kicks in and the team estimates become better as they learn more. I've also added a specific slant not included in the 2004 *PMBOK* in that the Quality (defect prevention) idea wraps the entire process.

While this generic diagram appears to illuminate some kind of *development standard*, the fundamental issue with utilizing the waterfall approach to all software development is that it simply doesn't work. The waterfall SDLC approach works best when you have a clear understanding of the all the components, parts, and pieces of your development initiative and the effort is de facto a low-risk proposition. The problem occurs when the organization tries to shoehorn this approach into every software development project and then wonders why the project runs into huge discovery and CR events, pushing out the timeline and driving up the costs.

The 2000 version of the *PMBOK* briefly referenced the Spiral Software, System Development Lifecycle Model (SDLM) that illuminated a different and effective alternative to the waterfall approach to software development.[1] It is unfortunate that this information was removed in the 2004 version—the 2000 version gave PMs a starting point to explore other SDLMs to determine which SDLM was most appropriate (and the most useful) for the projects they were implementing. These are important concepts to cover for a PM engaged in IT project management.

Therefore, in the following you will find a basic list of SDLM types that were never touched on in the 2000 or the 2004 versions of the *PMBOK*, with a few more thrown in for good measure. Reviewing these SDLMs will at least help point you in the right direction based on what kind of project scenario you are facing.

## THE EIGHT BASIC SDLMS PLUS ONE

In order to be consistent with standard terminology and concepts in the industry, the elements below are consistent with the following specifications:

- IEEE/EIA 12207.0–1996, 12207.1–1997 and 12207.2–1997 (i.e., ISO 12207)
- ISO/IEC 15288

There is no single SDLM that is the best one to use in every project situation. There is no *best model*—the best model is one that helps you successfully complete the project based on what you are attempting to do. Use the correct model and your chances of success increase dramatically.

Let's take a look at the short list of eight plus one*:

1. Waterfall
2. Iterative/Agile
3. Spiral
4. Evolutionary
5. COTS
6. Rehosting
7. Reengineering
8. Maintenance/Repair
9. *Automatic Application Generation (4 GL)

Here are brief descriptions of each model and what they are designed to help you accomplish:

1. **Waterfall.** In a pure waterfall implementation, activities are implemented in a *finish-to-start* relationship in that a subsequent activity is not started until the current activity is finished. Usually there will be Phase Gate reviews at the end of each activity held by management to determine if the project is ready to advance to the next activity. The driver for the waterfall approach is documentation. In other words, any interim deliverable is not the software or hardware, but the documentation representing the current activity—for example, Project Plan, Business Requirements, Technical Requirements, High Level Design, and the like. The key element to understand is that the system is not delivered in stages or increments, but is delivered to the customer at the completion of all project activities in one large, big-bang monolithic delivery. This can be a big problem, especially if the client is shocked by what is delivered ("This is not at all what I

imagined it would be . . . "). The waterfall model works well when the following conditions are met:

a. The project team is working with familiar technologies.
b. Requirements are well understood from the start of the project.
c. The project is well supported by management.
d. The users of the system are engaged and are active participants in the project process.

Waterfall works best when errors can be found early in the project lifecycle and are relatively inexpensive to fix. The issue with the waterfall approach is that it is an inflexible, compliance-driven model that is highly change averse.

2. **Iterative/agile**. There are a number of effective incremental approaches to software development that include proprietary and nonproprietary approaches. A partial list of these *agile* approaches include RUP, XP, Crystal, and Scrum. The iterative/incremental approach has been shown to be very effective in an environment where speed and flexibility are essential; where the projects being undertaken include high-risk product and process development; and where the big risks must be mitigated up front in the process. I've heard some PMs state that the iterative approach is nothing but a series of miniwaterfall iterations. Mechanically, that may appear to be what is occurring if you are on the outside looking in at the process; however, it also shows a deep misunderstanding of how iterative/agile processes really work and what they are. Iterative development is a true rethinking of the software development process that at a very high level can be summarized with the following idea: Software development, contrary to what most people believe, is not performed on an assembly line, but has to be inspected, tested, and corrected/adjusted *as the issues occur*. From one perspective, it is Lean Six Sigma meets software development. In another respect, it is Shigeo Shingo's idea of 100% source inspection applied to software development. Using Scrum as an example, some of the key elements to understand are:

a. Work is performed in short time-boxed increments (15–30 days) called *sprints*.
b. The work is prioritized so that the most critical elements can be addressed first.
c. If there are elements not completed in the sprint, they go into a backlog that can be reprioritized by the customer and the development team for the next sprint.
d. A working, tested, "shippable" component is delivered at the completion of the sprint that the customer/client can use and deliver feedback to the development team. It is here that the feedback can be used to make adjustments for the next sprint.
e. Each sprint utilizes what was built before and adds on to the delivered product—thus each iteration is continually being tested as each shippable increment is created.
f. Documentation is created as a collaborative effort between the customer and the developer. The important point is that documentation is not etched in stone and something by which project team compliance is measured. The process is not about compliance to a methodology—it's about delivery and putting useable product into the customer's hands.

   As a result, the entire software development process changes from one of a compliance-driven, change-averse approach requiring an extensive scope definition process, an extensive risk assessment process, a top-heavy change management process, and constant recalibration of the budget and the timeline, to one of:

g. Defining what is most important to the customer up front
h. Reprioritizing needs as they change (and they always do)
i. Putting a working model in the customer's hands so that they become participants in the development process instead of throwing the requirements over the wall and hoping they get what they asked for in 10 months
j. Each iteration expanding on the functionality delivered so the customer participates in the product taking shape

    k. Budget expended incrementally so that the customer clearly sees the relationship between what was spent and what got built

    l. Change managed incrementally and as part of the time-boxed iteration

   m. Documentation created and modified as the product evolves

      Figure 4.2 is a diagram of one approach to implementing an iterative development cycle.

3. **Spiral.** The spiral model is a risk-oriented DLM that breaks a software-intensive project into a series of subprojects. Each subproject addresses one or more of the major risks until all major risks have been mitigated. After the risks are mitigated, one or more additional subprojects are performed to fully develop the software. The spiral model is a relatively complex DLM when compared to the others. The ever-widening radial increments depict cumulative cost incurred in accomplishing the steps to date and each quadrant measures the progress made in completing each cycle of the spiral. With the Spiral model, activities are initiated near the center of the diagram. The diagram in Figure 4.3 is an example of the spiral model combined with an incremental approach (from Barry Boehm's 1988 article, "A Spiral Model of Software Development and Enhancement").

4. **Evolutionary.** The evolutionary model is particularly useful when the system requirements and associated technology are changing rapidly and/or not well understood. In this case, the customer will not be able to commit to a set of requirements because they may not understand the application. Like the incremental/iterative model, it produces a progressively elaborated, incremental build of the system, in which the customer is a participant. With this approach you cannot easily plan the work effort, estimate all costs, and create the schedule for entire project at the outset. This is because the scope of the deliverable and the number of iterations needed to complete the deliverable are not known or well understood at the commencement of the project. Contract vehicles used in this

**Figure 4.2**

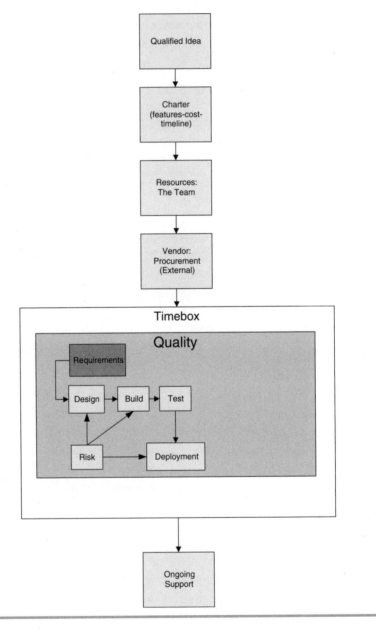

## Incremental Project Implementation

**Figure 4.3**

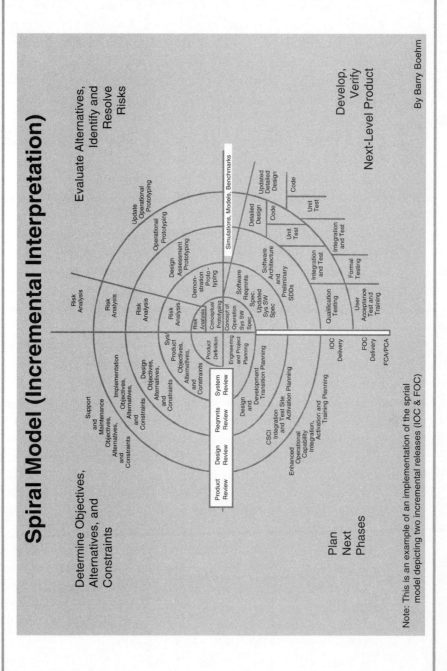

Spiral Model (Incremental Interpretation)

By Barry Boehm

Note: This is an example of an implementation of the spiral model depicting two incremental releases (IOC & FOC)

instance are generally of the Cost Plus or Time and Materials variety. You may also want to place each iteration under a separate contract. From a technical perspective, it may be very difficult to develop an architecture robust enough to adequately support all of the evolutions of the product. This may then lead to major architectural changes to the product and significant cost growth as the product evolves.

5. **COTS.** The commercial-off-the-shelf (COTS) integration model is fundamentally a purchased DLM that contains most of the functionality required by the organization. If a large percentage of the customer's needs are already addressed in the "vanilla" implementation of the software, all that remains is a small customization and configuration effort to implement the system. This type of system is usually selected as the result of an RFP process by which a number of COTS products are evaluated and matched against the organization's internal requirements. It also means that the organization had determined through a *buy-or-build analysis* that it was better to buy in this instance. The product finally selected is usually the one that meets and/or exceeds customer expectation on the key requirements. Notice the use of the term *key requirements*—while the output of this process is a system that will likely meet many of the customer's requirements, it will be unlikely to meet *all* of them. The system functionality being developed is driven by what is available in existing COTS products. If a capability is not supported by a COTS product, that capability is left out of the system being developed; thus as many requirements are satisfied as possible given the constraints of the COTS products. The COTS integration DLM starts with an activity to determine the initial system objective. Once the initial system objective is defined, a formal evaluation of the COTS product is performed using three simultaneously implemented key criteria: (1) domain analysis, (2) requirements analysis, and (3) architecture design. Domain analysis means that competing COTS products in the segment are identified, benchmarked, and analyzed for use in your proposed system. Proper due

diligence must be performed, which should include interviews with other customers of the COTS vendor as well as marketplace evaluation of the product to evaluate the efficacy of the solution. (Vendors will almost always offer you the spindoctored version of their "outstanding" solution, not empirical data on their implementations or the overall quality of their products.) Make sure you observe these products in action, to truly understand their capability. Requirements analysis is conducted in conjunction with domain analysis to map the customer needs and requirements against the existing feature set of the COTS software to determine what the system can support. The Architecture design produces the overall architecture of the system as it is proposed for your environment and is based on the initially selected COTS products. An initial selection of the COTS products is the outcome of these three simultaneous activities.

6. **Rehosting.** The software *rehost* model is used when your customer wants to move an existing legacy software system from its current platform to another platform—for example, from an IBM 390 to a cluster of Sun Fire X4600 servers. This migration can involve changing the current hardware, development language, and/or operating system. The reason for this migration is typically based on the need for a technology upgrade or high maintenance costs associated with the current system. For example, unavailability of hardware, excessive downtime, or a version of an operating system no longer supported by the vendor will drive a rehosting scenario. In order to make continual upgrades to the system, the operating system may need to be replaced. A key point in the rehost model is that the same functionality is retained from the initial system when migrating to the new system. The basic functionality and overall design of the rehosted system should be essentially the same as that of the initial system. While software rehost projects can add some functionality to the newly upgraded system, this type of activity is usually reserved for a reengineering DLM.

7. **Reengineering.** The reengineering model is best utilized when your customer is considering replacing an existing system with a new and functionally enhanced system. This model consists of performing a reverse-engineering activity prior to implementing one or a combination of the other DLMs. What it generally means is that you have an old system that has been functioning well for 25 to 30 years that at this point requires an upgrade, only you discover upon examination that:

   a. Any documentation for how to maintain the system has been lost or misplaced.

   b. All the resources that maintained the system have left the company.

   c. All of the original coders of the system are dead.

   Once the system is reengineered, this project will frequently turn into a rehosting project or in some cases a brand-new development. The reverse-engineering process involves studying the actual system to extract the requirements, architectural design information, and any potentially reuseable components. When conducting reverse engineering, you must consider what items from the existing system will be reused. The options are basically two: (1) Reverse engineering can go all the way back to the requirements level; thus nothing beyond the requirements is used in the development of a new system; or (2) reverse engineering can produce design information to include identification of existing components to be reused in the new system. Interestingly, a re-engineering effort can turn into a rehosting project once the initial system functionality is well understood. The organization may look for ways to enhance the initial software functionality by moving the software onto a more robust platform, thus reducing costs and improving performance.

8. **Maintenance.** This model is used by projects to fix defects or to implement modifications and enhancements in production systems. Typically, inputs to the maintenance model are known as trouble tickets or problem reports that describe software bugs or implementation defects in the system, as well as

requests for minor system enhancements. These minor modification or enhancement requests come in a variety of forms ranging from something as simple as a problem report to a request for proposal (RFP) on a task order contract. Maintenance problems are generally addressed in the form of a service level agreement (SLA) that details the level of response based on the needs of the customer. Response times range from immediate response for a critical system due to a system failure to normal criticality timeframes for resolving minor bugs or installing updated software or replacement parts. For example, on a software-intensive system, the software might have a standard update cycle occurring every 6 months. Normal criticality would mean that the fix could wait till the next six-month build was delivered. Contrast this with a critical response, which is an "all hands on deck" scenario requiring a fix to be delivered as soon as possible. A critical system is defined as one that will cause the business substantial financial loss or has severe regulatory penalties attached in the event of a failure.

9. **Automatic application generation/4GL.** This approach uses *rapid application development (RAD)* tools for the development of software. Examples of rapid application tools that fit this model include Powerbuilder, Dataflex Object Oriented 4GL, IronSpeed, PowerVista, Proc-Blaster, and scores of others. If you are interested in these tools, go to http://www .artofprogramming.net/development/dev_caserad.html for a short list of CASE, RAD, and 4GL software tools. The key to understanding this specific lifecycle model is that the deliverable software product is generated primarily by the RAD tool. This approach is not really different from the previously listed DLMs—it basically uses the same principles that exist in other DLMs, such as the incremental, COTS integration, and evolutionary models. What makes it different is the degree of automation that is happening within the model. In reality, the same DLM processes as previously outlined are still being performed; the difference is that they being performed rapidly and concurrently by the RAD tool(s). The strong advantage

with the 4GL (fourth-generation language) model is the speed at which a system can be implemented for your customer's use. The RAD tools enable development to proceed very quickly after requirements have been defined. The second key element is the degree to which the customer is involved in the development process and how fast they see the implications of their decisions in a working system. Typically, there are many iterations of requirements with customers in this type of lifecycle and you could easily combine the 4GL approach with agile/iterative methods.

Of the above SDLMs, the ones typically utilized for new development are the waterfall, iterative/agile, spiral, and evolutionary models. The grid in Figure 4.4 summarizes the important aspects of each.

Once again, there is no single best model to use when developing software—it depends on what you are attempting to accomplish. However, a key aspect to making the initial determination on which approach to use seems to dwell on the risk levels associated with the project. The higher the risk, the more you may want to employ iterative/agile approaches to development. All the data on software

**Figure 4.4**

| MODEL | Requirements Defined First | Multiple Development Cycles | Multiple Customer Deliveries | Process Driver |
|---|---|---|---|---|
| Waterfall | Yes | No | No | Well understood |
| Incremental | Yes/No | Yes | Yes | Risk reduction improved quality |
| Spiral | No | Yes | Yes/No | Risk reduction |
| Evolutionary | No | Yes/No | Yes | Requirements not well understood |

projects points to a much higher success rate when utilizing iterative approaches. One way to find out is to get some reasonable approximation of the risks your project may face to help you determine which SDLM is the most appropriate.

I frequently ask organizations if they use some kind of risk-assessment matrix in the planning phases of their projects to get some idea of which SDLM is the most appropriate—most do not. If you work for one of those companies that do not use this approach, feel free to copy the grid/questionnaire in Figure 4.5 and try it out. It may be very illuminating.

Answer each question in the grid to the best of your knowledge. If there is doubt, choose the pessimistic answer (the higher-scoring answer). How to score the grid will be shown at the completion of the questionnaire. While this is not an exhaustive listing, understand that it does include some of the more significant risk elements in a project.

Fill out the questionnaire by totaling the numbers placed in each column; total all the *1*s, *5*s, and *10*s. Then add up the totals of all the totals and divide by 39 (the number of questions in the questionnaire). The following criteria can be used to perform an overall evaluation of your project risk:

Low Risk: 1.00–3.24

Medium Risk: 3.25–6.24

High Risk: 6.25–10.00

This tool can be used to surface your project issues up front in the process so that the project team can brainstorm ideas on how to address the issues and reduce the project risk, while also determining the best SDLM to use for the project.

One final word about agile approaches: They are growing, they work, they produce better products, and customers are more satisfied with the result. While the agile approach is not a magic bullet, it does address how customers and software engineers actually get work

**Figure 4.5**

| Question | 1 (Low) | 5 (Med) | 10 (High) |
|---|---|---|---|
| Human Factors | | | |
| 1.1 Project length:<br>3–6 months (Low)<br>6–12 months (Med)<br>>12 months (High) | | | |
| 1.2 Deadline:<br>Doable (Low)<br>Some risk (Med)<br>Very aggressive (High) | | | |
| 1.3 Possibility of scope creep | | | |
| 1.4 Team size:<br>1–5 (Low)<br>6–12 (Med)<br>>12 (High) | | | |
| 1.5 Customer/project team interaction:<br>Daily (Low)<br>Monthly (Med)<br>At start and end only (High) | | | |
| 1.6 Project budget:<br>Realistic (Low)<br>Contingency reserve (Med)<br>Complete SWAG (High) | | | |
| 1.7 Executive support risk (Lowest is best) | | | |
| 1.8 User support risk (Lowest is best) | | | |
| 1.9 Cultural change risk (i.e., does the project significantly change the way people will work when implemented?) (Lowest is best) | | | |

| Question | 1 (Low) | 5 (Med) | 10 (High) |
|---|---|---|---|
| 1.10 Learning curve risk (Lowest is best) | | | |
| 1.11 PM authority:<br>    Projectized (Low)<br>    Matrixed (Med)<br>    Functional (High) | | | |
| 1.12 Experienced PM risk (Lowest is best) | | | |
| 1.13 PM dedication:<br>    Focused on this project<br>        only (Low)<br>    50% focus on this project<br>        (Med)<br>    < 50% focus on this project<br>        (High) | | | |
| 1.14 Project plan:<br>    Realistic, peer reviewed and<br>        approved (Low)<br>    Progressively elaborated<br>        (Med)<br>    No discernable plan (High) | | | |
| 1.15 Project priority:<br>    Critical—high<br>        visibility (Low)<br>    Moderate (Med)<br>    Low (High) | | | |
| 1.16 Project lifecycle:<br>    Defined and enforced (Low)<br>    Defined not enforced (Med)<br>    Not defined (High) | | | |
| 1.17 Team availability:<br>    Dedicated project team (Low)<br>    Key personnel committed<br>        (Med)<br>    Unknown (High) | | | |

*(Continues)*

**Figure 4.5 (Continued)**

| Question | 1 (Low) | 5 (Med) | 10 (High) |
|---|---|---|---|
| 1.18 Team location:<br>Co-located (Low)<br>One site (Med)<br>Multisite (or state) (High) | | | |
| 1.19 Team skill set:<br>Understands all technologies<br>(Low)<br>Requires some training (Med)<br>Unfamiliar technologies (High) | | | |
| 1.20 Dependence on vendors:<br>10% or less (Low)<br>11–30% (Med)<br>>30% (High) | | | |
| 1.21 Vendor quality:<br>Verified dependable (Low)<br>Meets most<br>deliverables (80%)<br>to spec (Med)<br>Unpredictable (High) | | | |
| 1.22 Management:<br>Responsive and focused (Low)<br>Usually responsive<br>but diffused focus (Med)<br>Thrown over the wall (High) | | | |
| 1.23 Issue resolution:<br>Issue log is tracked and<br>managed (Low)<br>Only high impact issues<br>are tracked (Med)<br>No issues ownership<br>or resolution timeframes (High) | | | |

| Question | 1 (Low) | 5 (Med) | 10 (High) |
|---|---|---|---|
| 1.25 User dispersal:<br>    Project focuses on a single<br>        department user group<br>        (Low)<br>    Between 2–4 user groups (Med)<br>    Five more user groups or<br>        market segments (High) | | | |
| **Technology** | | | |
| 2.1 Development<br>complexity risk<br>(Lower is best) | | | |
| 2.2 Development methodology<br>employed?<br>    Standardized and enforced<br>        (Low)<br>    Some repeatable elements<br>        (Med)<br>    Little to none (High) | | | |
| 2.3 Reuse employed?<br>    75% (Low)<br>    50–75% (Med)<br>    <50 % (High) | | | |
| 2.4 Software:<br>    4GL only (Low)<br>    COBOL, Java, C++, etc. (Med)<br>    New or ASM (High) | | | |
| 2.5 Software deliverable:<br>    None or COTS (Low)<br>    Reuse (Med)<br>    New development (High) | | | |
| 2.6 Data conversion:<br>    None (Low)<br>    Minimal (Med)<br>    Entire system or unknown<br>        (High) | | | |

*(Continues)*

**Figure 4.5 (Continued)**

| Question | 1 (Low) | 5 (Med) | 10 (High) |
|---|---|---|---|
| 2.7 System complexity—deliverable:<br>　　Single system (Low)<br>　　Multiple system—one site<br>　　　(Med)<br>　　Multiple Systems—multisite<br>　　　(High) | | | |
| 2.8 Change Control Utilized?<br>　　Programmatic (Low)<br>　　Manual (Med)<br>　　None (High) | | | |
| 2.9 Configuration management?<br>　　Programmatic (e.g., Clear<br>　　　Case) (Low)<br>　　Manual (Med)<br>　　None (High) | | | |
| 2.10 Hardware:<br>　　Use Existing infrastructure<br>　　　(Low)<br>　　Some new infrastructure (e.g.,<br>　　　single server or workstations)<br>　　　(Med)<br>　　Significant new infrastructure<br>　　　(e.g., multiple fully loaded<br>　　　racks fully fault tolerant)<br>　　　(High) | | | |
| 2.11 Testing:<br>　　Use existing infrastructure<br>　　　(Low)<br>　　Existing infrastructure—<br>　　　new process (Med)<br>　　Now infrastructure and<br>　　　processes (High) | | | |

| Question | 1 (Low) | 5 (Med) | 10 (High) |
|---|---|---|---|
| 2.12 UAT (user acceptance testing):<br>    Rigorous UAT review (Low)<br>    Some review of feature set<br>       (Med)<br>    Little or no review (High) | | | |
| 2.13 Handoff to support:<br>    Disciplined, documented<br>       handoff (Low)<br>    Some key elements of the<br>       deliverable are reviewed<br>       with the support<br>       organization (Med)<br>    Little or no support team<br>       interaction (High) | | | |
| 2.14 System documentation:<br>    Detailed, verified via<br>       configuration management<br>       (Low)<br>    Documentation—minimal<br>       verification (Med)<br>    Ad-hoc documentation (High) | | | |
| Total Score: | | | |

done in the information technology space. At some point soon, the approach will be the predominant way you run software projects. See Chapter 5, Principle #9, for more information on agile approaches.

## NOTE

1. *A Guide to the Project Management Body of Knowledge,* 2000 Edition, pp. 16–17, PMI, 2000.

# Chapter
# 5

# The Hitchhiker's Guide to Project Management

"Anyone who is capable of getting themselves made President should on no account be allowed to do the job."

—Douglas Adams, *Hitchhiker's Guide to the Galaxy*

AFTER A NUMBER OF years of managing and leading programs and projects, it seems that most IT projects can be defined as:

*primarily an endeavor initiated by people who can't describe what they want, constructed by people who can't describe what they do, and delivered to people who can't understand what was built.*

There are numerous variants on the preceding statement, but they generally point to a similar end; something in the project scope gets missed, requirements are misinterpreted or reinterpreted, and the end result is not what the customer was expecting.

Here are a few tools, precepts, principles, and guiding concepts to help you navigate the minefield of managing high-risk, high-intensity, confrontational, and otherwise high-stress projects and yet continue to keep an even emotional state, get some sleep, and function with a level head while others around you are bouncing off the walls in crisis mode. While some of the principles may appear to be tongue-in-cheek observations, they always address an underlying issue. Truth is usually more hilarious than fiction, and always remember: Comedy is a very serious business.

Notice that there are *no rules*. Rules are for sports that are administered by referees. Managing a project is not an athletic event, contrary to what most CEOs and sales types would have you believe while attending the biannual or quarterly corporate review. There are certainly parallels, but that's as far as it goes.

## HITCHHIKER'S TOOLS

Here is a brief listing and description of some of the most useful *thinking tools* you can have in your PM arsenal of problem solvers. These tools have been developed over the course of 70 years by quality practitioners and pioneers across the world:

**The Five *Whys*.** These are useful in determining an underlying or root cause of a failure or core problem. Continue to ask *why* when an explanation for an event is offered until you reach the proverbial "I don't know." When the ultimate answer is, "I don't know," that's where the real investigation begins.

**The Eight Wastes.** These are described as the "Seven Wastes" in the previous chapter, plus one:
1. Waste from overproduction
2. Excess transportation
3. Excess inventory
4. Waiting time
5. Processing waste
6. Wasted motion
7. Waste from production defects

**8.** Underuse of the worker's creativity or problem-solving abilities
Review your business processes and see where these wastes can be removed.

**Rolled Throughput Yield (RTY).** This is especially useful when your company uses a business process with many steps. This useful computation shows the likelihood that your order, insurance claim, or manufactured part will roll through your process defect free.

**Monte Carlo Analysis** (statistical probability analysis on steroids). The beauty of statistics is that it works. Where statistics gets a bad rap is when every manner of spin-doctor claims he has used "scientific statistical methods" to validate whatever position he is attempting to prove. Monte Carlo is a valuable scheduling probability tool as well as an excellent risk-assessment probability tool. See Chapter 10.

**Decision Tree Analysis.** This is useful in computing probability of investment return based on different approaches compared side by side in the decision tree. Numerous scenarios can be executed simultaneously and their potential paths predicted. This is particularly effective in estimating investment potential in projects. See Chapter 11.

**Analytical Hierarchy Process (AHP).** The AHP is used by international governments and major corporations in the decision process. It is very helpful in areas when the decision is complex, or can involve two or more groups in conflict over an issue or decision. See Chapter 9.

## HITCHHIKER'S PRINCIPLES

The following set of principles is offered in no particular order. They could be organized into groups, but then, due to time constraints or stress, you might skip over some really useful information. Hence, you'll just have to deal with each as it comes. Section 2 of this book is the organized part—so if you want to dispense with the precepts and go straight to the tools, feel free to dive right in there.

*Principle #1:* **If your project process is more work than the actual *work*, you need to rethink and simplify your process.**

The world is littered with proprietary processes and methodologies developed for businesses that are primarily designed to generate sales for the vendor rather than actually help the customer. One of the processes that comes to mind is *Method/1*, a project process developed by the now-defunct Arthur Andersen. The documentation for the process took up an entire bookshelf that was longer than a person's outstretched arms could span. You would have been lucky to have read through this anchor weight of volumes in two years' time, much less to have been able to put it to use.

In every interview conducted, every user of the system had the same thing to say about it: "I'm not doing my job anymore—I'm doing Method/1." The only people that did have something positive to relay about the process were usually those who had something to do with its purchase and had a stake in looking good to their superiors: "Of course the process is good—I recommended it!"

Some highly skilled practitioners argue that methods are only a crutch for the incompetent and that they should be dispensed with altogether, since they encourage "replacing insight with ritual."[1]

Use the hitchhiker's heuristic here: If the process helps you do a better job than you could do without the process, use the process providing that it generates increased value to the customer. Then continue to use the process until changes in customer needs force you to reevaluate and either change or abandon the process.

*Principle #2:* **If rework and break/fix processes are included in your project budget as the "cost of doing business," you are cooking the books and fooling yourself.**
   *Corollary #1:* You can recover 15–40% in manufacturing costs and 50–80% in service industry costs by eliminating the "hidden factory."

Armand Feigenbaum, the inventor of Total Quality Control and a contemporary of Deming and Juran, wrote about something he called the "hidden plant" in which he states:

*[T]here now exists what might be called a "hidden plant"—amounting to 15 percent to as much as 40 percent of productive capacity, depending upon the particular capacity. This is to . . . rework unsatisfactory parts, to replace products recalled from the field, or to retest and reinspect rejected units.*[2]

In the Six Sigma process, this is called the *hidden factory*.

This means that the business expends time, energy, and dollars as the normal cost of doing business to address the scrap, rework, inspections, recalls, and all the additional work that the business performs due to nonconformance issues. In software development terms, this is expressed as what I call the *50% pad*. This is a heuristic used by IT team leaders to create time estimates based on the concept that whatever the original estimate is for the task, pad it by 50% to cover rework, errors, and general contingency so that the project doesn't go over budget or schedule. If the team does an exceptional job and money is saved because the project comes in ahead of schedule and/ or under budget, the manager can attribute it to her outstanding management skills and her extraordinary team, and thus look good to her superiors and justify her existence. (That *sizzling* sound you hear is the sound of the books being slow-cooked under the watchful eye of the group manager or team leader.)

Be warned: This is an area no one in the business wants to talk about. The pad is something the group considers its *safety net*. In reality, it is nothing more than pure waste. In an age where CYA (Cover Your Ass) is more important than the customer, you may experience outright hostility when attempting to identify the hidden-factory areas of the business.

Unfortunately, the company's accounting system is completely blind to hidden-factory problems. In this case, how do we eliminate the waste of the hidden factory? You first must bring hidden-factory activity into the light of day. This can be done by utilizing a simple tool from the Six Sigma toolbox, called Rolled Throughput Yield (RTY). Let's say you have a manufacturing or ordering process that takes 250 steps to complete and, for the sake of argument, each step is accurate to the 99.9% level. This means that the probability of going through each process step without generating an error is 99.9%. This sounds great and might make you think you have a high-quality, fundamentally sound process—that is, until you do the math and find out something very different. The RTY formula is represented thus:

$$\text{Defect-free probability } \%^{(\text{of steps})}$$

This would play out as: $0.999^{250}$ or 99.9% to the 250th power. This yields:

$$\text{RTY} = 77.9\%$$

Ouch! So, the probability of your manufacturing or ordering process delivering a defect-free result from end-to-end is only 77.9%. Would that be good enough for you if you were processing online orders for books or rolling automobiles off the assembly line? Most would cringe when they see such a result, but it is a typical result for most businesses. Unless you are looking for it, you will never find it.

---

HITCHHIKER'S HEURISTIC: The RTY is a relatively rapid method for determining the final defect probability of a process consisting of many steps.

---

*Principle #3:* **American management never measures true resource utilization.**

*Corollary #1:* Resource-leveling your MS Project plan will send the project timeline somewhere west of the dark side of the moon.

*Corollary #2:* If you are on salary, management doesn't care if you are resourced at 40 hours a week but actually have to work for 55 hours. It will still be reported as 40 hours.

*Corollary #3:* See Principle #2.

In the IT environment, the 40-hour week is virtually nonexistent. I have worked in environments where management claims that they do not want to burn out the team by working them 55 to 65 hours a week, but this statement is by-and-large a fiction unless you happen to work in a parallel universe where people actually do what they say and say what they do. This is one reason why project managers will rarely resource-level a Gantt chart in any one of the project management software programs now available (e.g., MS Project$^{TM}$, SureTrak, and so on). In most cases performing the resource leveling is meaningless.

Users have the option of setting up the workday length in an MS Project Plan to be whatever length they require. However, management will usually have project managers set up the standard 40-hour week on the Gantt chart. This is because most developers who work for the company are not hourly, but salaried workers, so that extra hours demanded by the job never show up on the timesheet as true resource utilization. There is usually some lip service paid to the notion that management *wants* to see the true resource utilization so that they can ascertain whether to increase headcount to balance the workload. (This "official statement" at a major telco prompted great hilarity from the salaried knowledge workers.)

This is, of course, the typical Big 5 formula:

- Get the best and brightest out of business school ("green-beans," as one Big 5 manager called them).
- Pay them a decent starting salary for someone just out of college (e.g., $75K/year).
- Work them 70 to 80 hours a week for two years. (This actually works out to between $18 and $20/hr for your Harvard MBA. Most people I know made more money tending bar to pay their way through college.)
- The kid then gets much-needed experience at the "world-class" Big 5 firm. (This is called "paying your dues.")
- After three to four years, the kid discovers that there are other jobs he can get at 50% better salary for 25 fewer hours per week and leaves with a very good credential from a top-tier firm.

On the other hand, consultants and contractors will always show true resource utilization—actual time worked—because they are hourly workers who are generally contracted at a high hourly rate, and the consulting firm (e.g., a Big 5 consulting firm) charges the customer back for each hour the consultant works (if it is a time-and-materials contract).

This is why when there are cutbacks due to downsizing, rightsizing, dumbsizing, or whatever other sizing estimate the company is using, the consultants are usually the first to go.

A CFO once told me that as long as the budget balanced, he didn't care how long anyone had to work to achieve the result. That was a telling insight given that the turnover in the professional staff was better than 25% per year. He was not connecting talent acquisition costs with the staff burnout rate. Neither was HR.

HITCHHIKER'S OBSERVATION: *Everything* costs the business something. The question is: Does your accounting system capture all the costs so that the business knows where its true bottom line exists? If it doesn't, your actual costs are unknown and unknowable. (Are you hearing that *sizzling* sound again?)

*Principle #4:* **There is no such thing as the *cost of quality*—it implies that the cost doing things right the first time carries an added expense.**

*Corollary #1:* It is always cheaper to do things right the first time.

*Corollary #2:* There is a *cost of doing business*. This cost is minimized by implementing quality processes that enable the business to "get it right the first time."

There is a cost of poor quality. It is reflected in the customers you lose and how many people are dissatisfied customers who will tell everyone they know about their bad experience with you. Here is an approximate ratio:

- Satisfied customers may tell 2 or 3 people about their experience.

- Dissatisfied customers will tell at least 10 people about their bad experience. This can go up dramatically depending on the level of outrage experienced by the customer with your company. If customers truly feel they have been ripped off, not only will they tell *everyone* they know, but will usually file a fraud complaint with the state attorney general's office or any other government agency that takes consumer complaints seriously.

Why does bad news get distributed at a 10-to-1 factor? Chalk it up to the laws of physics and, specifically, entropy. When left alone, processes will deteriorate to a state of maximum chaos unless there is greater effort working against the forces of entropy.

Typically, businesses infuriate their customers because of two primary elements: (1) defects and (2) delay:

- Defects in the form of mistakes made in service, delivery, billing, adjustments, product quality, and so on
- Delay in terms of receipt of product or service, getting issues resolved, having to repeatedly call the business to get the same issue resolved, and so on

These elements are discussed in some detail in Chapter 6, "Your Customer Is Talking—Are You Listening?"

*Principle #5:* **Don't go after low-hanging fruit just because it's there. It draws focus to the "trivial many" instead of the "vital few."**
*Corollary #1:* Only collect what adds value for the customer.
*Corollary #2:* Following the line of greatest advantage is always more profitable than following the line of least resistance unless they are the same (*very rarely*).

I've heard so many managers use the term *low-hanging fruit*. It refers to the things you can do on your project that are easy to accomplish. Managers like this approach because it shows forward motion and shows that the team is accomplishing *something*. I was on a telecom project that was initiated to reformat the customer telephone bill with more useful information. In order to make the bill easier to understand, some of the low-hanging-fruit was to fix:

- The position of the company logo on the bill
- Changes in the bill font
- The spacing of the elements on the page

Of course, the looming technical issue that needed to be solved was how they were going to pull all the information they needed from various databases and assemble it onto the bill in a coordinated manner. Not all the systems were updated in the same way and some of the information would not be in synch for the current bill. It was a logistical problem that needed to be solved before the project would work at all.

And yet, the manager was exhorting us to capture the low-hanging fruit—the things that had little-to-no customer impact and added no real value for the customer.

---

HITCHHIKER'S HEURISTIC: Ask yourself if the activities you are performing add customer value or are increasing your overhead. And if it's *overhead*, it goes *overboard*.

---

*Principle #6:* **When implementing a process improvement in the company, a clear barometer of the *state of management competency (SMC)* is usually reflected in the average number of Dilbert postings found in the work area. The *Dilbert indicator* will help anyone charged with process improvement or Six Sigma activities to obtain a quick read on what they are up against:**

- *One Dilbert posting per cubicle:* Workers think management is basically okay and makes occasional errors (no one is perfect).
- *Two to three Dilbert postings per cubicle:* Management is missing the boat in certain areas of the operation.
- *Four to five Dilbert postings per cubicle:* Management is clueless in most areas of operation.

☐ *Six or more Dilbert postings per cubical:* Workers are wondering how the business has not yet spontaneously combusted—a state of maximum dysfunction and managerial incompetence.

This may appear far-fetched, but as a general heuristic it seems to work with a high level of accuracy. There are several reasons for this, but the one that seems to stand out is the mistaken approach taken by the business that people doing the work for the company need to be *managed*.

In the last 30 years or so, the business environment has largely shifted from the command-and-control model to the *knowledge worker* model—the people doing the work are not performing mindless assembly-line work; they are highly educated and highly skilled and frequently smarter than their management counterparts. Telling a knowledge worker *how* to do a job is like trying to teach a dolphin how to swim—you're already hopelessly outclassed. Telling the knowledge worker *what* to do might now raise questions such as: "Why are we taking that approach?"

If you are the project manager on a team of high-performing professionals, give some thought as to how you might motivate this team. The usual team-building activities will not work. The typical steps that are said to occur when assembling a team—the "forming-storming-norming-performing" notions—may not apply, either.

Peter Ducker's insight in this area supports this notion. His take on the present-day knowledge worker is that it is not enough to simply throw money and stock options at people; management must be aware that knowledge workers want to participate in the decision process of the business. It means offering them social recognition and social power, and turning them from highly paid subordinates into partners. A financial incentive alone actually motivates the knowledge workers to cash in their options at the most opportune moment—companies whose primary agent of employee motivation is financial typically have the greatest turnover:

*IBM once had the largest alumni association in the world. No longer . . . those two alumni associations which were the largest—Procter & Gamble and IBM—those alumni love their ex-companies. Microsoft alumni hate Microsoft. Precisely because they feel that the one thing it offered them was money and nothing else, they resent all the publicity that goes to the top people, to one top man, and they don't get recognition. Also they feel the value system is entirely financial, and they see themselves as professionals. Maybe not scientists but applied scientists. So their value system is different.*[3]

If one of the challenges on your next project is team-building, you might keep the above in mind.

---

HITCHHIKER'S OBSERVATION: High-performing teams require leadership, not management. You manage *processes*, but you lead *people*. If you are in a position of leading a high-performing team, your best bet is to stay out of their way. Help them with the obstacles they face, defend the team when the company president starts chewing them out, asking when such-and-such will be delivered, but never tell them *how* to do their jobs—you're not qualified.

---

*Principle #7:* **Any CEO or company president who publicly claims that the company's first responsibility is to its investors needs to be fired—immediately.**

I've had people tell me that their leadership has made statements like this in their quarterly meetings—what a frightening prospect. How would you react if you were a customer of that company?

The business's first responsibility is to its customers. Investors are just along for the ride. If you were smart enough to invest in a company whose goal is to stay in business by putting its customers first, you will probably be in for a pleasant trip.

Here's what happens when you put the customer first. This story is a legend in the retail business and I've had it verified by several employees of the company, so it is not apocryphal.

A lady went into Nordstrom's in Anchorage, Alaska to return a set of snow tires she claims to have bought there. (You heard it right— snow tires.) The store manager took her for a tour around the store and showed her all manner of clothing, shoes, furs, suits, evening gowns, sportswear, underwear—but no snow tires. The lady insisted she had bought the snow tires there and wanted her money back—$400—because they were defective.

In fact, she was correct. Another business had occupied that space before Nordstrom's took it over and that business sold, among other things, snow tires. Unfortunately, that company had either moved or gone out of business and were nowhere to be found. In most cases, and with most other businesses, management would have been polite but firm, and would have told the lady—sorry, we don't sell snow tires and can't refund your money.

At this juncture, you should know something about the Nordstrom's employee handbook. It states the following: *Rule #1: Use your good judgment in all situations. There will be no additional rules.*

The manager of Nordstrom's in Anchorage did just that and followed Rule #1: He (1) found a place that would get her a set of reliable snow tires and (2) *refunded her money!* Outrageous, you say? Not at all; it's amazing what can happen when you put the customer first. The lady came back to Nordstrom's and spent thousands of dollars on merchandise, ebullient about the high quality of service she had received, and evidently told all her friends about it, as well. I can't think of better publicity or a better story to tell about your company—it is one of the reasons why *I* am a Nordstrom's customer.

Would an *investor* have made the same decision?

---

HITCHHIKER'S HEURISTIC: Take care of your customer and use your good judgment in all situations.

---

*Principle # 8:* **If your project's budget and timeline is based on the REBE[4] approach, any and all budget and schedule variances are meaningless.**

As a consultant, I was asked to review the budget for an investment area of a large bank that manages over $2 trillion in assets. It appeared that they were $5 million over budget on an original budget of $17 million and the team administrator was in something of a panic. After some review of the spreadsheet, a glaring error was discovered: One of the budget areas had been double-counted, inflating the budget an additional $3.4 million. (This is why it is a good practice to lock down cells on an Excel spreadsheet, especially where computing the totals is concerned.) Once the correction was made, the overage was about $1.6 million or within 10% of the planned budget; however, this was still some cause for concern.

My question to the team lead was this: "What is the basis of estimate for your projects?" The response was the proverbial deer-in-the-headlights look. It turned out that the business would gather sometime in October to hash out what would be done for the upcoming year and would do a complete shoot-from-the-hip estimate on every project. The next question was, "If your basis of estimate is a fiction, then how can the variance mean anything?" Once again, it was the deer-in the-headlights look. "Well, we're over budget," was the response. This is akin to the guitarist Nigel's response in the film, *This Is Spinal Tap*, when asked why he simply didn't renumber the settings on his amp: "This amp goes up to 11."

The sad part of this scenario is that many businesses do their estimating this way. The usual excuse is that it takes too long to do a bottom-up estimate. The real reason is usually that the business area *prefers* to finance all of its projects via the slush-fund approach because it gives them the flexibility to address constantly changing business requirements.

Of course, the larger the project, the more difficult it is to deliver an accurate estimate. As a software project goes out further than 6 months—a year to 18 months or two years—the future becomes much more difficult to predict. It also becomes the victim of galloping "scope creep"—the heaping of additional requirements on a project that had already locked-down the project scope some time before. For a large software project with a $10M budget, your chances of project success—coming in on time and on budget—are about zero.[5] One of the most telling, cautionary tales of what happens when the project is too large (among other things) is related in the IEEE Spectrum article, "Who Killed the Virtual Case

File?,"[6] which clearly demonstrates how the FBI blew $170 million on a software project with no usable code to show for their efforts.

How do we address the staggering failure of large, poorly estimated projects? The answer lies in the implementation of Principle #9.

> *Principle #9:* **Iterative development is the best risk-mitigation and product-delivery strategy for a software project.**
> *Corollary #1*: Software project estimates are rarely correct.
> > *Earned value* is very difficult to compute on software projects.
> *Corollary #2:* Smaller is better.

PMI devotes a good chunk of the *PMBOK* to reviewing and showing PMs how to compute *earned value* in its many forms. Earned value computation is used as a method for showing the PM exactly where the project stands from a schedule and budget perspective. It gives a precise readout at any given time in the project whether you are over, on, or under budget and over, on, or behind schedule. Thus it is a useful tool in helping the PM keep the project on track and on target, and can help point out where corrective action needs to be taken.

MS Project has the ability to compute earned value on a Gantt chart and reports can be created showing the earned value on a project right up to the minute. As we mentioned in Chapter 1, the earned value formula as described in the *PMBOK* gives the user two metrics that denote the financial and schedule health of the project; the CPI (cost performance index) and the SPI (schedule performance index). CPI tells you if you are over or under your budget and SPI tells you if you are ahead of or behind your schedule.

These indexes are computed by means of the following simple formulas:

$$\text{CPI} = \frac{\text{EV}}{\text{AC}} \quad \text{and} \quad \text{SPI} = \frac{\text{EV}}{\text{PV}}$$

where:

> EV = Earned Value (what you're *supposed* to get for what you spent)
>
> AC = Actual Cost
>
> PV = Planned Value (that is, the planned budget—the estimate)

If the CPI or the SPI are equal to or greater than *1*, this is a good thing.

The derivation of the earned value is a bit of a problem for many because budgets are measured by (1) what you planned to spend and (2) what you actually spent. So how does earned value fit into the equation? It represents the notion of the *value* you were supposed to get for what you spent. It means that you understand what a certain amount of completed work is *supposed* to cost.

Example: If you wanted a low brick wall to frame the front of your primary residence—something 150 feet long, 4 feet high, and 18 inches deep with a 6-foot space in the middle to accommodate a walkway and shrubbery on each side, you might see something like this from the bricklayer:

> Job length: 2 weeks
>
> Materials cost: $1500.00
>
> Hourly labor rate: $40.00
>
> Anticipated total cost − materials + labor (*planned value*): $5,200
>
> Contract basis: Time and materials

In terms of earned value, this means that you are expecting $1,600 of labor to get done per week and you are expecting 50% of the job to get done each week.

If you want to look up the costs for a specific construction job, the *R.S. Means—Building Construction Cost Data* reference can give you this information with prices based on:

- The specific job
- Geographic location
- Low-Medium-High price estimates based on the skill of the crew or price ranges in the area

For the bricklaying job, if a week went by and exactly half the work were done, your CPI formula would look like this:

$$\text{CPI} = \frac{\text{EV}}{\text{AC}} \quad \text{or} \quad \frac{\$1,600}{\$1,600} = 1$$

In other words, you were supposed to get $1,600 of value and that's exactly what you spent, thus your CPI = 1. That is, you got a dollar's worth of value for every dollar spent. Let's look at some alternative scenarios:

- If it took the bricklayer 50 hours instead of 40 hours to do half the work, your AC would be $2000.00. Computing for CPI and SPI:

$$\text{CPI} = \frac{\text{EV}}{\text{AC}} = \frac{\$1,600}{\$2,000.00} = 0.80$$

  In other words, you are getting $0.80 of value for every $1 you spent.

$$\text{SPI} = \frac{\text{EV}}{\text{PV}} \quad \text{or} \quad \frac{\$1600}{\$1,600}$$

  In other words, the earned value didn't change and the planned value didn't change—your project is still on time: Half the work was accomplished in one week.

  However, you overspent because the work took longer in total hours than it should have, so the CPI shows that you are over budget but the SPI shows that your schedule is still on track.

- If one week elapsed, but the bricklayer was a fast worker and got 60% of the work done in 40 hours instead of the expected 50%, your earned value would be 0.6 × $3200.00 or $1,920. Computing for CPI and SPI we now get:

$$CPI = \frac{EV}{AC} = \frac{\$1,920}{\$1,600} = 1.2$$

$$SPI = \frac{EV}{PV} = \frac{\$1,920}{\$1,600}$$

A CPI of 1.2 means you are earning $1.20 in value for every $1 spent.

An SPI of 1.2 means your project is 20% ahead of schedule.

Try to do the same for a software project and the ground becomes much more unstable. There is no R.S. Means cost guide for software projects. In fact, there is *no such guide in the software industry*. There are estimating tools used in software, such as the function point analysis, COCOMO, and others, that attempt to give the professional estimator a handle on how to do this for a software project. Yet this still does not give us a handle on what software tasks are *supposed* to cost.

**Comparative Example:**

- How long will it take and what will it cost to sheetrock and tape a 30-foot by 15-foot room with 10-foot ceilings using standard half-inch wallboard? Go to R.S. Means. You can put together an estimate in a few hours.

- How long will it take and what will it cost to set up an Oracle database that will interface to my Product Ordering web site to capture customer information and ordering information? It depends on whom you talk to. Consider the following:
  - What you thought was a simple request is now a major project.
  - You will now be asked for an explicit set of business requirements (BR).
  - You and the technical team will have to sign off on the business requirements.
  - The technical team will take the BR and translate the business needs into technical requirements (TR).
  - You and the technical team will have to sign off on the technical requirements.

- □ The technical team will then create a high-level design (HLD). They will ask for your input—you may or may not know what they are talking about.
- □ You and the technical team will have to sign off on the HLD.
- □ The HLD will then be translated into a detail design (DD), which is technically beyond the understanding of the customer. You will have to take it on faith that Development knows what it is doing. Development approves and signs off on the technical design unilaterally.
- □ The signoff on the BR, TR, and HLD is required before any actual coding on your project starts. This is so that the developers can cover their behinds in case *you* had a different interpretation of what the work was supposed to be than the developer's interpretation of the work.
- □ Several months may go by, at which point you will be told that a working model of the project is ready for review. If you like what you see, you'll be happy. If not (e.g., "This doesn't look or function at all the way I imagined it . . . "), you will probably request that changes to the final product are necessary to make it (1) usable and/or (2) marketable in your environment. Of course, any changes you request at this point require a formal *change request* that has additional dollar and time impacts on your project.

I once priced the above scenario and got a range of prices from $250K to $2.75M from six different vendors. The preceding scenario is how most software projects work. If you have forgotten how many challenged software projects are still being cranked out by the Fortune 500, review the section on the *CHAOS Report* in Chapter 1. The preceding scenario is also typical for anyone implementing the waterfall approach on software projects.

What is the earned value for the work? That's a good question; you can ask 10 people and get 10 widely varying answers. No one knows what the work is supposed to cost. In fact, the most consistent answer I've ever gotten on any software project is this: "Here's our estimate if everything goes right and there are no interruptions" (!).

Here are some of the top elements that prevent you from determining earned value on a software project:

1. The development resources also troubleshoot production problems—you cannot predict when a key resource may be called away from development to address a major production outage. This adds time and dollars to your project schedule.

2. Management may pull a key resource away to address a C-level's pet project.

3. An unknown, undocumented error in the software your team is using causes a delay in completion of critical milestones in your project. The team burns cycle time troubleshooting the problem.

4. Most of the development team consists of employees who are in the *exempt* category; they are paid the same salary whether they work 40 hours or 60 hours. (See Principle #3.) True resource utilization is not measured.

We can go back and forth with the earned value question, but one gnawing issue remains. This approach presumes that measuring dollars expended against planned or historical values is the only way you can compute earned value. However, Deming warned against running a business by visible figures alone—too much is left out in that analysis. Sure, you came in on time and on budget, but was the result what the customer was expecting? And that's the rub. Does the assessment of the dollars alone speak to the quality and the usability of the deliverable? In most cases, it doesn't. Maybe a better approach to determining earned value would involve an assessment, from the customer's perspective, of whether the delivered product met the needs of the users and to what extent it did so.

It is also interesting to note that in 1985, the U.S. DOD (Department of Defense) adopted a waterfall-based software development standard, which it abandoned for iterative methods due to high failure rates with the former. It is even more interesting that over

20 years later most Fortune 500 businesses have yet to get that message.

How does one avoid the pitfalls of the monolithic development process? The best way thus far is to utilize *agile development* approaches:

- Build small working prototypes.

- Engage the customer immediately in the process and involve them in the co-creation of the work.

- Elaborate the requirements over time. The *PMBOK* states that a project is a progressive elaboration. How about actually doing it? Changing business needs or marketplace demands may necessitate changes in requirements and the development team may have to quickly and nimbly respond to those changes.

- You don't know what you don't know. This approach allows you to mitigate the big risks in your project up front and abandon the costly, time-consuming, top-heavy and monolithic change management and risk management processes for an empirical process. It is Deming's Plan-Do-Check-Act idea applied to software development.

- Utilize time-boxed deliverables that are clearly scoped; 30-day iterations will give you 12 major deliverables in a year and will be much closer to what the customer wanted. The smaller time slice of a 30-day iteration from design to rollout is much simpler to scope and manage in terms of budget and schedule. Also understand that implementing a monolithic re-quirements-gathering process is, de facto, a flawed process. The process as it exists in the waterfall mentality assumes the customer knows exactly what they want and can describe it in terms clearly enough so that development can go off and build it. This is fundamentally an illusion. Customers change their minds or are impacted by market pressures. Putting usable product incrementally into the hands of the customer allows requirements to evolve and allows the customer to make adjustments as the product evolves—without penalty or finger-pointing.

- The project *manager* now becomes the project *leader* and helps the team meet its goals and focuses primarily on removing obstacles so the team can get its job done.

- Assemble the right team from the start. Hollywood has understood this for years: Casting is 90% of the job. Putting the right people on the team will get you a long way to a successful implementation.

- Champion technical excellence—if people need training, make sure that they get it.

- Let testing help to drive development. Use of automated testing and configuration tools at the completion of each iterative sprint will keep bugs to a minimum and promotes building quality into your process and addressing problems as they occur (the "lean" 100% source inspection approach), instead of inspecting quality into your process at the end of the cycle (where they are the most expensive to fix). You will be amazed how few bugs are manifested in your final testing when your project is complete.

- Incrementally improve your process on each iteration: Plan-Do-Check-Act.

Figure 5.1 shows the fundamental difference between the waterfall approach and an agile approach.

To expand your horizons on iterative development concepts, there are several excellent works on Agile/Lean project management and software development that bear mentioning here:

The U.S. army did studies on earned value and found the following to be true 100% of the time: At the 20% point into your project schedule, check the earned values for SPI and CPI. At that point in time, your CPI and SPI will not vary more than ±10% of that value from that point forward. In other words, if your CPI is .85 and your SPI is .87, your project will *never* come back to a CPI and an SPI of *1*.

# Figure 5.1

**Assembly Line Approach (Waterfall)**

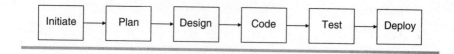

Initiate → Plan → Design → Code → Test → Deploy

---

**Command-and-Control Model (Waterfall);**

- Requirements are etched in stone.

- Change averse: If scope varies from original plan, requires top-heave formal change management process.

- With high-risk projects, you don't know what you don't know—"discovery" can trigger extensive change management activities.

- Defects found late in testing require rework at high expense.

- Quality is "inspected" into the process, just prior to release (monolithic testing).

---

**Empirical Approach (Agile/Iterative)**

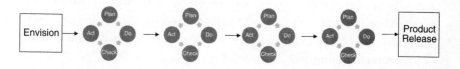

Envision → [Plan–Act–Do–Check] → [Plan–Act–Do–Check] → [Plan–Act–Do–Check] → [Plan–Act–Do–Check] → Product Release

---

**Empirical model (Agile/Iterative: Plan–Do–Check–Act);**

- Requirements evolve as more is learned about the project.

- Usable product is delivered to the customer with each iteration.

- High-risk elements are mitigated in early iterations.

- Process is not change averse—customers can change their mind without penalty. "Discovery" engenders adaptability and flexibility of responses.

- Testing occurs in each iteration. Defects are fixed as they occur (zero quality control). Each iteration integrates the functionality from the last and the integrated product is tested each integration and each iteration.

- As a result, quality is continually designed into the process. The customer does not receive the product as a big surprise but has participated in the product's creation and approved the deliverables as they evolved.

> HITCHHIKER'S HEURISTIC: Don't bother with earned value unless you know what things are supposed to cost and you are keeping accurate historical data on your software projects. It is useful in a traditional waterfall approach where process and project elements are well understood. However the higher the risk, the less likely the waterfall DLM will work and the more we need to evolve a broader definition of earned value from the customer's perspective: Is the product of the process useful and does it meet the customer's needs?

### Principle #10: *The Apprentice* is not about project management.

*The Apprentice* is an interesting phenomenon in the so-called *reality* TV genre—most people think it is about business and project managers. I forced myself to watch five consecutive episodes, against my better judgment, and started to dissect the show critically. There actually is something to be learned here, but not what you would expect. What became clear is that: (1) *The Apprentice* doesn't resemble any business I have ever dealt with—except the ones that failed, and (2) there isn't a project manager I have seen on the show that deserves the title of "Project Manager." Several things should be obvious after even one viewing of *The Apprentice*:

- The format was developed by a master of the TV Soap Opera genre. Let's be somewhat realistic here: Putting 10 type-A, hyperthyroid lunatics in a room together to solve a problem or complete a task is like pouring water on magnesium—a sure formula for fireworks. While it might be fun to watch once or twice, it becomes fairly predictable and boring on repeated viewings. If the goal of your project is only to produce the biggest, loudest fireworks you can, assemble all your project teams this way.

- If Don Trump ran his day-to-day business the way he runs the TV show, he would be quickly out of business.

- For any task, someone on the "losing" team will always be fired. In one instance, the task was to sign up "subscribers" for some service. The winning team signed up 52 to the losing team's 47. Of course, someone on the losing team got fired by Mr. Trump. Well, here's a news flash for you: Anyone who would fire a team lead/PM for bringing in better than 48% of the company's business is an idiot. By this logic, Avis should simply give up because they're only "Number 2" even though they have made quite a reputation for themselves by "Trying Harder." The business they bring in is certainly not chump-change by any standard.

- It's just TV, and it's a sitcom at that! This program just kept getting funnier and funnier. It is an interesting mix between what happens when Moore's Law collides with Murphy's Law.

After five episodes, the saturation point was reached. Outside of being a predictable, junior-high-school-mentality treatment of how "real business" is done, the double-dealing, backstabbing, and generally disingenuous nature of the participants became predictably obnoxious and not recommend viewing on a weekly basis.

---

HITCHHIKER'S CAVEAT: If you are a PM on a project that is causing you angst, loss of sleep, lots of worry, and lots of confrontation, I recommend that you watch an episode or two of *The Apprentice*. You will feel much better about your life. However, if it looks similar to your day-to-day project operations, start asking the people on your project team if *they* watch *The Apprentice* on a regular basis. Anyone who needs to create this much drama in their daily work activities has got other issues that need to be addressed by a mental-health professional!

---

*Principle #11:* **Don't implement tools until you understand *what* you are doing.**
  *Corollary #1:* Implementing tools before you understand your system and define your processes will help you fail faster.
  *Corollary #2:* A fool with a tool is still a fool.[7]

In this respect, most IT types are the same as professional engineers; they like to tinker with their toys—if they are a PE or an EE and work for a manufacturer, then the computerized shop equipment, hardware tools, bench testing gear, and so on are things they like to fool around with. For IT types, the toys are servers and software applications. Given enough time and money, they think that they are smart enough to figure out and solve any problem. This is by and large true, given unlimited time and unlimited budget. Unfortunately, we function in a world where we do not have the luxury of unlimited time and budget. Most software engineers would be wise to take their cue from Eleanor Roosevelt, who was once quoted as saying, "Learn from the mistakes of others; you won't have time to make them all yourself."

A brilliant example of this concept occurred recently. I was brought in as a consultant to help implement Microsoft Project Server for a large bank. One of the development groups was in sore need of a project management tool. One of the team leads implored, "Give us *anything* that we can use to track our projects. We have nothing. . . . " The organization had rolled out Microsoft Project Server 2003 and the development group was anxious to get their teams trained and up to speed on Project Server, which they hoped would be the answer to their prayers.

In a series of successive interviews with team leads in the development organization to ascertain the requirements for how the group would actually use the tool, one of the team leads had a very different take on projects for his team. "Projects are *evil*," he stated simply. Being a PMI-certified project manager, naturally my curiosity was piqued. "Please elaborate," I asked with great anticipation.

What transpired over the next 25 minutes was an enlightening discussion that illuminated:

- Why the strict waterfall approach was not working for his team
- Why projects did not work for his team
- Why the traditional waterfall approach has nothing to do with how software developers actually do their jobs
- Why the Project Server tool would add yet another layer of bureaucracy on an already-overbureaucratized environment
- Why resource-leveling a project timeline was a joke

- Why no one would use the Project Server tool even if it were implemented and people were trained

This was the first indication that there was something of a disconnect going on, but it wasn't until my interviewing process got around to the end users—the business—that the other shoe finally dropped. In an interview with one of the main business users, he began laying out a series of business needs around the practice of project management. As he progressed, it was clear that the organization was wrestling with:

- How do we implement project practices at the enterprise level?
- What PM skill sets are needed?
- What should the PMO look like?
- How should the business interface with the development organization to implement projects?
- How will we effectively track resource availability so that we can plan upcoming projects?

It should be mentioned at this point that I was hired by the development VP to help the development organization get up to speed on MS Project Server—clearly the development organization was my customer. Yet from what the business liaison was telling me, the organization hadn't figured out what it was doing with project management.

I asked my usual innocent question when this situation presents itself:

"Why are you attempting to implement a complex tool like MS Project Server when you are not sure if it will help you achieve your organizational goals for project management?"

BUSINESS LIAISON: "My point exactly. I don't know why we're doing this. It appears development is just doing anything to get some kind of process around the problem, but it's not helping us."

That's when the real problem dawned on me.

"Wait a minute," I asked. "Who's the customer here?"

BUSINESS LIAISON: "Well, *we* are."

"That's interesting," I replied, "I was just hired by the VP of development, who thinks that *he's* the customer!"

The previous scenario is not uncommon. There are numerous case studies from personal experience that follow the same modus operandus. In each case, the business thinks that implementing the tool first will do their thinking for them. In reality, this is a formula for negative returns on investment, if not outright failure.

---

HITCHHIKER'S OBSERVATION: Elaborating project management for an organization is first and foremost a *thinking* process. Once the organization understands how it will manage projects, *then* it may be time to look at software tools that will aid the organization in realizing its goals. The tools are only *enablers*; they do not do the thinking for you. Do your thinking first; *then* go shopping for tools.

---

*Principle #12:* **There are no "quick fixes" to your project problems.**

*Corollary #1:* Performing a true root-cause analysis can be somewhat painful for the organization.

*Corollary #2:* Performing a series of quick fixes or workarounds for your problems is simply putting a band-aid on a symptom—the core problem is never addressed.

A director at a company in which I was also a director was always looking for a quick fix to some software or network problem. "Hey, one of the utilization reports isn't coming out right—can you put in a quick fix for the next manager's meeting?" Management liked that approach because he wasn't trying to "solve world hunger"; just patch up that leaky boiler with some chewing gum and duct tape so we can keep this barge afloat and moving forward!

Of course, over the next few months, the problem reemerged in various forms because the real problem was never addressed. This is what happens when management makes the mistake of identifying the symptom as the problem. I made a point of removing the phrase *quick fix* from my vocabulary as a result. It is never a *fix* and it is anything but *quick*—the quick fix usually exacerbates the situation. It becomes particularly painful when management attempts to improve the system before they have first stabilized the system or understand if the system is in a state of control. This is what Deming referred to as "tampering with the system by management."

So if your goal is to be in a state of developing consistent work-arounds utilizing rubber bands, duct tape, paper clips, squirrels, or what-have-you to solve the immediate fire drill of the moment, read no further. You won't find the quick fix here—no "Tips & Tricks," no "Fast Track to Instant Project Success."

If you want your projects to have the reputation of "Built to Last" instead of "Built to Spontaneously Combust," you would do well to remove the quick-fix concept from your vocabulary and your business process as well.

---

HITCHHIKER'S HEURISTIC: When anyone on the project team, be it management or a team member, is looking for a quick-fix to a problem, starting digging into the issue—the underlying cause is usually much deeper than any quick fix can cure. You don't need a quick fix; you need a quick method to help you zero in on the problem so that you don't get bogged down in analysis paralysis.

Use the Five *Whys* approach as utilized in Six Sigma, or what Kepner-Tregoe calls "questioning to the void."

---

*Principle # 13:* **If you are not in the software business, don't build software—buy it.**

A number of businesses get tripped up over this principle.

As Robert X. Cringely so deftly asserted:

*Unless you are operating a software company, software should not be central to the way you view your business. It's just a means to an end. And to be classed as truly successful, the means should be quietly efficient and close to invisible as you can get.*[8]

**Figure 5.2**

| Project Size | People | Time (months) | Success Rate |
|---|---|---|---|
| Under $750K | 6 | 6 | 55% |
| $750K–$1.5M | 12 | 9 | 33% |
| $1.5M–$3M | 25 | 12 | 25% |
| $3M–$6M | 40 | 18 | 15% |
| $6M–$10M | +250 | +24 | 8% |
| >$10M | +500 | +36 | 0% |

The Standish Group once again through its empirical studies collected the information shown in Figure 5.2 on software project success in relation to project size and duration.[9]

Yet in spite of this telling information, there are those businesses that attempt to build software when it is not their core business. This occurs when there are developers in-house who are currently charged with performing application maintenance, but who are really itching to do some hard-core development and convince management that they can "handle it easily."

There are also a number of businesses that get roped or finessed into paying for the creation of custom software, much to their detriment. This usually occurs when the technical sales team from some Big-Time Consulting Firm convinces the client's management that Big-Time is imminently qualified to create a custom-built solution for its client. After all, look at all these impressive credentials and its extensive client list!

This occurred on a project I managed in the public sector for a major city government agency in Chicago. The agency was attempting to upgrade its operations center and dealt with a vendor it had used in the past. The vendor proposed a shrink-wrapped solution for its client. For those that don't know, a shrink-wrapped solution means that the solution is not customized software—it is prebuilt and you simply install it, much like Microsoft Office or similar software products. This is generally a good thing for the client because a shrink-wrapped solution has usually been out on the market for awhile and many of the usual kinks and bugs have been corrected. At that point, you are left with a system that is generally very stable and operates to customer expectation.

In this case, however, one month into the signed contract, I got wind that all was not well with the Prime Contractor's sub—the actual group responsible for the shrink-wrapped solution. It turned out the subcontractor's solution was essentially vaporware and the sub was relying on the contract to fund their first commercial build of the solution.

What did the Prime Contractor do at that point? *It offered up a completely custom-coded solution for the city agency!* Never mind that the city agency did not have the programming talent in place to maintain a custom-coded solution or that they would be roped into a long-term support agreement that would have joined the city agency and the vendor at the hip for years to come and at huge expense.

My response to the Prime was, "You will create a solution made of existing software components readily available in the marketplace and will now function as a systems integrator." The advantage to assembling the project in this manner is that each of the companies providing part of the solution *did* have shrink-wrapped components that could be installed and brought online. The agency CIO liked the approach as well. When we were through with the redesign, only 10% of the solution needed to be custom coded.

The interesting part of this exercise was this: All of the shrink-wrapped components worked extremely well and according to specification. The most problematic part of the effort continued to be the custom-built 10% component, long after the shrink-wrapped components were already in place and functioning.

Do yourself a favor: If software is not your business, focus on your core business and leave the software to someone else. Developing software is a long-term R&D endeavor that requires patience and dollars. Buy shrink-wrapped software whenever possible, and only support development if you can mitigate the risk:

- Negotiate with the development company for a cut rate on development if the product developed can be used by the software company to create a new line of business or salable product for the software. You are in effect helping them pay for their own development while getting the benefit of the newest, latest, and greatest software.

- Negotiate your first release of the code as a *work-made-for-hire*, while allowing the development company to continue to enhance and market subsequent releases of the product, offering you the upgrades at a substantial discount.

---

HITCHHIKER'S HEURISTIC: Don't ever buy version 1.0 of *anything* unless you:

- Must be the first one on your block to have one
- Are highly adventurous and not risk averse to any potential negative outcomes
- Are dying of curiosity and just have to find out what it is!

Wait until the product has been out a few years and has stabilized in the marketplace—at least to version 2.0 or 3.0. After that, find other businesses that are customers of the software company and ask them how it's going. If the software is functioning as advertised and meets your needs, invite them in for an RFP or buy the shrink-wrapped product.

---

*Principle #14:* **The management of any company that consistently uses the *bell curve* to evaluate employees' performance either has abdicated its responsibility, or has no objective measure by which to evaluate employee performance.**

I have gotten into some rather drawn-out discussions and outright arguments with HR types when I bring this up in seminars. I will probably get hate mail on this one, but the issue needs to be broadly addressed by businesses. While large organizations depend on metrics and measurements to guide their improvement activities, it all goes out the window when it comes to evaluating the work of the employee.

The *annual review* is a sacred cow of most HR departments and any breach that attempts to assail the process is met with pure ornery contempt and a sense that the trespasser is treading on sacred turf. However, anyone who has been through this process in most Fortune 500 companies—at least 80% of them—have emerged from the review embittered, frustrated, frequently shocked, and usually resolved to find a better place to work. HR will maintain that the review is a reality check that most employees dislike because it points out the employee's weaknesses, shows where they could use improvement, and quite frankly offers criticism of the employee's performance. Part of the review process will also have a section focused on how well the employee took criticism.

This may be news to you, but the "employee review" has been dead for some time now—it's just that no one has bothered to bury it yet. It needs to be shredded along with other arcane notions such as Frederick W. Taylor's "principles of scientific management," the idea that "mutual funds are the best investment vehicle," and the Puritan Ethic.

In reality, the *annual employee review* has done more to decimate teamwork, diminish employee productivity, create resentment, kill pride in workmanship, and lower individual self-esteem than any other single management blunder. Its creation was a direct result of the application of Frederick W. Taylor's *scientific management* concepts and it has done more damage to the employee-management relationship than any other manmade employee productivity improvement idea since the invention of the galley-slave.

As a former Director of Development, Senior Program Manager, and Senior Project Manager, I have witnessed the devastating effects of the employee review first hand. From a project management perspective, the employee review is a broken process due to the unreliability of the users who input the data, and it is a failure from the quality perspective because the "metrics" gathered in the process are usually fraudulent or subject to severe tampering.

I used to think of the annual review in the same way I thought about New Year's resolutions. I'd look over what I did the year before, look at what I had accomplished, look at what didn't work so well, think about what I could do to improve it, and then set some new goals for the upcoming year. This seems like a reasonable thing to do: Celebrate your successes, get motivated to make some improvements, and look forward to another year of great ideas, interesting projects, working with interesting people, and doing some good in the world, while also making a good living doing it. Sounds like a plan to me. I could motivate and inspire a lot of people with a plan like that.

Unfortunately, most businesses in the Fortune 1000 don't use the employee review in this manner. From speaking with various associates and employees that I have interviewed in scores of businesses, the employee review is used for the following:

- Setting the employee's bonus based on the review ranking
- Setting the employee's salary increase based on review ranking
- Denying the employee a bonus or salary increase based on review ranking
- Getting rid of someone the company doesn't like (for whatever reason)
- Initiating some form of punitive action against the employee based on the results of the review
- Giving the HR department something to do besides administer the healthcare plan for the company
- In the event of a legal action by an employee toward the company for cause (e.g., sexual harassment or discrimination), using HR employee records and employee reviews as evidence against the disgruntled employee

Some of you reading this might think that some of these examples are far-fetched or unusual—in fact they are much closer to reality than most HR departments will ever admit. Let's see what the concepts of forced ranking and employee evaluation by the annual employee review actually do to the employee and how this ultimately hurts the business.

# WHY THE EMPLOYEE REVIEW PROCESS CAN'T POSSIBLY WORK

The five-level evaluation criteria are used in conjunction with the bell curve to deliver the one-two punch that is used to distort any value the employee may have provided the business. This is where pseudoscience meets backroom corporate politics. It is pseudoscience, because using the normal distribution gives the rating process an air of scientific accuracy, unfettered by human emotion or manipulation. In reality, it is an insidious form of manipulation, taking a marginally useful tool and turning it into a dagger that the business can use to plunge into the backs of the employees they don't like. Here is how it is typically applied.

## Pseudostatistics

The normal distribution is applied to the people in the department. If there is a team of let's say 50 programmers, team leads, and architects, the normal distribution will be applied to the entire team. (Don't laugh, I've had at least 20 or more people from 20 companies tell me this is *exactly* how the company applies the bell curve.)

Based on a normal distribution, which looks like the diagram in Figure 5.3, certain percentages of people will be rated as a *1* (Top Performer), *2* (Exceeding Job Requirements), *3* (Meeting Job Requirements), *4* (Below Job Requirements), or *5* (Not Meeting Job Requirements). There are no exceptions. Loosely based on standard deviation divisions inside a normal distribution, approximately 60% of the team will fall in the middle or get ranked a *3*, approximately 15% of the team will fall in at a *2* level, another 15% falls in at a *4* level, another 5% of the team will fall in with a *1* ranking, while the final 5% of the team will be ranked a *5*.

Since the department is usually given a pool of bonus money to distribute to the team at the end of the year, the money is distributed based on the employee's ranking. Therefore, in order to make the team fit the curve, employees are ranked on the Criteria Grid so that the criteria rankings will line up according to the normal distribution

**Figure 5.3**

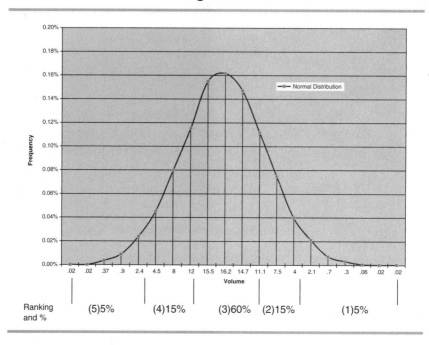

shown in the figure. In other words, 2 or 3 of the 50 employees will get a rating of 5—*not at all meeting the job requirements*.

*The glaring illogic with this approach is that it guarantees that employee failure has been built into the system.* Think about it. Two or three of the employees will be evaluated as *not at all meeting the job requirements regardless of their actual performance.* It would indeed be a dark day if you happened to be one of the three singled out by the business for such an honor!

In spite of what a company may publicly say about the value of its employees to the business, it is clear that any organization applying the method described above to evaluate an employee does not really value its employees at all.

Since the approach builds a certain percentage of guaranteed employee failure into the rating process (with this method, *someone has to fail*), it not only reflects a serious flaw in how the evaluation is performed but it also points to serious problems in the hiring process, which also puts the HR department directly on the hook. After all, how did such an "incompetent" pass muster through the drawn-out hiring/interviewing process? It has been documented in numerous trade periodicals that a bad hire costs a company more than the new hire's salary for an entire year. The upshot of this approach is that the business may lose a valuable and capable employee and make your HR department appear somewhat incompetent.

You may find it interesting to note that many managers with whom I have discussed this issue have come back with the same buck-passing, copout: "What are we supposed to do? The company tells us that this is how we have to perform the evaluation. We can't be perfect, and anyway, it's better than nothing."

Is that really true? Based on what most employees have to endure, *nothing* would be a more useful option than what passes for policy at most companies.

The following scenario actually occurred at a major U.S. brokerage—now defunct (bought out by a bigger dog).

The employee, we'll call him "Bob," finishes his freshman year at the brokerage. We'll call it that, because the CIO stated in a meeting of the entire IT department that many people first experiencing the furious pace at Paine-Webber might not do as well on their employee review. There may be a few areas where the employee needs to shoe up their effort, get more on the ball, put in longer hours, and be more responsive to the business's needs. After all, this is an intense environment that requires a level of commitment above and beyond most jobs. A lot of people have to gear up to the needed level of performance.

Bob takes this to heart and puts out the effort. At year-end, the review is performed—Bob is evaluated in 30 areas on the 1-to-5 scale. To his amazement, nothing is less than a *3*, meaning that in every area Bob met the requirements of the job. In fact, the scale played out like this:

- Level 1 scores: 6
- Level 2 scores: 18
- Level 3 scores: 6

You don't have to be a math genius to see that when you average these score together, Bob showed a solid *2*, meaning that overall he exceeded the job requirements during the performance year! This was quite a feat for a new guy on the block who was told to expect some fairly harsh evaluation.

His manager reviewed his performance and said that he was quite impressed with Bob's performance his first year on the job—most people don't do that well the first time out. After all 30 process areas were reviewed, the manager said, "Great job, Bob, we're going to rank you a *3* for the year!" Bob was shocked. He inquired how that could be when the scores averaged to a solid *2*. The manager stated that, unfortunately, there were people with the company who had been there over 5 years and if they didn't get their *2* there would be a revolt of sorts, not to mention some bad blood in addition. Bob inquired what method was used to come up with the ranking. The manager said that the bell curve was used.

Here is where the conversation got interesting. Bob posited, "What if you had 35 crackerjack programmers on your staff, all meeting or exceeding the job requirements. Are you saying that a few of these would have to be ranked as not at all meeting the job requirements (a score of *5*) because the bell curve tells you that you must? The manager said unfortunately, that would be true.

Bob said, "Okay, I understand," and left the manager's office, without complaint or criticism. Thirty days later he quit to everyone's amazement. Why had Bob quit? Bob had been *bell curved* and realized there was no possibility of getting a true evaluation of his accomplishments based on this evaluation approach.

## Management Is Responsible for the Working Environment

The reality about employee ranking is this: The employee ranking merely measures how well the employee can function within the environment management has created (i.e., it is really measuring management's effectiveness in training, leading, and setting a good example for the employees). It has very little to do with the employee.

Here is what American quality guru W. Edwards Deming had to say about the employee review, employee ranking, and the merit system:

> *Ranking is a farce. Apparent performance is actually attributable mostly to the system that the individual works in, not to the individual himself. . . . Ranking creates competition between people, salesmen, teams, divisions. It demoralizes employees. Ranking comes from failure to understand variation from common causes. . . . The so called merit system introduces conflict between people. Emphasis goes to the achievement of rank, merit, not on the work. The merit system destroys cooperation. . . . The aim of anybody under the merit system is to please the boss. The result is the destruction of morale. Quality suffers. . . . Judging people, putting them into slots, does not help them do a better job. . . .* The ranking of people indicates abdication of management. *[emphasis mine]*[10]

In effect, by ranking the employee, management is actually ranking its own effectiveness in leading its internal workforce. Unfortunately, there isn't an executive I have ever spoken to who has ever owned up to this idea. It's not that they are covering up for some inadequacy—they simply don't understand the connection.

To summarize, the current employee review process:

- Guarantees some level of employee failure
- Fails to truly capitalize on the employee's strength
- Suboptimizes the organization by forcing employees to compete against each other for rank, merit pay, and incentive pay
- Hides the true cause of employee success or failure: management

## WHAT TO DO ABOUT THE BROKEN EMPLOYEE REVIEW PROCESS

There are a series of steps that, if taken, will start turning around the negative effects of the employee review.

1. Admit the process doesn't work and train everyone, particularly senior executives, in the understanding of process variation and how to understand the difference between *specific causes* and *common causes* of variation in a system.

2. Make it corporate policy that everyone one is properly trained for his or her job.

3. Abolish ranking, the bell curve, competitive merit pay, and incentive pay (remember *piecework?*) as the company's primary method for evaluating employees.

4. Institute a program of discovering your employee's real strengths and work to help the employee improve those strengths.

5. If you want to find out how well you employees are doing, ask your customers, not the employee's manager. Start basing any evaluation criteria on customer satisfaction. The employee's manager doesn't sign his paycheck—your customers do.

6. Evaluate the entire team, not just individuals, and share any profits or bonuses with the team equally.

7. Monitor the effects of executive training on the overall improvement in employee performance—as executives create a saner work environment, employee performance will also improve.

*Principle #15:* **Offshoring your quality problems doesn't work and it may not be cheaper, either.**
   *Corollary #1:* Onshoring via the use of the H1-B or L1 visa program is another form of indentured servitude.
   *Corollary #2:* Automating a bad process helps you fail faster but more efficiently.

Offshoring is a phenomenon that goes back a long way in U.S. business. After all, given that hardware and equipment knows no nationality, a business can usually find qualified, educated offshore workers to do the same job for less money. We have seen this in the proliferation of offshore confabs that make IC chips and CPUs in Malaysia and the like.

However, does this work well for organizations that offshore customer service or software development functions? At this point, there are a few successes and a considerable mess based on the consensus of opinion from those in the trenches who are actually dealing with offshore/onshore projects. With many offshore projects we observe that many offshore IT shops in India and elsewhere claim a CMM/CMMI (Capability Maturity Model Integration) assessment level of 4 or 5. What does this mean? Below is a briefly summarized representation of the levels of the CMMI model:

*Level 1—Initial Level.* This is where most businesses start. Their projects are typified by intense heroic effort, consistently running in fire-drill mode, working project teams to burnout, and frequently running over budget by working 12+ hour days to meet deadlines. Good work can be done; it's just a miracle if you can repeat it.

*Level 2—Managed Level.* All project processes—Requirements Management, Project Planning, Project Tracking and Oversight, Software Quality Assurance, Software Configuration Management, and Vendor Management—are brought under project management control. The software managers for a project track software costs, schedules, and functionality; problems in meeting commitments are identified when they arise. The project's process is under the effective control of a project management system, following realistic plans based on the performance of previous projects. Generally, a company will pilot a few projects at this level to gain an understanding of the CMMI and get control of its work.

*Level 3—Defined Level.* All Level 3 projects can be summarized as standard and consistent because both software engineering and management activities are stable and repeatable. This process capability is based on a common, organizationwide understanding of the activities, roles, and responsibilities in a defined software process. Studies by the SEI have shown that any company that has reached a CMMI Level 3 can typically show a *400–800% ROI from implementing CMMI.* At this point, the lessons learned from the Level 2 projects have now been codified into a companywide standard and the Level 3 company has now institutionalized the processes from end-to-end and top-to-bottom in the entire organization

*Level 4—Quantitatively Managed Level.* Organizations functioning at this level can be summarized as predictable because the process is measured and operates within measurable limits. This level of process capability allows an organization to predict trends in process and product quality within the quantitative bounds of these limits. Management has clear visibility into all processes and can make sound decisions based on this visibility

*Level 5—Optimized Level.* Level 5 organizations analyze defects to determine their causes. Software processes are evaluated to prevent known types of defects from recurring, and lessons learned are disseminated to other projects. In other words, defects are frequently found and addressed before your customer knows there was a problem at all. The company works at consistently optimizing and streamlining its own processes. The company is looking down the road 5 to 10 years to see what technologies need to be retired and what new technologies need to be integrated with the business process. A CMMI Level 5 company operates with the goal of producing defect-free software, the first time, every time. By the time it has achieved CMMI Level 5, the results keep getting better. NASA and Telcordia function at this level.

In looking at the CMM claims made by offshore companies, my research has uncovered the following:

1. Offshore companies claim to be CMM certified. This is *impossible.* Here is what the SEI says about "CMM certification" (reprinted from http://seir.sei.cmu.edu/pml/):
   □ The terms "SEI certified" and "CMM certification" are simply incorrect since there is no such thing.

- □ The SEI does not certify organizations.
- □ The SEI only licenses and authorizes lead appraisers to conduct appraisals.
- □ Neither the SEI nor any other organization is a "certifying authority" of the results from an appraisal.
- □ The SEI does not confirm the accuracy of the maturity levels reported in published listings and has no intention of doing so.

□ The main intended goal and purpose of the models and appraisal methods developed by the SEI is for *self-improvement*. The outcome, which is entirely dependent on the organization that follows these practices, is to raise the level of quality of the products developed with a better ability to predict the time and budget needed to develop the product. *The goal focuses less on a perceived business advantage and more toward the ability to reliably develop products in a repeatable fashion with continual improvement versus doing the same in a chaotic state.*

□ Maintaining a certain maturity status is a continuous process. Therefore, once a certain level is reached, appraisals are still necessary to know if the maturity is being maintained over time.

2. Stateside businesses that have implemented offshore solutions have found that members of offshore firms have cheated on certification tests or pushed back project risks on the American teams to deal with the fallout. I spoke to several QA resources from a large U.S. insurance company that discovered a group of Indian programmers from a well-known offshore CMM Level 4 company cheating on a written Java programming test. "The test results were filled out by 75 people identically, right down to the commas, periods, hyphens, and question marks. It turns out they had taken the test home for the weekend and performed a *group answer session*. When we questioned one of the programmers about this, his response was, "I cheated, so what? Everyone does." Another well-known CMM Level 5 IT company in India refused to honor specific terms of its contract

with a privately held Fortune 300 American engineering firm. As one resource told me, "These guys refused to be on the hook for delivering *anything*." When the team told the Indian company that it was in breach of the contract, the Indian company responded that it would be "changing the contract."

3. The offshore view of customer service is different—in the United States, if the customer is dissatisfied with an outcome, the vendor will ask what it can do to fix the problem. With the offshore companies such as in India, their attitude is: "You gave us your specs and we built what you asked for. If it is not what you wanted, that is your problem." An associate working a major offshore deal for a Fortune 300 company has encountered this attitude on several occasions from CMM Level 4 and Level 5 companies in India.

4. Communication: You're not just dealing with a different culture; you're dealing with a culture that has a very different understanding of what your requirements actually mean. I spoke with an engineer at a U.S. Fortune 30 company who stated when he first tried the offshore approach the results he experienced were unpredictable and varied—all this from an advertised CMM Level 5 company in India. He said, "In short we asked for a banana and got an apple. Then we asked for a banana again and instead we got a strawberry. We literally had to open up an offshore office in India and hire the programmers directly into our organization before we achieved any control over the result. They could not, or would not, understand our requirements. You'd think that after drawing a picture somebody would get it."

5. A CMM Level 4 or 5 company is supposed to offer very clear ideas on how to improve a client's software process by significantly decreasing software defects and increasing productivity for software development projects. Here's the reality one associate observed at a major U.S. pharmaceutical company at which she is a project manager: "The offshore CMM 5 development resources just stated, 'Just tell us what to do and we'll do it.' You know, that's not why we hired them. They're the CMM 5 company—don't *they*

have some idea of what needs improvement? That's why we hired them in the first place. If we have to tell them what to do, we could just as easily do the work ourselves."

6. In the November/December 2003 issue of the *IEEE Software* journal, an article entitled "Software Development Worldwide: The State of the Practice" documented a survey of 104 software projects in India, Japan, Europe, and the United States. The participating Indian companies included four CMM Level 5 assessed businesses: Motorola India Electronics, Infosys, Tata Consulting, and Patni Computing. The performance information shown in Figure 5.4 was surveyed and tabulated. Note the following:

☐ No. of new lines of code/(avg. no. of staff × no. of programmer-months).

☐ No. of defects reported by customers in 12 months after implementation/total source LOC. We adjusted this ratio for projects with less than 12 months of data.

   The defect rates shown below are per 1,000 lines of code. The error rate per 100,000 lines of code is respectively:

☐ Japan—2

☐ Europe—23

☐ India—26

☐ United States—40

## Figure 5.4

| Table 3 Performance data | | | | | |
|---|---|---|---|---|---|
| | India | Japan | US | Europe & other | Total |
| Number of projects | 24 | 27 | 31 | 22 | 104 |
| Programmer LOC/MO | 209 | 469 | 270 | 436 | 374 |
| Median defect rate per/KLOC | .263 | .020 | .400 | .225 | .150 |

*Source:* Reprinted from November/December 2003 *IEEE Software.*

Not only did India place third in the code error-rate category, but it is also interesting to note that Indian companies averaged the *lowest Median output—new lines of code per programmer per month—of all the compared regions.*

In other words, India, the country that has claimed to produce more CMM/CMMI Level 5 assessed companies than the rest of the world combined, has the lowest code productivity and is third behind Japan and Europe in the number of errors per 100,000 lines of code. (As of 4-17-2003, 75 of 116 CMM Level 5 assessed companies are from India. See: http://seir.sei.cmu.edu/pml/index.asp.)

At this point, you may be wondering why the huge fanfare about CMM when it is clear that Japan, without the benefit of implementing the CMM, has produced the most productive programmers and the most error-free code in the world. The reason: Japanese companies started implementing the quality processes brought to them by Americans W. Edwards Deming and Joseph Juran from the early 1950s and for the last 50 years have built entire industries on quality standards that continue to evolve and that are second-to-none in the world. It is no surprise they are leading the pack in programming as well; after all—how many Japanese programmers do you see working in the United States? Unfortunately, the United States is still trying to get the message, which is why most U.S. businesses are importing CMM/CMMI processes from a third-world country instead of looking in their own backyard and taking advantage of processes that were invented here and funded by the DOD. Did we forget to mention that much of the CMM was inspired by the quality works developed by Deming, Juran, Philip Crosby, and Watts Humphrey?

An interesting wrinkle in the consulting business is the proliferation of H1-B visa resources that has been occurring for the last 10 years. U.S. businesses are claiming that we need additional help in the IT area because there are simply not enough qualified local resources to handle the workload at IT shops in the United States.

I have recently noted with great interest the public press releases from software giants Microsoft and Oracle. Bill Gates of Microsoft and Oracle VP Robert Hoffman have implored the U.S. Congress to raise the H1-B visa limits and allow more foreign IT professionals into the United States because American businesses are hurting for help so desperately.

It is a curious thing to watch a grown man who has more money than God whining to Congress about why he can't get IT resources at dirt-cheap prices to build the next iteration of Windows XXX. In reality, companies that make this claim simply do not want to pay qualified U.S. IT professionals to do the work—and the U.S. resources *are* out there.

Let's follow this through to its logical and absurd conclusion. If U.S. business is correct in this claim, then how did this occur? It is simply this: When enough work is offshored to India, China, or anywhere else and many computer trade publications state that hiring in the American IT industry is down, college graduates look in areas where they can make a living. Thus fewer people go into IT as a career choice. In essence, if we are to believe the rantings of IT industry leaders, then it should be clear to the reader that the IT industry has manufactured its own shortage. Why are we not instead seeing incentives to put our own citizens back to work in information technology? The reason is outlined below.

The very dark side to the H1-B/L1 visa program does not surface until one talks to the H1-B/L1 resources and discovers a very different scenario. U.S. businesses are not only ignoring the qualified U.S. resources, they are using the H1-B resources in a way that can be described only as a modified "slavery deal" or form of indentured servitude. As a former Director of Development dealing with "consulting firms" that offered H1-Bs as contract help, I found out that there were so many middlemen taking a cut from the H1-B resource that for a $95/hour contract, the consultant was frequently making in the range of $20/hour while the rest was going to the middlemen as overhead/markup. The upshot is that the customer still pays the same rate it would be paying for a qualified U.S. resource, except that using the H1-B resource allows the customer to pay the body shop a larger percentage of the rate! It looks more and more like the H1-B is a scam perpetrated by middlemen and used-car salesmen to cut themselves in for a bigger share of the "gift that keeps on giving" (a weekly cut of the resource's rate) while adding no value to the overall system. I have heard the same or similar stories from numerous stateside IT resources on an H1-B visa.

The L1 visa program is even more insidious. It was created to allow multinational companies to temporarily transfer employees with specialized skills from their foreign subsidiaries or parent companies to work on projects in the United States. The L1 visa has two subcategories: L1-A for executives and managers, and L1-B for workers with specialized knowledge. L1-A status is valid for up to seven years; L1-B status is good for up to five years.[11] However, a loophole allows IT consultancies with operations overseas to import foreign workers and then contract them out to U.S. companies, which are not required by law to pay L1 visa holders prevailing U.S. wages. In other words, U.S. businesses can pay an L1 visa holder working in the United States an offshore bill rate, whereas H-1B visa holders must be paid at prevailing U.S. rates. According to the Bureau of Citizenship and Immigration Services, the stock of L1 visa holders in the United States rose from 75,315 in 1992 to 328,480 in 2001. U.S. employers of L1 visa holders do not have to pay the $1,000 fee required for H-1B visas.

In Florida, Siemens was accused of replacing U.S. workers with foreigners who had L1 visas employed by Indian and U.S. firm Tata; the Tata workers were paid $36,000 a year, well below the prevailing wage. Siemens contracted with Tata for software maintenance, and Tata sent a team to Siemens, transferred as much of the work as possible to its Indian subsidiary, but brought Tata workers from India on L1 visas to work at Siemens.[12]

L1s don't pay U.S. federal income tax, either.

In short, the H1-B/L1 visa programs are a wonderful tax-evasion vehicle for U.S. businesses while simultaneously putting U.S. IT workers effectively out of business.

Do you want to know who is playing in the L1 arena? The top-20 list appears in Figure 5.5, courtesy of the U.S. Senate, 2007.

**Figure 5.5**

| Rank | Company | Headquarters | Primary Employment Base | L-1 Visa Received |
|---|---|---|---|---|
| | | Top 20 L-1 Visa Users | | |
| 1 | Tata | Mumbai, India | India | 4887 |
| 2 | Cognizant Technology Solutions | New Jersey | India | 3520 |
| 3 | IBM | Armonk, New York | USA | 1237 |
| 4 | Satyam | Hyderabad, India | India | 950 |
| 5 | Wipro | Bangalore, India | India | 839 |
| 6 | Hindustan Computers Ltd. (HCL) | Noida, India | India | 511 |
| 7 | Deloitte & Touche LLP | New York, New York | USA | 512 |
| 8 | Patni Computer Systems | Mumbai, India | India | 440 |
| 9 | Intel Corporation | Santa Clara, California | USA | 394 |
| 10 | Kanbay | Chicago, Pune, Hyderabad, and Chennai | India | 329 |
| 11 | Honeywell International | Morristown, New Jersey | USA | 320 |
| 12 | Hewlett Packard | Palo Alto, California | USA | 316 |

(Continues)

**Figure 5.5 (Continued)**

| | | Top 20 L-1 Visa Users | | |
| Rank | Company | Headquarters | Primary Employment Base | L-1 Visa Received |
|---|---|---|---|---|
| 13 | Infosys | Bangalore, India | India | 294 |
| 14 | Accenture | Hamilton, Bermuda | | 291 |
| 15 | Caritor | San Ramon, California | India | 231 |
| 16 | Schlumberger Technology Corp. | Netherlands Antilles | | 214 |
| 17 | Oracle Corporation | Redwood Shores, California | USA | 176 |
| 18 | Syntel | Troy, Michigan | India | 171 |
| 19 | PricewaterhouseCoopers | New York, New York | USA | 168 |
| 20 | Microsoft | Redmond, Washington | USA | 169 |

HITCHHIKER'S HEURISTIC: If you are going to work with a claimed CMM/CMMI-assessed offshore company, do yourself a favor and do the following with any company claiming a CMMI assessment level of 2 or above:

1. Ask them, What was your last published assessment level?

2. Ask them, When did that occur? (If the assessment is over two years old, you have the right to insist that they get reassessed for that level. After two years, the assessment is out of date, according to the SEI.)

3. You have a right to ask for and receive a copy of the company's CMM assessment documenting the strong areas and the areas still needing improvement.

4. You have a right to know:
   a. Who performed the lead assessment?
   b. Who was on the assessment team?

   Ask to directly question any of the assessment team about the assessment.

5. You have a right to question the vendor on specifics of its improvement processes regarding its customer interactions:
   a. What were the productivity improvements?
   b. By what percentage did the defect level drop?
   c. How much money has this saved you or how much have your earnings increased?
   d. Can your customers verify this?

   Ask for a customer list and do some of your own checking.

6. Ask the vendor what specific improvements have been made internally to its *own* product or processes as a result of its CMM/CMMI activities. You can demand specifics: metrics and written verification.

Finally, if you think of yourself as an ethical player, find out if your onshore/offshore resource is on an H1-B or L1 visa. If it's an H1-B, make sure you are not getting raked over the coals by the body shops that are keeping the rates inflated to stuff their own pockets. I never met any business leader who thought his mission in life was to increase overhead. If you find out you are dealing with an L1, you can be sure that most of what you are paying is going to be overhead. In either case, find out from the resource what their situation is and act accordingly.

*Principle #16:* **If you are wasting more than 30 minutes a day screwing around with an MS Project (or any other) Gantt chart, you are not managing your project.**

Sure, the Gantt chart has its uses. It has computational abilities and can compute timeline changes, perform *what-if* scenarios, compute earned value, perform resource leveling, track and manage the critical path in a project plan, and a host of other bells and whistles. That's all well and good.

Now let's ask the following. Does MS Project or any other Gantt chart tool:

- Negotiate with line managers for critical resources?
- Analyze and quantify risks in your project?
- Determine which software architecture is the best?
- Define which risks are learnable or are completely random?
- Negotiate the best resource price with a vendor?
- Help you build a high-performing team?
- Decide which DLM is best for the project you are going to be starting?
- Identify how to incrementally improve your project process?
- Determine which tools to use to ascertain whether your time estimates will actually deliver the most accurate probability for success?
- Help you decide whether a resource needs guidance or needs to be removed from the team?

These questions speak to decisions that confront project managers at some point in each project. They cannot be delegated to a software tool.

Gantt charts are good for basically two things: listing the tasks in your WBS down to the work package level, and mapping out timeline scenarios graphically to see how your critical path may be impacted if the length of any of your tasks changes. MS Project is basically

Excel on steroids. It can do some specific types of computations well, but it is severely limited. When I really need to calculate anything in a project such as resource utilization, burn rate for resources, profit margins, or task completion probabilities, or perform any statistical analysis of the data, Excel is more than adequate. For performing a DOE analysis, my first choice is Minitab.

By the way, if you said *yes* to any of the above questions, you might consider a lifetime membership in the Flat Earth Society.

## NOTES

1. Graham McLeod, *Managing Methods Creatively*, University of Cape Town, February 1992.
2. Armand Feigenbaum, *Total Quality Control, Third Edition*, pp. 46–47, McGraw Hill, 1991.
3. Peter F. Drucker, *Managing in the Next Society*, pp. 24, 26, St. Martin's Press, 2002.
4. REBE: Rectally Extracted Basis of Estimate (pronounced *ree-bee*), © 2005, Richard J. Perrin.
5. *Source:* The Standish Group.
6. Harry Goldstein, "Who Killed the Virtual Case File," *IEEE Spectrum*, September 2005.
7. Ken Barnhart, *MS Project Server Seminar*, Occam Systems, November 2003.
8. Robert X. Cringely, *Inc.*, February 2003.
9. The Standish Group.
10. W. Edwards Deming, *Out of the Crisis*, MIT Press, 1986.
11. http://en.wikipedia.org/wiki/L-1_visa.
12. http://migration.ucdavis.edu/MN/more.php?id=82_0_2_0.

## REFERENCES

*Agile Project Management*, Jim Highsmith, Addison-Wesley Professional, 2004.

*Agile Estimating and Planning*, Mike Cohn, Prentice Hall PTR, 2007.

*Managing Agile Projects*, Kevin Aquanno, Multi-Media Publications, 2005.

*Agile and Iterative Development: A Manager's Guide*, Craig Larman, Addison-Wesley Professional, 2003.

*Agile Project Management with Scrum*, Ken Schwaber, Microsoft Press, 2004.

*Agile Software Development with Scrum*, Ken Schwaber and Mike Beedle, Prentice Hall, 2001.

# Chapter
# 6

# Your Customer Is Talking—Are You Listening?

"Nothing travels faster than the speed of light with the possible exception of bad news, which obeys its own special laws."
—Douglas Adams, *The Hitchhikers Guide to the Galaxy*

**M**OST PROJECT TEAMS and PMs, like many businesses, seem to forget that the customer is the one that writes the check. The project team is trying to please the project sponsor, senior executive, or some other executive, and unless the project is an internal company project with internal customers, your actual customer is somewhere outside the company. Make sure this fact stays firmly implanted in your thoughts as you forge ahead implementing whatever project you have been charged with leading.

Most employees think they are paid by their company. The check or direct deposit has the company logo on it, after all. But in reality that payment is only a passthrough—the money is actually being paid by the customers of the business. I have had interesting conversations with various C-levels who continue to promote and sustain the following arcane concepts:

- Accountants and CFOs claim that inventory is an *asset.*
- Accounting systems continue to ignore the hidden factory in the business.
- The annual review is seen as a key tool used to help the employee improve.
- Customer service (that ignores the customer) is a "key component in our business success."

There are many companies that regularly dump on their customers. They never state that in their advertising—on the contrary, they state that their customers are their reason for being. Of course, they have to *say* it or no one would deal with them. In reality, the level of customer service over the last five years has consistently and dramatically diminished, particularly in the service sector: banking, computer system manufacturers, telcos, and credit card organizations, to name a few.

Since the mid-1990s, many U.S. businesses, faced with rising costs and competition, have offshored millions of U.S. jobs, citing their inability to "remain competitive" unless the work can be offshored for less. What management is really saying is that they are unable to solve their internal quality problems and offshoring is the magic bullet that will bring their businesses back into profitability.

In reality, the CEOs, whose salary and bonus are tied to the stock price of the business, fire thousands, sell off subsidiaries for short-term gain, pocket a huge bonus, slap a new coat of paint on the business, sell or merge the business with a larger competitor, and then take this movable feast to another company where they wash, rinse, and repeat the process (e.g., "Chainsaw" Al Dunlap—Sunbeam).

In the book, *Pay Without Performance,* the authors state the following reasons why CEOs get away with jacking up their compensation while delivering less and less to shareholders and society at large: While the boards of directors at publicly held companies are supposed to bargain at arm's length with CEOs and negotiate a compensation package that serves the interests of the shareholders, most publicly traded companies that do not have a controlling shareholder frequently do not exercise the necessary control to prevent runaway CEO compensation.

Presented below is a partial listing of issues that confront the investor/shareholder:

- Directors on a board are virtually reassured of being reelected on a yearly basis without opposition. Dissatisfied shareholders who attempt to dislodge an existing director by putting forth their own candidate have met with significant obstacles. In an empirical study performed between 1996 and 2002, challenges to the board's slate were virtually nonexistent—fewer than three per year for firms with a market cap greater than $200M.[1]

- CEOs have a powerful, if not a deciding, influence over the board nomination process. A 2002 survey discovered that of the S&P 1500 companies that had a nominating committee, only 50% of those operated independently of CEO influence.[2]

- CEOs used influence to make the design of option plans advantageous to them. Since stock option plans are not tightly linked to executive performance, they enable managers to "reap windfalls from stock price increases that are solely due to market and segment forces beyond managerial control."[3]

- A CEO who doubles as Chairman of the Board will usually get a higher compensation package.

- CEOs leaving a company—for whatever reason—may receive gratuitous payments and benefits at the expense of the shareholders and at very little cost to the directors on boards that approve such compensation packages. The CEO can exert influence that can "prevent acceptance of offers that are attractive to shareholders but harmful to the CEOs themselves":[4]
  - □ Webvan CEO George Sheehan resigned shortly before Webvan declared bankruptcy. He had a $6.7M loan forgiven in exchange for $150,000 in Webvan stock.[5]

- Bank One CEO John McCoy, pushed out in 1999 for poor performance, got his friends on the board to cook the books and arrange a departing $10.3 million cash payment, a $7.5 million "Special Recognition" award for his "service" in 1997 and 1998, plus a $3 million annual pension starting in 2001.
- Retirement benefits are paid in the form of an instrument called a *SERP* (supplemental executive retirement plan). A SERP is called a "defined benefit" plan because it guarantees fixed payment to the executive for life. All of the CEOs in the S&P ExecuComp database have defined-benefit plans.[6] No matter how poorly the company or its investments perform subsequent to the CEO's departure, the CEO is guaranteed the negotiated cash stream for life. The most insidious part of this arrangement is that the SERP is designed to increase executive compensation "off the radar screen of shareholders."[7] Some directors have voted to adopt SERPs after being assured the dollar amounts contained therein will not be reported to the public and that the awards plan will *not* be tied to company performance.[8]

The ultimate problem becomes a system that allows the CEO to put self-interest ahead of the interests of:

- The customer
- The employees of the company
- The shareholders of the company

The ultimate issue in the simplest terms represents abdication of responsibility by senior management. The continuing retention of command-and-control-type management that is typified by top-heavy bureaucracy and authoritarian (and sometimes sociopathic) management continues to do tremendous damage to the American workforce. From what we have seen in the previous examples, being a CEO in the S&P 1500 coupled with the collusive efforts from boards of directors grants the CEO a license to steal.

In short, 60 to 70 years of quality leadership and pioneering has largely gone ignored by executive management in the United States. Here is what the quality experts have to say about the state of U.S. business:

- W. Edwards Deming: "For the most part, most unemployment is created by management."

- Joseph Juran: "During this century (20th), very few of our (U.S.) companies became world leaders in quality."

- Philip B. Crosby: "The cost of quality is the expense of doing things wrong. It is the scrap, rework, service after service, warranty, inspection, tests, and similar activities made necessary by nonconformance problems."

How did we get here? Some possible causes are:

- Inability to compete globally without offshoring.
- Inability to market the business for real growth.
- No commitment to kill internal bureaucracy.
- No commitment to institutionalize innovation.
- No commitment to let the best ideas win. Best ideas are usually politicized into uselessness. Peter Drucker noted that if a great idea makes its way up the corporate hierarchy, the concept of the idea is diluted by half while the noise (misinterpretation) doubles for every level it moves up the corporate communication chain. If your idea has to go through five levels of bureaucracy, it will be diluted to 6¼% of what it was while the noise level jumps by a factor of 16. Your idea will bear no resemblance to what it was by the time it reaches the president or CEO.
- Lip service paid to:
  - Mission
  - Vision
  - Quality—continuous improvement

- □ "Our people are our most valuable asset" (a crock—see below)
- □ Ultimately: the customer

If we can translate what we see in the financial or business columns, most CEOs are a combination of:

- □ A used-car salesman
- □ A complete sociopath
- □ A criminal

Figure 6.1 is a reprint of part of an actual e-mail—minus any identifying corporate markings—sent out to an entire business unit at a major telco, demonstrating how much the business actually cares about employee contributions to cost savings.

Assuming that the savings is real and not funny money, that is, not a ploy to convince a SOX (Sarbanes-Oxley) auditor that your company has actually implemented tangible improvement processes, the preceding note is insulting, to say the least. I don't know about you, but if I had just saved a company over $2M in measurable improvement and they handed me a gift certificate for $300, my first response would have been, "It looks like you guys need this money more than I do," and the gift certificate would have been returned. My second response would have been to find a job where the business actually values the contributions of its employees.

A number of colleagues and seminar participants have confirmed that the above example is the rule and not the exception in most businesses. In fact, the way in which businesses treat their own employees is usually a strong indication of how they treat their customers, as well.

How do most businesses treat their customers? *They vomit on them.*

## Typical Vomiters:

- Airlines
- Telcos—local/long distance/cellular

## Figure 6.1

_____ has a goal for 2006 to achieve a total computer optimization savings of $12M. Included in this goal are the following targets:

- Mainframe Target—$6.5M
- Midrange Target—$3.5M
- Teradata Target—$2M

As of the end of June, _____ has achieved 113% of its goal, with $13.5M in annual savings.

This notice is to provide recognition to those individuals who have achieved cumulative optimization savings of $500,000 or more for 2006, as a result of their initiative and execution. We applaud them for their significant contributions toward our optimization goal!

| Recognition |
| --- |

*Congratulations go out to the following individuals for reaching cumulative optimization savings of $2,000,000 or more. In recognition of his efforts, this employee will be awarded gift certificates which total $300.*

*Congratulations go out to the following individuals for reaching cumulative optimization savings of $500,000 or more. In recognition of their efforts, these employees will be awarded a gift certificate of $100.*

- Utilities—oil and gas, electrical
- Computer systems manufacturers
- Insurance companies—particularly health insurance
- Auto dealers
- Banking/credit card/brokerage/mortgage company
- Your government (once you've heard the Seven Deadly Words, it's usually all over)[9]

These businesses all use the same approaches in dealing with their customers, which are called TVMs (*target vomiting methodologies*). Here are a few TVMs with which you may be familiar:

- *The Stall:* There are endless phone menus that must be navigated or bypassed before you ultimately (hopefully) get to the service you need.
- *Official Party Line:* "It is our policy that. . . . "
- *You Screwed Up:* "We don't handle that here. . . . "
- *By the Book:* "It's one week out of warranty—sorry."
- *Water Torture:* They make you (the customer) repeat information to a CSR (customer service representative) after you had already dialed it into the system.
- *It's Not My Fault:* "Our systems are down right now. . . . "
- *Don't Interrupt Me:* You attempt to convey your issue to the CSR but are consistently cut off or are not given a chance to speak.
- *Dead End:* At no point are you given the option to talk to a live human being. The entire system is automated. The real message: You are not a valued customer.

These TVMs are frequently combined—for example, the "You Screwed Up, Water Torture, Stall" method. This is where the customer is repeatedly asked for the same information while being bounced to new phone menus and more CSRs, who tell them they need to call a different number, because "we don't handle that here. . . . "

For example, while the major telcos figure out ways to increase the ability of their systems to handle customers through an automated voice menu system—after all, it's much cheaper than paying a human being—the customers, sick of being puked on, fight back. At a lockdown meeting at a major telco where speech scientists were discussing how to move the company's under 20% automated response rate to about 40% or more, I asked a simple question:

*How do you twist the customer's arm to use your interactive voice response (IVR) system, when all they have to do is go to www.gethuman.com? The web site shows you how to bypass every voice menu in the Fortune 500 and directly reach a human being so you can get your problem addressed.*

*If you infuriate the customer enough they will do an end run around you—the customer is not stupid, there is simply a limit to what they will endure. Telcos, airlines, insurance companies, and the like are increasing the use of systems of this type and they do not work very well—they are simply increasing customer frustration and wasting customers' time.*

What happens if it's worse than that? Recently I was on a call—an interview—with a representative of a BC/BS holding company that managed several state Blue Cross/Blue Shield plans. They were looking for ways to "improve the customer's IVR experience." After the usual round of questions, the interviewer asked if I had any questions. The question was, "Many of my colleagues who work in healthcare state that if the industry does not fix its financial model we will have issues for quite some time. What is your opinion?" The interviewer went in to a 10-minute dissertation on insurance companies, doctors, pharmaceutical companies, and hospitals. At no point did the interviewer mention the word *patient*. Since I thought that was a glaring omission, I asked, "Well, who is the customer?" The interviewer, without missing a beat, stated, "That depends on who you talk to." Is it any surprise that the healthcare industry does not know who its customers are? Apparently this BC/BS holding company does not.

There are three reasons why businesses treat their customers and employees badly, lose business, and lay off thousands:

*Reason #1:* Managerial incompetence

*Reason #2:* Managerial incompetence

*Reason #3:* Managerial incompetence

And there is no fourth reason.

If we are to believe the "models for quality" figures offered by Joseph Juran, this describes more than 80% of the so-called leadership populating the upper echelons of the Fortune 500, which usually include the three reasons listed above. I could offer case studies experienced first hand or by associates at AT&T, Blue Cross/Blue Shield, MCI, BP, Sears, Northern Trust, Houghton-Mifflin, HSBC, Allstate, AC Neilson, and so on, but at this point it would simply be throwing gasoline on the fire.

Why bother discussing these elements in a book about project management? In many cases, if you are a PM dealing with a customer, you *are* the company to that customer. There may be a significant disconnect between the company's official party line and what it actually practices.

If you find yourself functioning as a project manager in such an organization, depending on how far up the corporate hierarchy you may be reporting, you may find it difficult to function within an organization that does not talk-its-walk and walk-its-talk. Yet, as a PM, your job is to continue to communicate data and facts to the organization in a professional manner, no matter how dysfunctional that organization may be. Stay focused, and if it is a balancing act you must perform, do so with personal and professional integrity.

Reporting that the emperor has no clothes might not make you too popular with the company's internal bureaucracy. However, *doing just that* will let the customer know that they can depend on *you* in spite of what the business is actually doing. There are those within your company as well as customers who will recognize and appreciate your efforts. Some of those individuals move on to other companies with positions of increased responsibility. If things don't work out at your present company, new opportunities will present themselves and some of those individuals will remember your good example. Keep your network alive and keep walking the talk.

## NOTES

1. Lucian A. Bebchuk, "The Case for Shareholder Access to the Ballot," *Business Lawyer* 59 (2003), pp. 43–66.
2. Burke, Davis, Loayza, Murphy, Schuchner, *Board Structure/Board Pay*, 49, 2002.

3. Lucian Bebchuk and Jesse Fried, *Pay Without Performance*, Harvard University Press, 2004.
4. Lucian Bebchuk and Jesse Fried, *Pay Without Performance*, Harvard University Press, 2004, p. 92.
5. Joann S. Lubin, "As Their Companies Crumbled, Some CEO's Got Big Money Payouts," *Wall Street Journal*, February 26, 2002.
6. Steven Balsam, *An Introduction to Executive Compensation*, Academic Press, 2002.
7. Cynthia Richson quoted in Liz Pulliam Weston, "Despite Recession, Perks for Top Executives Grow," *Los Angeles Times*, February 1, 2002.
8. Glenn Howatt, "Health Partners Ex-CEO Reaped Board's Favors: Secret Deals Contributed to $5.5 Million Package," *Minneapolis Star Tribune*, January 17, 2003.
9. The Seven Deadly Words: "I'm from Washington—I'm here to help."

# Chapter
# 7

# Negotiating the "Quality Quagmire"

"The big corporations are suddenly taking notice of the web, and their reactions have been slow. Even the computer industry failed to see the importance of the Internet, but that's not saying much. Let's face it, the computer industry failed to see that the century would end."
—Douglas Adams

W E HAD QUALITY PROCESSES in the mid-to-late 1940s here in the United States. The U.S. Army was one of the largest implementers of SQC (System Quality Control) processes in the world. American quality guru Dr. W. Edwards Deming was instrumental in setting up and helping the army to implement these processes. Then World War II ended, and when the dust cleared, U.S. industry found itself in the enviable position of being the only power in the world with industrial capacity that had not been severely crippled or completely blown up.

The world needed goods, and the U.S. could produce them. As a result, the quality message got lost in favor of U.S. industry's new battle cry, "quantity!" When you're in the catbird seat, you can get away with almost anything, and this worked for a while until U.S. industry started experiencing an unscratchable itch—something they had not noticed in quite some time—something called *competition.*

While American business had, for the most part, abandoned quality processes in favor of dumping goods on the market as fast as they could produce them, the competition was at work implementing the quality concepts brought to them by Dr. W. Edwards Deming and Dr. Joseph Juran. The competition was Japan. Chrysler was the first to feel the pinch in 1979—as Japanese imports began to flood the U.S. market, Chrysler's old and unproductive plants couldn't compete with Japanese quality methods and processes. With the Flint/ Detroit area facing a 17% unemployment rate in the late 1970s/early 1980s, the U.S. auto industry had to rethink its modus operandus. Here is an example of what occurred:

In 1982, GM closed its Fremont plant, which had the worst productivity and absenteeism record in the company. In 1983, Toyota and GM reopened the same plant and hired back the same workers. New United Motor Manufacturing, Inc. (NUMMI) was managed by Toyota-trained management. They borrowed widely from Frederick Taylor in areas of work measurement, but with one major difference. Instead of industrial engineers, small work teams were formed and trained in work measurement and analysis methods. Workers designed their own jobs, and continually worked to improve their own performance. *In two years, the same facility, with the same workers, was operating at twice the productivity and quality—better than any other GM plant.* Absenteeism and drug abuse on the job had virtually disappeared, and the plant was being expanded.[1]

One would think that the U.S. automakers would have gotten the message across the board, but unfortunately, it didn't happen. When W. Edwards Deming, the man who taught Japan about quality, was brought to GM at the behest of the CEO Roger Smith (remember the film *Roger and Me* by Michael Moore? *That* Roger Smith) to teach GM how to implement quality processes, Roger Smith got up and left the room as Deming was about to begin his talk. The story goes that

Deming followed him out the door. When Smith turned and asked Deming why he had left the room, Deming replied that he thought Roger wanted him to follow to show him something. Smith replied that he had some critical business to attend to and that Deming needed to stay behind and deliver the quality message to the troops—the presidents, VPs, and directors—in the other room. Deming's response illustrates why most CEOs still don't get it when it comes to implementing quality. Deming replied that the message had to be delivered to the CEO (Roger Smith) or it would not be delivered at all.

It is interesting to note that, in the 1990s, Chrysler implemented a remarkable turnaround, becoming the most profitable car company in the *world* and giving Toyota some real angst. Chrysler was the only American car company that was giving Toyota serious competition! Chrysler created vehicle product development centers modeled after Honda and turned the old functional organization into a *product-driven* organization. Unfortunately, the merger of Daimler and Chrysler, purported to be a merger of equals, was nothing more than an out-and-out takeover by Daimler. By 2000, Chrysler was once again on the verge of bankruptcy and barely breaking even.[2]

Since U.S. businesses have largely failed—from a business, business ethics, and software development standpoint—to implement process quality coherently, a number of quality initiatives have been developed over the last 25 years that work in compliance with the standards developed by the International Organization for Standardization (ISO):

- *The Capability Maturity Model (CMM)* was initiated and developed at the Software Engineering Institute at Carnegie Mellon University in 1984 and funded 100% by the DOD. It is in compliance with ISO 9000 and ISO 15504.

- *The Capability Maturity Model Integration (CMMI):* This is a continuation of the CMM with the advent of two maturity processes: *continuous* and *staged*. Both have been subdivided into four progressively elaborated processes that have broadened the reach of the software development process.

- *The Project Management Institute,* started in 1969, achieved ISO 9001 certification of its project framework (*PMBOK*) in 1999.

- *ITGI:* The IT Governance Institute was founded in 1998.

- *CobiT:* The information technology standard for security and IT control practices—published in 1996—complies with ISO 17799.

- *SOX (Sarbanes-Oxley Act):* "What?! Quality *legislation?*" This is the first of its kind in the United States.

In addition, there are other commercial, proprietary processes in current use for quality improvement, which include:

- *Six Sigma:* A Joseph Juran consulting assignment at Motorola brought about the creation of the Six Sigma process, which was released and trademarked by Motorola in 1982.

- *Rational Unified Process (RUP):* For control of software development processes—released by the Rational Corporation in 1998. Rational Corp. is now owned by IBM.

- *ITIL (Information Technology Infrastructure Library):* This is the unified standard for *IT service management.* It provides documentation on the planning, provisioning, and support of IT services. ITIL is a registered trademark of the Office of Government Commerce (OGC) for the British government.

Due to the catastrophic failure of Enron and the outrageous financial malfeasance that occurred at WorldCom and Global Crossing, publicly traded corporations now have to prepare for audits and verification of financial and IT controls at an unprecedented level. After all, the last message Wall Street wants to send investors is that the market is rigged. The Sarbanes-Oxley Act (SOX), enacted in 2002, became law as of November 2004, and imposes a higher burden of proof on businesses for financial and IT controls. SOX compliance virtually requires that high levels of quality process improvement be implemented to satisfy the provisions of the Act.

Given the bewildering array of processes, I frequently get calls from consulting companies that are looking for people with quality process backgrounds. Hiring managers are jumping up and down stating that they need a "Six Sigma Black Belt," who has "implemented CMMI up to Level V," is "ITIL certified," with "five years' CobiT implementation experience," "SOX experience," and so on. It's what is called the *purple squirrel syndrome*—looking for an impossible amalgamation of skill sets that management thinks they need because someone read an article in *Computer World* or *CIO*.

When managers talk about the various methodologies mentioned above, they discuss them as though they are each a distinct and separate entity (e.g., "I need a Six Sigma Black Belt, a CMMI specialist, a CobiT specialist, and, oh yeah, and a PMP to manage the whole thing").

Unfortunately, what has happened is that these quality processes have been reduced to a series of labels and buzzwords identified by recruiters and management alike who seek to buy the label without understanding the content.

---

KEY CONCEPT: All of these processes and frameworks operate on quality principles and processes that are *not unique* to each framework—they are *common* to each framework. The consistent thread that runs through all of these methodologies is project management.

---

What businesses need are people who are experienced in the understanding of fundamental quality principles and the elimination of process variation—how to measure it, how to reduce it, and how to infect the organization with the quality bug so that quality becomes everyone's responsibility—*especially management's responsibility*.

The number-one reason why implementing a quality transformational change in your organization will (or won't) work is if management (read: the CEO or the president) leads the charge and takes ownership of the process and the outcome. Management is responsible for this transformational change. Management is also responsible for all the common causes in process variation—only management can fix these problems.

The news to most people is that the ISO-compliant and proprietary processes enumerated above are all fundamental quality processes and all based in some way on the work of Deming, Juran, Ishikawa, Shingo, Akao, Taguchi, Kano, Feigenbaum, and Crosby.

The success of Six Sigma and more recently Lean Six Sigma is due to CEOs such as Jack Welch and others implementing and achieving success with the process. In reality, the Six Sigma process is a repackaging of quality tools and processes that have all been around for over 30 years—some of them for much longer than that. That's not necessarily a bad thing. There is some benefit to the practitioner of quality tools and implementation to have a process that has collected and exemplified the use of the tools via a framework whose focus is improving the bottom line—get rid of delay and defects and boost profitability at the same time. Some of the tools of Six Sigma have the following pedigrees:

- SPC was developed in the 1930s by Walter Shewhart.
- Ishikawa's book, *Guide to Quality Control*, delineating the use of the "Seven Quality Tools," was published in 1968 by JUSE (Japanese Union of Scientists and Engineers) and includes descriptions and instructions on the preparation of flowcharts, control charts, Pareto diagrams, cause-and-effect diagrams, scatter diagrams, checksheets, and histograms.
- *Poka-yoke* (mistake proofing) and just-in-time were developed by Shigeo Shingo between 1961 and 1964.
- Principles of *kaizen* (continuous improvement) have been used in Japan since the 1960s.
- QFD (Quality Functional Deployment) was first put to use by Dr. Yoji Akao in the early 1960s.
- Genichi Taguchi's "loss function" was developed in the 1970s.
- Design of experiments (DOE) has been written about and documented in books and scientific journals for over 100

years. Sir Ronald Fisher, statistician, created DOE *factorial* concepts during the 1920s in the area of agriculture with great success, and modern DOE was born.

- The FMEA (Failure Modes and Effect Analysis) discipline was developed by the U.S. military and first documented in Mil Spec MIL-P-1629 in November 1949.

While Six Sigma has gained traction in the United States, understand that companies like Toyota, Kobe Shipyards, and Sony, and scores of other Japanese companies, have achieved the highest quality levels in the world without Six Sigma, CMM, CMMI, CobiT, ISACA, ITIL, RUP, PMI, or any other framework being marketed under the guise of any "www.quality.R.us.org." Japanese business leaders took the work that Deming and Juran brought to Japan in the early 1950s and began elaborating quality processes that transformed how business was done in Japan. Case in point: Of the top-five-selling passenger sedans in the United States, four of them are Japanese. And they did it without the benefit of or input from a Six Sigma Black Belt replete with Magic Decoder Ring and Secret Handshake.

Leave it to American Management to create a "Quality Tower of Babel" and add layer upon layer of needless complexity to an improvement process. If you review all the processes, you will see that project management concepts are fundamental and are a common thread that runs through *all* the quality processes—ideas like managing scope, budget, requirements, change control, quality, risk, human resources, vendors, and timeline are fundamental to *all the methodologies.*

When all of the proprietary approaches are distilled to their essentials, we are left with two ideas that drive the success of any of the quality processes:

1. Disciplined scientific method—tools and techniques
2. Disciplined engineering—systems thinking

As far as moving your organization to quality, understand this: It doesn't matter *what* you call the quality process—TQM, Six Sigma, CMMI, CobiT, ITIL, RUP, or Green Eggs and Ham.

Hey, maybe you would get *better results* if you *called* it "Green Eggs and Ham"—after all, what is the book about?

It's about a frumpy-looking individual who absolutely refuses to try green eggs and ham because they *look weird, sound weird,* and don't appear very appetizing, no matter how much Sam-I-Am tries to persuade the frump to take a bite. However, once the frump tries a sample, he finds that he *likes* green eggs and ham— that he would eat them here and there; he would eat them *anywhere*. The book is really about having a transformational experience, an epiphany if you will, and emerging changed as a result of the experience. Quite a feat and only 50 words were used. The *outstanding* bonus you achieve with the GE&H approach is that it's already written at a level that most CEOs can understand and "vision" types like to keep it simple.

What if you substituted the term *quality* for "Green Eggs and Ham"?

Let's not get *too* excited! That's usually a bit of a stretch for most people. We had better reconsider this or the CEO's brain might explode.

Our problem has been that we have a lot of information, but no expertise in helping us get to and hold onto quality.

We are suffering from the knowing–doing gap. We know what to do but for some reason we don't do it. Only very few companies do. Why?

One possibility is the *change-or-die syndrome*. Given that you just found out from your cardiologist that if you don't immediately dump the fast-food diet and start eating salads and protein, start exercising, and reduce your stress level, you will suffer a major heart attack and die within one month, the odds are 9 to 1 *against you* actually doing anything about it. This has been confirmed in numerous medical studies performed over the last 50 years.[3]

"What!" you say? After reading the odds, any *rational* person would do what was necessary to save one's own life. Unfortunately, it seems that most of us aren't very rational. After reading the odds and considering what most people do—absolutely nothing—you must come to one of the following four conclusions:

**1.** We are too stupid to get it.

**2.** We just don't give a damn—we're all going to die someday, anyway.

**3.** We think it won't happen to us—it will happen to someone else. (After all, when the doctor tells us something we don't like, we usually ask for a second opinion.)

**4.** It's just another scare tactic to try and sell us something that won't work.

Consider this a wakeup call. Your worst nightmare is about to come true, but you probably won't recognize it. Your nightmare will come dressed up as a new job offer, a promotion, or even an opportunity to work overseas on some *fabulous* offshore deal with a company from China or India.

I've talked to many businesspeople about this and there is considerable debate on which of the four conclusions outweighs the other three. However, no matter which theory you subscribe to, the result is the same. You thought you could solve your quality problems by offshoring them, merging the company, implementing massive layoffs to cut costs, or whatever. After all, the same work gets done a whole lot cheaper and your business reaps the benefits. You couldn't solve your quality problems yourself, so you moved your pile of garbage under someone else's window with the full and optimistic expectation that *they* would fix it for you!

It's reminiscent of that philosophical question about a tree falling in the forest, but with a new twist: If you move a stinking pile of low-quality garbage from under your window to an IT company in Bombay, and you are not there to smell it—does it still stink? It's certainly a question to ponder for the ages. Anyway, you offshore the work and eventually go out of business—not because you offshored the work, but because the quality of service your customers are receiving from the Bangalore/Bombay/Shanghai crews is so poor, your customers have decided to deal with companies whose customer service reps they can *understand*.

Interesting scenario, don't you think? It happens every day.

So, if you are the one-of-nine that wants to do something about it, and you really want to understand what is going on in the "World of Quality," I've attempted to break down the various groups—be it the Software Engineering Institute (SEI), American Society for Quality (ASQ), I-Six Sigma, or whatever dot-com or dot-org has entered into the fray—into understandable segments that can be appreciated by the general public. As they say in baseball, you can't know the players without a scorecard:

*Quality Factory:* The business makes a high-quality product and is in excellent tune with its customers. Profits are high, production is high, and mistakes are very few and far between. Management is leading the charge because they are keyed into and knowledgeable about quality principles and processes. Quality truly is "Job #1," but you'll never see that in their advertising because they don't have to say it. It will be obvious in the products they turn out.

*House of Quality:* This is a misnomer for Yoji Akao's Quality Function Deployment process developed in the late 1960s, otherwise known as the *Voice-of-the-Customer*. It is a cornerstone of the quality improvement process that helps a business understand what the customer really needs, what the customer is really asking for, and the fitness for use of the designed product. In other words, if the business finds out how the customer actually intends to *use* its product(s), better product(s) might be designed.

*Quality Condo:* Various teams in the business are working to internally develop quality standards that help them get through the day and produce a *good-enough* quality product to keep management off their backs. They hit their numbers and meet their quotas and that's all they do. Don't ask for anything beyond that. Management thinks they need to keep an eye on these guys in case someone tries to put something over on them, but basically thinks they can be kept in line with threats of offshoring and staff reductions. The technologists have barricaded themselves into the condo behind locked doors and the doorman at the front of the building (the QA department) refuses to let management in unless they first remove their shoes.

*Quality Tenement:* The company is loaded with people that have taken training and read about every quality process under the sun but have never been permitted to implement anything. However, because the company has paid for "quality training," they now consider themselves a "Quality Organization." The CIO, however, is still wondering why all the money they spent on the quality training hasn't turned into increased productivity, increased sales, and lower defects. However, firing all the people they had trained would show senior management that the program had been a failure, so everyone is kept on and continues to deal with issues in fire-drill mode. Management approves because with all the activity and churn, it looks like those "damned IT goons" are finally earning their keep.

*Quality Bunker:* Quality is managed by a "Quality Control" team. People working in the business who encounter one of this team in the hallway will immediately turn in the other direction to avoid contact of any kind. They produce reams of paper and lots of policy statements—which everyone ignores because implementing the policies slows work to a crawl. The QC manager is viewed by workers as a variant of a Nazi torture doctor who resembles Lawrence Olivier in *The Running Man* ("Is it safe?"). Everyone hates the Quality Department.

*Quality Landfill:* Who needs this quality stuff? Anyway, *we* didn't invent it, so get rid of it. A major U.S. insurance company in Illinois prepared for a CMMI Level 2 assessment by coaching their employees on exactly what to say to the auditor so that there would be no variance in the answers. They produce a lot of documentation they will never use, just to say they have it in case an auditor ever checks up on them, and continue with business as usual. (They really didn't have the quality processes in place—they just wanted the rating.) However, because of the accumulation of large quantities of printed paper and binders, large pockets of methane are beginning to form in various areas of the facility.

*Quality Outhouse:* No matter what you do, it all winds up in the same place anyway! A major American oil company successfully completed a CMM Level 2 assessment; however, as the result of a merger, when the buying company took control, the purchasers decided the CMM assessment wasn't worth the paper on which it was printed. They took almost two years' worth of process and documentation and literally threw it into the dumpster. The company then offshored its IT work to India and the execs gave themselves big bonuses for having thought of it. Their customers continue to pay record prices for oil and gas, not to mention that the worst oil refinery explosion in the United States in 25 years at a Texas City refinery in 2005 was probably just a glitch.

*Quality Dungeon:* People are hired into a major telco because they are certified as project managers, and have CMMI experience and Six Sigma experience. All employees are exhorted in slogans and in an unstated-yet-implied attitude that the company should be reaping great rewards because the business was smart enough to bring these quality geniuses into the company. No quality training, support for the hired quality experts, or management support of any kind is provided by the company. Management has issued press releases that they have "installed quality" in the business. After two years, the company decries its "investment" and fires all the quality experts it hired because nothing has improved—in fact, things have gone from bad to worse—but the company puts out a press release stating that it spent $150M on "research and development." The company's stock price goes up $5 a share. Wall Street is fooled, investors are happy; but customers are already puking in their shoes because they are locked into contracts that will bankrupt them if their service gets any worse.

*Quality Crypt:* A small utility room in which all the quality process documentation the company developed is kept. Occasionally, a new employee or contractor is directed to the room when they inquire about methods and procedures. The room is small, poorly lit, and smells of mildew—one corner contains the decomposed, skeletal remains of the last QC manager. This "snipe hunt" is gleefully plotted by the company's longtime employees, who gather outside the crypt door and respond with great hilarity upon seeing the expression on the newbie's face when first emerging from the crypt.

And then there are the various "quality personnel":

*Quality Practitioner:* Someone who attempts to apply the quality principles, techniques, and tools that have been successful over the last 70 years, and meets with success—in spite of management's insistence that they are overhead and will have to continue justifying their existence to the business.

*Quality Zombie:* Has read every book about the failed or quack business processes of the last 50 years, including MBO (Management by Objectives), MBR (Management by Results), MBWA (Management by Walking Around), and MBE (Management by Exception), and can spout endlessly about why these methods don't work, but has never implemented a successful quality process anywhere.

*Quality Homeless:* Has taken every ASQ course and passed every certification there is to be had, but cannot find a job because she is overqualified for everything.

*Quality Roadkill:* What happens to a member of the QA organization who dares to state that the emperor has no clothes. Usually, these are the most knowledgeable members of the QA department and the first people to be threatened by the business when they find issues with the last product release and refuse to sweep it under the rug. The company releases the product anyway, and, as sales drop, the CFO engages in a cost-cutting frenzy—guess who gets fired first?

*Quality Prostitute:* A business that will sell you any "quality process," libraries of books and methodologies, or consulting that your business thinks it needs to satisfy and placate unhappy customers and investors. The vendor shows up, bearing consultants with impressive credentials, slick-looking binders, and lots of training. Customers are brought in when all this is going on to show them just how much the business is "committed" to implementing quality improvement. The temporary euphoria from all this activity and churn is followed by a severe letdown when, in a very short time, nothing is implemented and everyone forgets the training because management is not committed to the process.

The somewhat tongue-in-cheek treatment from the preceding listing underscores a particularly vexing issue: U.S. companies, particularly in the service arena, are having great difficulty making the transition to the product-driven, customer-focused model that Japan & Co. seem to understand very well.

What I hear from most businesses is that changing the corporate culture will take quite some time, and that these things must be implemented slowly and deliberately. To all the businesses that think the move forward to quality and customer loyalty needs to happen on a slow and deliberate path—consider the following:

- By the time you have gotten around to implementing quality and surpassing customer satisfaction for your business, you will have ceased to exist.

- The way to catch up quickly is to seek out those who have trod the path before you and implement drastic changes in how you think your business should be run.

- Institute consistency of purpose—if you are running in a two-year cycle where your star executives who are interested only in the fast track up the corporate ladder are managing your critical business projects, stop right now. You had better be thinking 5, 10, and 20 years ahead. Too many companies start initiatives implemented by the "new VP" only to have that VP move on two years later, and the key projects that were started fall by the wayside. I call this "management by sounding smart" without any follow-through. It's just like a baseball swing—no follow through, no home run.

Ultimately, if you are not willing to change what is not working, on a dime, and do what you need to do to succeed, don't expect to be here in 5 or 10 years. In 2001 I made the rash prediction that GM and Ford might not exist (or exist in significantly different forms) by 2010 because of their refusal to implement key improvements in their quality and reliability. Here we are in 2007 and the following has occurred:

- Toyota has moved into the #1 slot in gross revenues, making it the top grossing car company in the world (and also one of the most profitable). Toyota is showing Net Tangible Assets in excess of $100B. If you check *Consumer Reports* for October 2007 (www.consumerreports.org), Toyota and Honda (including Lexus and Acura) have 24 "Recommended Plus" vehicles out of a total of 55 across all car manufacturers and models!

- GM is mortgaged up to its ears. As of June 2007 the balance sheet shows Net Tangible Assets of larger than *negative* $3.5B.

- Ford is the least productive of the "Big 3," showing Net Tangible Assets of larger than *negative* $8B and running at only 79% of capacity (GM ran at 90%, Chrysler at 94%, and Toyota at 106%).[4]

As I said to some employees at a large telecommunications company whose projects were consistently over budget and far beyond their due dates: "You had better pray with every fiber in your being that Toyota does not decide to go into the telecommunications business, because if they do, they will be scraping you off the ground in 5 years like just so much roadkill."

# NOTES

1. Paul Alder, "Time-and-Motion Regained," *Harvard Business Review*, January/February 1993, pp. 97–108.
2. Jeffrey Liker, *The Toyota Way*, McGraw-Hill, p. 83, 2004.
3. "Change or Die," *Fast Company*, September 2005.
4. David Welch, David Kiley, and Stanley Holmes, "How Mulally Will Tackle Ford's Problems," *BusinessWeek*, September 7, 2006.

# Section
# 2

# Technical Tools for Quality Management, Risk Management, and Financial Management

# Chapter
# 8

# Critical Chain
# Project Management

CRITICAL CHAIN PROJECT MANAGEMENT (CCPM) is based on the *theory of constraints* developed by Dr. Eliyahu Goldratt. Simply put, CCPM is a project timeline approach that will cut your project durations by 25–50%. After hearing this, most CTO/CIO/CFO types tell me I am lying and go about their business. However, this approach requires that you move out of your traditional comfort zone, forget about what you thought you knew about managing projects, and get prepared to have the traditional project model turned on its head. This is another one of those mind-altering processes that will change the way you look at work from this point forward.

What is CCPM? To understand that better, let's look at the way a typical project is managed. You're the PM on a team that is rolling out a new system that uses some prebuilt software components, has a good bit of new development, and has to integrate with an existing system.

You have a deadline nine months out (39 weeks) that is etched in stone because there are some regulatory compliance issues that must be addressed by that time, so ultimately your project's primary constraint is the timeline.

You have assembled an experienced team that consists of system architects, network architects, certified Java and C++ developers, DBAs, and Online Documentation and Test. There are a few greenbeans who are apprenticing to more experienced team members. These folks are out of school with CS degrees and can code, but they have never worked in a full-blown production environment—this is their first job. You have engaged the testing organization up front because, in your experience, you know that to fail to include the testing/QA team until the code has been completed is a recipe for disaster.

You hold a team kickoff, review the high-level scope, impart management's expectations to the team, and give the team five business days to come up with their estimates while you take a week to develop the initial schedule. You are thinking that with the team's experience your schedule will probably coincide with the team's estimate fairly well, so, with minor adjustment, the schedule will be about 80% in the bag.

Then you get a reality check. At the next team meeting all the team leads bring their estimates and, instead of receiving a confirmation of the schedule estimate, you receive the following:

- 3 weeks—Business requirements elaboration
- 1 week—Peer review and signoff
- 5 weeks—Technical requirements elaboration
- 1 week—Peer review and signoff
- 3 weeks—High-level design (all teams)
- 1 week—Peer review and signoff
- 5 weeks—Detail design (all teams)
- 1 week—Peer review and signoff
- 12 weeks—Coding and unit testing
- 3 weeks—Integration testing
- 12 weeks—System testing

- 3 weeks—UAT and end-user training
- 2 weeks—Operational readiness testing
- Deployment

Instead of 39 weeks, your project is now sitting at 52 weeks. Shocked by the estimate that increases your schedule by one-third, you ask the teams why their estimates are so far off the expected timeline for the project. After all, management figured that this project would not possibly take longer than nine months; why the big discrepancy?

One team lead suggests that we should have started sooner if management wanted to finish by the required due date. Another states that the estimates are accurate given how projects are generally implemented in this organization and that there is no slack in the timeline. The project manager (you) digs a little deeper. How did the teams arrive at the estimate?

They used a PERT followed by a Monte Carlo analysis and based their outcomes on an 80% confidence factor. This means that there was an Optimistic, Most Likely, and Pessimistic estimate fed into a PERT formula and then the result was fed into a Monte Carlo to derive a probability for completing the tasks by a certain time with an 80% confidence factor. The above schedule is what they got.

Instead of exhorting the team to "work smarter" and "cut the fat out of this estimate to bring it in on time," you remember that a colleague had gotten remarkable results on a project by using something called CCPM (Critical Chain Project Management) and you call her up and ask her if she would be up for a short consulting assignment to help the project team. She agrees and an initial fact-finding session is set up with the team leads.

Your colleague—we'll call her Athena—sits down with the team and starts in asking the following questions:

- How many projects including this one are you working on right now?
- How many projects including this one are your team members working on right now?

- What are the key issues that contribute to your pessimistic time estimates?

- What are the most time-constraining impediments to getting your job done on this or any other project?

- If there is one overriding process that you would fix that causes you the most pain on all your projects, what would it be?

Athena collects the answers from the team leads and prepares a report for you and her to review later in the day. The report summary appears in Figure 8.1.

Athena noted that all the team leads and their teams were multitasking to juggle conflicting needs. The other constant was that they were continually padding estimates to account for the anticipated *undesirable events*, many of which are mentioned in the summary. The typical pad was 50% due to elements that were beyond the control of the team or the team leaders.

How can CCPM help? Athena explains that CCPM is based on the theory of *constraints*, which is a process that focuses on improving a business system. There are six fundamentals that need to be understood and where TOC can help:

1. Any system has a constraint that limits its output.

2. Before we can improve the system, we must define the system's global goal and the measurements that will enable us to judge the impact of any subsystem on the goal.

3. Each system has a "weakest link" (constraint) that limits the success of the entire system.

4. Therefore, system thinking is preferable to analytical thinking in managing change and solving problems.

5. The undesirable effects (UDEs) the team is experiencing are caused by a few core problems:
   a. Core problems are almost never superficially apparent— they are manifested through a number of UDEs linked by a network of effect–cause–effect.

**Figure 8.1**

| Question | Architects | Leads | DBAs | Online Documentation | Test |
|---|---|---|---|---|---|
| How many projects including this one are you working on right now (concurrently)? | 5 | 6 | 8 | 9 | 4 |
| How many projects including this one are your team members working on right now (concurrently)? | 3 | 4 | 4 | 6 | 2 |

| What are the key issues that contribute to your pessimistic time estimates? | |
|---|---|
| Architects | Conflict with management about architectural direction |
| Leads | ■ Resources pulled to work on production issues or emergencies.<br>■ VP reassigns resource for pet project.<br>■ Experienced resource suddenly quits—time is lost retraining. |
| DBAs | ■ Long lead times to obtain needed hardware.<br>■ Volume estimates are never accurate and need to be redone. |
| Online Documentation | ■ User indecision on what is needed in online documentation.<br>■ Difficulty setting up time with developers to capture essentials. |
| Test | ■ Unclear requirements traceability matrix.<br>■ Some requirements untestable on present platform—new test beds are needed, This eats up valuable test time. |

*(Continues)*

**Figure 8.1 (Continued)**

| Question | Architects | Leads | DBAs | Online Documentation | Test |
|---|---|---|---|---|---|
| What are the most time-constraining impediments to getting your job done on this or any other project? | | | | | |
| Architects | ■ Too many meetings.<br>■ Clients changing direction in midstream. | | | | |
| Leads | ■ Too many meetings.<br>■ Too many change requests due to missed requirements. | | | | |
| DBAs | ■ Lack of effective tools.<br>■ Constantly changing requirements. | | | | |
| Online Documentation | ■ Unavailability of developers for information. | | | | |
| Test | ■ Management pressure to certify software without performing complete tests. | | | | |
| If there is one overriding process that you would fix that causes you the most pain on all your projects, what would it be? | | | | | |
| Architects | Setting up a 5-year architectural blueprint for the business and have the business follow through. | | | | |
| Leads | Management: Let us do our jobs and stay out of our way. | | | | |
| DBAs | Obtaining a world-class toolset to help us automate drudgery so we can focus more on the design. | | | | |
| Online Documentation | Join us at the hip with development so we can do our jobs correctly. | | | | |
| Test | Enough time to properly and ruthlessly test. | | | | |

   b. Elimination of individual UDEs gives a false sense of security and usually ignores the underlying problem.

   c. Core problems are usually perpetuated by a hidden or underlying conflict.

   d. Solution of core problems requires challenging the assumptions of the underlying conflict and invalidating at least one.

**6.** Most system constraints usually trace back to a flawed policy rather than to a physical constraint.

Athena suggested that we look at two core UDEs that are causing our difficulties right now by examining two work scenarios (Figure 8.2).

With Scenario #1, three tasks are taken on sequentially—one unit of throughput can mean a week, 10 days, a month, or any unit you devise. When the first task is completed, the second task is started and worked to completion. In Scenario #1, at the end of two units of throughput, two of the three tasks are completed. In Scenario #2, at the completion of two units of throughput, we don't know where we are with tasks A, B, or C.

When I ask developers or team leads the Scenario #2 question (Where are we with the three tasks?), the answer I usually receive is that the tasks are 80% complete and they stay that way for quite some time. It seems at some point in the schedule tasks are *always* 80%

**Figure 8.2**

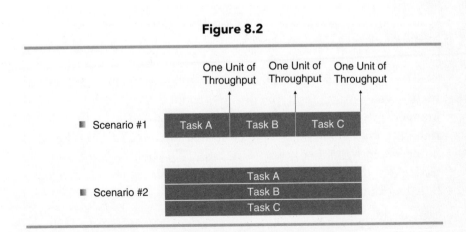

complete. The assumption with Scenario #2 is that there is no time lost dropping one task and picking up another—this is the fundamental precept behind multitasking. However, if we look at statement 5d listed above we must challenge the assumption of the underlying conflict—the assumption that multitasking is an effective way to accomplish work.

So, our first identified system constraint is *multitasking*. In reality, multitasking is the absolute worst way to get work accomplished:

- Multitasking burns up cycle time as resources drop one task in order to get "in flow" (completely engaged and concentrating on their process) with another.

- Studies done on software engineers show that interrupting a resource that is in flow to work on something else (an emergency, another project issue, etc.) will take minimally 45 minutes to an hour for them to get back into flow on their original task.

- If you are interrupted four times in one day, half your day has been shot simply attempting to get back into flow on your original task.

- In Scenario #2, none of the tasks complete until the third week (if that)—we have no idea what the merge bias impacts may be on your task timelines at this point.

> *Core Constraint #1:* We must remove the multitasking constraint and allow people to focus exclusively on their task at hand—no interruptions!

The second core UDE is has to do with how estimates are created; in this case estimates typically are padded 50% to address unplanned events and unscheduled interruptions. If everything went right, the work could be completed in half the time. CCPM takes this into account by taking the built-in buffer for each task and concentrating it at the end of the task stream. A graphic representation looks like the example in Figure 8.3.

**Figure 8.3**

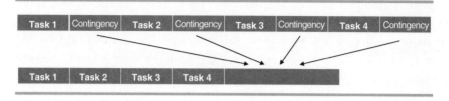

By concentrating the uncertainty in the four tasks at the end of the critical path in a single continuous buffer we derive the following bonus:

- Less total project time.
- Concentrating the contingency at the end of the project path reduces the likelihood that it will be overrun by a large amount.

To make this work, we have to challenge more assumptions and conventional thinking, such as the assumption that resources can be pulled off their assigned tasks at will by management to address a VP's pet project, a production issue, a missed requirement by the business, and so forth. It means that:

- A resource starts work on a task as soon as input is received.
- The resource focuses on that task 100% to its completion—no contingency time utilized.
- Pass on the task output as soon as it is completed to the next resource.

---

*Core Constraint #2:* Remove the excess contingency that increases each task and reduce task completion time as a result. Concentrate the contingency in a buffer at the end of the timeline.

---

For example, look at Figure 8.4. Notice that the CCPM approach reduces the entire project timeline by 25%, even if the buffer at the

## Figure 8.4

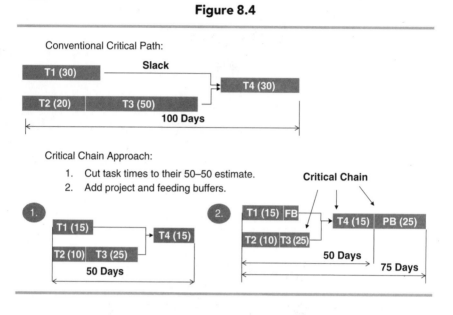

Conventional Critical Path:

Critical Chain Approach:
1. Cut task times to their 50–50 estimate.
2. Add project and feeding buffers.

end is completely exhausted. Project managers using this approach expect 50% of the tasks to spill into the buffer, so the usual panic that sets in is replaced by a reality check and some sense of the actual velocity needed by the team to complete the work.

Unfortunately, this approach is usually met with hostility by management or panic by the development team. The developers feel their padded estimate gives them a safety net and that they will be blamed by management for not hitting their deadlines. However, the real mind shift has to occur with management. Stop multitasking and get rid of the pad for each task. This approach challenges some deeply held beliefs about how work must be performed and frequently reflects either flawed thinking or a flawed internal policy.

Just so that you know this is not smoke and mirrors, there are several companies in the Chicago area that are utilizing the CCPM approach and are not disclosing who they are because the CCPM approach is yielding a competitive marketplace advantage for these organizations.

# Chapter
# 9

# The Analytic Hierarchy Process

IN EVERY PROJECT, decisions need to be made: selecting the right equipment, choosing the best vendor to supply parts, selecting the most secure wireless technology, the best training for the lowest price, and so on. Most decision processes involve setting up some kind of grid that shows the decision criteria, assigning each criterion a specified weight (i.e., how important it is), and matching various products against each criterion to deliver an overall score. A typical example of this type of grid is shown in Figure 9.1. In this case, we are evaluating four copiers.

Notice each criterion is given a weight, that is, its relative importance compared with the other criteria on a scale of 1 to 10, *1* being the least important and *10* being the most important. Each product is then scored against each criterion on a scale of 1 to 10 to show how well each product scored compared to the others. Then the *weight* is multiplied by the *score* to produce the *weighted score* for each criterion. Add up the weighted scores for each product, and the one with the highest score wins—or so it's supposed to go.

This type of decision process is problematic for several reasons:

**Figure 9.1**

| Criteria | Weight | Ricoh | | Xerox | | Oce | | HP | |
|---|---|---|---|---|---|---|---|---|---|
| | | Score | Weighted Score | Score | Weighted Score | Score | Weighted Score | Score | Weighted Score |
| Speed | 10 | 9 | 90 | 10 | 100 | 9 | 90 | 7 | 70 |
| Ease of use | 8 | 6 | 48 | 9 | 72 | 7 | 56 | 10 | 80 |
| Paper capacity | 7 | 8 | 56 | 9 | 63 | 8 | 56 | 8 | 56 |
| Two-side print capacity | 8 | 8 | 64 | 9 | 72 | 9 | 72 | 7 | 56 |
| Ease of maintenance | 7 | 8 | 56 | 9 | 63 | 9 | 63 | 6 | 42 |
| Autostaple? | 5 | 6 | 30 | 6 | 30 | 9 | 45 | 7 | 35 |
| Power consumption | 5 | 5 | 25 | 5 | 25 | 7 | 35 | 9 | 45 |
| TCO | 9 | 7 | 63 | 9 | 81 | 7 | 63 | 7 | 63 |
| Total Points | | | 432 | | **506** | | 480 | | 447 |

- It is too easy to skew the results based on someone's personal agenda. Maybe someone has a preference for Oce because a good friend is the CFO of the company.

- Only *quantitative* elements can be compared. There is no way to assess qualitative elements ("It's easy to use") and quantitative elements ("Which machine holds more paper?") in the same grid.

- The criteria are not weighed against each other; therefore, there is no way of determining if the weight ranking of the selection criteria is consistent. (Is auto-stapling really as important as the power-consumption of the copier?)

- There is no way of knowing whether the entire selection process is logically consistent.

Enter the *Analytic Hierarchy Process (AHP)*—a decision-making process developed in the early 1970s at the Wharton Business School by world-renowned mathematician, Thomas L. Saaty. Unlike a lot of decision-type matrixes producing the standard weighted averages, this process is a bit different and certainly unique among decision processes.

It enables the users to make decisions in complex environments, with people who may be in disagreement or outright conflict, and enables users to consider not only measurable attributes of a problem, but individual preferences in considering the solution to the problem. It enables decisions based on varying levels of fact, expertise, competing and organizational agendas, and using criteria that do not easily lend themselves to simple comparisons—that is, it handles qualitative and quantitative possibilities simultaneously!

Not only does it enable decision makers to handle the ubiquitous comparison of apples-to-oranges, but I have seen it work in every conceivable circumstance that requires a decision, and the beauty of the process is that it requires no special skill or significant training to enable it to function as a useful decision tool. No PhD is required to learn it or use it.

In short, we need a decision process that:

- Is simple in its construction
- Is workable with groups or individuals
- Is intuitive
- Promotes consensus and/or compromise
- Is relatively simple to master

Why is it called a *hierarchy process?* Because it is fundamental to the nature of human thinking—humans are good at classifying and organizing elements of a problem into different levels. We fundamentally create two types of hierarchies to describe our natural world: (1) structural hierarchies, which break complex systems down in descending order, and (2) functional hierarchies, which decompose complex systems based on the relationships of the parts to each other.

An example of a *structural hierarchy* would be how we classify life on planet Earth: Kingdom, Phylum, Class, Order, Family, Genus, and Species. (Remember Biology 101?) An example of the *functional hierarchy* might involve a conflict over the best way to improve a baseball team's performance. You have the major stakeholders (the owner, the manager, pitching coaches, hitting coaches, trainers, physical therapists, team doctor, the players), the stakeholder objectives (get more hits, improve fielding, improve pitching, ultimately win more games), and some potential outcomes (improved pitching has the highest chance of improving overall team performance, followed by improved hitting and better fielding).

The approach taken to construct a hierarchy depends on the kind of decision that needs to be made. The following list represents some of the widely disparate areas in which decision makers can implement the AHP:

- Selection of the best family car
- Which general contractor to use for building your dream house
- Selection of the best marketing strategy for a business
- Which graduate school provides the best possible all-around education

- What is the best approach for irrigating the Sahara desert to produce crops

- Which defense system provides the greatest security against terrorism

- Which boat cruise provides the best features for the purchase price

- What is the best approach for solving the city's school bussing issues

- Determination of the best jazz band to emerge in the United States in the last five years

- How to evaluate and best utilize the players on a baseball, hockey, basketball, badminton, or swimming team

In each case, the decision makers would create a listing of criteria that addressed their most important considerations in the selection process and would then apply these criteria to each potential solution. In some instances, and depending on the complexity of the problem, the main criteria may be broken down into subcriteria for more detailed consideration. After the hierarchy has been created, it is important to note that the process is not etched in stone—on the contrary—the decision makers may choose to recast their criteria based on their initial thinking and rerun the hierarchy. The AHP not only helps decision makers discover answers; it illuminates what questions they should be asking to help solve their problems as well. In almost every instance, asking the right question will point to where the answer lies.

For the purposes of refining our decision-making processes, we will devote our study to the *functional hierarchy*. Let's run an example of an AHP to demonstrate how it might work.

## THE NEW-CAR AHP

The family needs a new car. There are certainly a number of choices they can make and a number of well-qualified contenders for the honor of being "The Family Transportation Vehicle of Choice." However, there are a number of criteria that need to be considered: some elements that can be measured and quantified (e.g., fuel economy, total cost of ownership, safety, etc.), and other elements that relate to how one *feels* about the purchase (e.g., "looks cool/my kind of style," "exquisite color," "elegant appointments," etc.). The decision process could become lengthy and quite emotionally heated: I once overheard a couple discussing a vehicle purchase at a car dealership as the wife was telling her husband, "Yeah, the car is safe and gets great mileage, but it looks evil. I mean, I wouldn't be caught dead driving that thing. It looks like 'Road Warrior' on steroids."

In this case, the AHP can compare those elements in a way that diffuses conflict and helps illuminate the most significant issues so that a decision can be made that everyone feels good about.

**Step 1:** Make a list of your decision criteria.

What are the most important elements to consider regarding the purchase of the new vehicle? Is this a vehicle purely for family transportation and vacations, or will it be used for some business activity as well? In this example, the family (we'll call them "the Smiths") needs a car for local errands, driving their two children to and from school, picking up groceries, taking the dog to the dog park to run around, and short-haul vacations within five hours' drive time that allow them to take swimming gear, camping equipment, and recreational games (e.g., volleyball set) along with them. Their criteria list includes:

- Good fuel economy (better than 25 mpg city/32 mpg highway)
- Safety (top 5 safety for front and side impact)
- Roominess (2 adults, 2–4 kids, 1 dog, recreational gear)
- Low repair frequency—low total cost of ownership (other than scheduled maintenance)
- Looks cool (This car is a head turner!)

"Looks cool" hardly seems to be a criterion that can be easily quantified—in fact, *cool* is largely in the eye of the beholder.

Everyone will have a different opinion on what looks cool. That's one of aspects of the AHP that makes it so useful; it allows the user to make comparisons not only based on elements that concern metrics, data, and facts, but also about completely subjective criteria—how they feel about something—all within the same decision grid.

**Step 2:** Rank the listed elements in pairs.

The AHP compares each of the criteria to each of the other criteria and then allows the user to rank each pair according to its importance. This pairwise comparison is called an *orthogonal array*. We will set up a grid consisting of two columns: A and B. The comparison being made in this case is shown in Figure 9.2.

Since there are five criteria, this listing shows that each of the criteria has been compared to each of the other remaining four criteria. Check the list and you will see that each criteria appears at least four times in the comparison in the figure. (We've highlighted/color-coded *economy*, *roominess*, *looks cool*, and *safety* as examples.) There are a total of 10 comparisons.

**Figure 9.2**

| A | B |
|---|---|
| Economy | Safety |
| Economy | Roominess |
| Economy | Low repairs |
| Economy | Looks cool |
| Safety | Roominess |
| Safety | Low repairs |
| Safety | Looks cool |
| Roominess | Low repairs |
| Roominess | Looks cool |
| Low repairs | Looks cool |

Now comes the interesting part. The mechanics of the AHP asks you to rate each pair based on the following number scheme:

- If A and B are of equal importance, they are rated a *1*.
- If A is more important than B, the rating is a *3*. (Conversely, if B is more important than A, the rating is *1/3*.)
- If A is strongly more important than B, the rating is a *5*. (Conversely, if B is usually strongly more important than A, the rating is *1/5*.)
- If A is very strongly more important than B, the rating is a *7*. (Conversely, if B is very strongly more important than A, the rating is *1/7*.)
- If A is always more important than B, the rating is a *9*. (Conversely, if B is always more important than A, the rating is *1/9*.)

Use even numbers, *2, 4, 6,* and *8,* if intermediate ratings are required.

We've filled out a sample grid in Figure 9.3 to show how the Smiths ranked the criteria that were important to them.

Notice that if comparing (A) *safety* to (B) *economy* yields a *3,* then comparing B to A yields the inverse, *1/3,* shown in the circles in the figure. This holds true for all the comparisons.

**Figure 9.3**

| Criteria: (B▶) (A▼) | Economy | Safety | Roominess | Low repairs | Looks cool |
|---|---|---|---|---|---|
| Economy | 1 | 1/3 | 3 | 1/3 | 1/5 |
| Safety | 3 | 1 | 5 | 3 | 3 |
| Roominess | 1/3 | 1/5 | 1 | 1/5 | 1/7 |
| Low repairs | 3 | 1/3 | 5 | 1 | 1 |
| Looks cool | 5 | 1/3 | 7 | 1 | 1 |

Also notice that when comparing the same criteria (e.g., *economy* to *economy*) the ranking always has to be *1*. Two identical entities will always have the same weight. Thus, all the identical entities in the grid are ranked as a *1* and highlighted in green for easy identification.

After the comparison and ranking of the criteria has been done, the *criteria scores* can be created. This can be easily accomplished by doing something you learned in the fourth grade: division.

To create criteria scores:

1. Take the first value (*economy*) in the first column and divide it by the sum of all the values in the column: $1/(1 + 3 + 1/3 + 3 + 5) = .081$.

2. Repeat the process for each cell in the column (e.g., $3/(1 + 3 + 1/3 + 3 + 5) = .243$, and so on).

3. Repeat the process for each cell in each column.

Finally, the *average of the criteria scores for each row* is calculated and also shown in the grid in Figure 9.4. The grid will now have the criteria scores shown in the figure contained in each cell.

The *weighted criteria averages* shown in the far-right column of the grid in Figure 9.4 give you an indication of which of the five criteria carry the most importance for the Smiths. In descending order, they are as shown in Figure 9.5.

**Figure 9.4**

| Criteria: (B▶)<br>(A ▼) | Economy | Safety | Roominess | Low repairs | Looks cool | Average (priority) |
|---|---|---|---|---|---|---|
| Economy | .081 | .161 | .053 | .060 | .037 | **.079** |
| Safety | .243 | .484 | .263 | .524 | .561 | **.419** |
| Roominess | .027 | .097 | .053 | .036 | .027 | **.048** |
| Low repairs | .243 | .097 | .263 | .181 | .187 | **.194** |
| Looks cool | .405 | .161 | .368 | .181 | .187 | **.260** |

**Figure 9.5**

| Safety | .419 |
|--------|------|
| Looks cool | .260 |
| Low repairs | .194 |
| Economy | .079 |
| Roominess | .048 |

Try it yourself! Figure 9.6 is a grid that has not been filled in, except for the identical entities (which will always be a *1*). See whether the five decision criteria carry the same weight in your own decision process.

**Step 3:** Narrow the field down to a short list of four or five vehicles.

Now the process gets *really* interesting. Pick the four or five vehicles that you would choose based on the decision criteria you have decided are important. The Smiths selected the following short list of vehicles for their comparison:

1. Volvo station wagon
2. Toyota Highlander hybrid SUV

**Figure 9.6**

| Criteria: (B▶)<br>(A ▼) | Economy | Safety | Roominess | Low repairs | Looks cool |
|--------------------------|---------|--------|-----------|-------------|------------|
| Economy | 1 | | | | |
| Safety | | 1 | | | |
| Roominess | | | 1 | | |
| Low repairs | | | | 1 | |
| Looks cool | | | | | 1 |

**3.** Ford Escape hybrid SUV

**4.** Honda Civic hybrid

**5.** Volkswagen Passat wagon

**Step 4:** Rank each vehicle against each of the decision criteria.

Basically, the grid is filled out five times (see Figures 9.7–9.16), once for each of the decision criteria; each vehicle is ranked on *safety, "looks cool," low repairs, economy,* and *roominess.* The same process is followed here as we performed when the decision criteria were ranked in one grid and criteria scores created in a second grid.

The Smiths ranked and scored each of the criteria against the short list of vehicles—here we go!

**Step 4:** Take the vehicle scores collected from each *vehicle scores* grid and multiply them by the *criteria averages* (from the decision criteria grid) to obtain a final ranking.

For example, creating the overall score for Volvo, combining all the criteria, yields the following calculation:

- Volvo Safety score (.375) * Safety criteria score (.419) +

**Figure 9.7**

RANK—Safety

| Criteria: (B▶)(A▼) | Volvo | Toyota | Ford | Honda | Volkswagen |
|---|---|---|---|---|---|
| Volvo | 1 | 2 | 4 | 2 | 3 |
| Toyota | 1/2 | 1 | 3 | 1 | 2 |
| Ford | 1/4 | 1/3 | 1 | 1/3 | 1/2 |
| Honda | 1/2 | 1 | 3 | 1 | 2 |
| Volkswagen | 1/3 | 1/2 | 2 | 1/2 | 1 |

## Figure 9.8

VEHICLE SCORES—Safety

| Criteria: (B▶) (A ▼) | Volvo | Toyota | Ford | Honda | Volkswagen | Average |
|---|---|---|---|---|---|---|
| Volvo | 0.387 | 0.414 | 0.308 | 0.414 | 0.353 | 0.375 |
| Toyota | 0.194 | 0.207 | 0.231 | 0.207 | 0.235 | 0.215 |
| Ford | 0.097 | 0.069 | 0.077 | 0.069 | 0.059 | 0.074 |
| Honda | 0.194 | 0.207 | 0.231 | 0.207 | 0.235 | 0.215 |
| Volkswagen | 0.129 | 0.103 | 0.154 | 0.103 | 0.118 | 0.121 |

## Figure 9.9

RANK—Looks Cool

| Criteria: (B▶) (A ▼) | Volvo | Toyota | Ford | Honda | Volkswagen |
|---|---|---|---|---|---|
| Volvo | 1 | 1/3 | 1/5 | 1/3 | 1/3 |
| Toyota | 3 | 1 | 5 | 3 | 3 |
| Ford | 5 | 1/5 | 1 | 1/4 | 1/3 |
| Honda | 3 | 1/3 | 4 | 1 | 1 |
| Volkswagen | 3 | 1/3 | 3 | 1 | 1 |

## Figure 9.10

VEHICLE SCORES—Looks Cool

| Criteria: (B▶) (A ▼) | Volvo | Toyota | Ford | Honda | Volkswagen | Average |
|---|---|---|---|---|---|---|
| Volvo | 0.067 | 0.152 | 0.015 | 0.060 | 0.059 | 0.070 |
| Toyota | 0.200 | 0.455 | 0.379 | 0.537 | 0.529 | 0.420 |
| Ford | 0.333 | 0.091 | 0.076 | 0.045 | 0.059 | 0.121 |
| Honda | 0.200 | 0.152 | 0.303 | 0.179 | 0.176 | 0.202 |
| Volkswagen | 0.200 | 0.152 | 0.227 | 0.179 | 0.176 | 0.187 |

**Figure 9.11**

RANK—Low Repairs

| Criteria: (B▶)(A▼) | Volvo | Toyota | Ford | Honda | Volkswagen |
|---|---|---|---|---|---|
| Volvo | 1 | 1/5 | 1/3 | 1/4 | 2 |
| Toyota | 5 | 1 | 7 | 1 | 3 |
| Ford | 3 | 1/7 | 1 | 1/7 | 2 |
| Honda | 4 | 1 | 7 | 1 | 3 |
| Volkswagen | 1/2 | 1/3 | 1/2 | 1/3 | 1 |

**Figure 9.12**

VEHICLE SCORES—Low Repairs

| Criteria: (B▶)(A▼) | Volvo | Toyota | Ford | Honda | Volkswagen | Average |
|---|---|---|---|---|---|---|
| Volvo | 0.074 | 0.075 | 0.021 | 0.092 | 0.182 | 0.089 |
| Toyota | 0.370 | 0.374 | 0.442 | 0.367 | 0.273 | 0.365 |
| Ford | 0.222 | 0.053 | 0.063 | 0.052 | 0.182 | 0.115 |
| Honda | 0.296 | 0.374 | 0.442 | 0.367 | 0.273 | 0.350 |
| Volkswagen | 0.037 | 0.125 | 0.032 | 0.122 | 0.091 | 0.081 |

**Figure 9.13**

RANK—Economy

| Criteria: (B▶)(A▼) | Volvo | Toyota | Ford | Honda | Volkswagen |
|---|---|---|---|---|---|
| Volvo | 1 | 1/3 | 1/2 | 1/3 | 1/2 |
| Toyota | 3 | 1 | 5 | 1 | 2 |
| Ford | 2 | 1/5 | 1 | 1/5 | 1/3 |
| Honda | 3 | 1 | 5 | 1 | 2 |
| Volkswagen | 2 | 1/2 | 3 | 1/2 | 1 |

**Figure 9.14**

VEHICLE SCORES—Economy

| Criteria: (B▶) (A ▼) | Volvo | Toyota | Ford | Honda | Volkswagen | Average |
|---|---|---|---|---|---|---|
| Volvo | 0.091 | 0.110 | 0.034 | 0.110 | 0.086 | 0.086 |
| Toyota | 0.273 | 0.330 | 0.345 | 0.330 | 0.343 | 0.324 |
| Ford | 0.182 | 0.066 | 0.069 | 0.066 | 0.057 | 0.088 |
| Honda | 0.273 | 0.330 | 0.345 | 0.330 | 0.343 | 0.324 |
| Volkswagen | 0.182 | 0.165 | 0.207 | 0.165 | 0.171 | 0.178 |

- Volvo Looks Cool score (.070) ∗ Looks Cool criteria score (.261) +

- Volvo Low Repairs score (.089) ∗ Low Repairs criteria score (.194) +

- Volvo Economy score (.086) ∗ Economy criteria score (.079) +

- Volvo Roominess score (.076) ∗ Roominess criteria score (.048)

Repeating this process for each vehicle and each criterion yields the final scoring for the Family Car Project, as shown in Figure 9.17.

**Figure 9.15**

RANK—Roominess

| Criteria: (B▶) (A ▼) | Volvo | Toyota | Ford | Honda | Volkswagen |
|---|---|---|---|---|---|
| Volvo | 1 | 1/3 | 1/5 | 1/3 | 1 |
| Toyota | 3 | 1 | 1/2 | 1 | 3 |
| Ford | 5 | 2 | 1 | 2 | 3 |
| Honda | 3 | 1 | 1/2 | 1 | 1/3 |
| Volkswagen | 1 | 1/3 | 1/3 | 3 | 1 |

**Figure 9.16**

VEHICLE SCORES—Roominess

| Criteria: (B▶) (A ▼) | Volvo | Toyota | Ford | Honda | Volkswagen | Average |
|---|---|---|---|---|---|---|
| Volvo | 0.077 | 0.059 | 0.079 | 0.045 | 0.120 | 0.076 |
| Toyota | 0.231 | 0.176 | 0.197 | 0.136 | 0.360 | 0.220 |
| Ford | 0.385 | 0.353 | 0.395 | 0.273 | 0.360 | 0.353 |
| Honda | 0.231 | 0.353 | 0.197 | 0.136 | 0.040 | 0.191 |
| Volkswagen | 0.077 | 0.059 | 0.132 | 0.409 | 0.120 | 0.159 |

In descending order of preference, the cars were rated as shown in Figure 9.18.

What is important to note is that given the above result, the Smiths may decide to:

1. Reevaluate their choices.

2. Change the criteria.

3. Reweigh the current criteria to change the criteria rankings.

**Figure 9.17**

| Criteria / Vehicles | Safety (.419) | Looks Cool (.261) | Low Repairs (.194) | Economy (.079) | Roominess (.048) | Average |
|---|---|---|---|---|---|---|
| Volvo | 0.375 | 0.070 | 0.089 | 0.086 | 0.076 | .202 |
| Toyota | 0.215 | 0.420 | 0.365 | 0.324 | 0.220 | .307 |
| Ford | 0.074 | 0.121 | 0.115 | 0.088 | 0.353 | .109 |
| Honda | 0.215 | 0.202 | 0.350 | 0.324 | 0.191 | .246 |
| Volkswagen | 0.121 | 0.187 | 0.087 | 0.178 | 0.159 | .138 |

**Figure 9.18**

| Toyota | .307 |
|--------|------|
| Honda | .246 |
| Volvo | .202 |
| Volkswagen | .138 |
| Ford | .109 |

**4.** Redo the entire process with any combination of the three elements above.

One of the important aspects of the process is that it can bring to light areas of interest that may not have been clear when the process was started. For example, after the car has been chosen based on the above criteria, the terms of the purchase or financing options may be something that needs to be considered before a *buy* decision is made. Other aspects, such as the reputation of the dealer, quality of the dealer's service division, proximity to the buyer's home (you may not want to travel 50 miles for a warrantied tune-up), or other factors may become more important after the initial evaluation is performed. The AHP can always be run again with different criteria or even additional criteria. One of the key values of the AHP is that it can clearly enlighten different points of view that are critical to the decision process.

## NEXT STEP: BEYOND THE BASICS AND A SLIGHTLY MORE COMPLEX AHP

Now that you've gotten your feet wet with a fundamental AHP, let's kick it up a notch—we'll introduce some new concepts, see what happens when the process becomes slightly more complex, and work through an exercise on how to handle it.

The next aspect that we will explore in the AHP is the concept of *consistency* and how it applies to the AHP.

What do we mean by "consistency"? If we are performing a comparison and say that we prefer peaches more than plums and plums more than bananas, then to be perfectly consistent we will always prefer peaches more than bananas. However, in real life, this does not always occur—that preference could change depending on the season, the day of the week, or some other circumstance. Since the relationship does not always hold true, this could lead to an inconsistent result—violating this consistency is something that humans do all the time!

How damaging is this inconsistency when performing the pairwise comparison in the AHP matrix? Given that we may not always be perfectly consistent in our judgments, we need to know if there is enough consistency in our judgments to validate the results of the AHP. Therefore, the AHP measures overall consistency via the use of a *consistency ratio*. The value of the consistency ratio should be 10% or less on a matrix of $5 \times 5$ or larger, 9% on a $4 \times 4$ matrix, and 5% on a $3 \times 3$ matrix.

Using the AHP we derived in the previous section, let's see if our *criteria weighting* for the Smiths' decision criteria created in Step 1 of the AHP was a consistently made decision.

Now compute the *consistency ratio*:

**Step 1:** Take the original *decision criteria rankings* and the *resulting criteria scores*, which yield the *decision criteria* (Figure 9.19).
The *criteria scores* are given in Figure 9.20.

**Step 2:** Using the *row sums* in the criteria scores grid, place the *average row sum* for each criterion in its matching column (shown in Figure 9.21), and multiply the *column average* by each selection from the decision criteria grid as shown in the figure.

**Step 3:** Now take the *column of row totals* created in Step 2, divide each row total by its corresponding *criteria scores average row sum* created in Step 1, and compute the average of the five numbers:

$$\frac{.482}{.094} = 5.112 \quad \frac{2.274}{.408} = 5.568 \quad \frac{.234}{.046} = 5.122 \quad \frac{1.098}{.200} = 5.487 \quad \frac{1.377}{.252} = 5.476$$

**Figure 9.19**

| Criteria: (B▶) (A ▼) | Economy | Safety | Roominess | Low repairs | Looks cool |
|---|---|---|---|---|---|
| Economy | 1 | .33 | 3 | .33 | .20 |
| Safety | 3 | 1 | 5 | 3 | 3 |
| Roominess | .33 | .20 | 1 | .20 | .14 |
| Low repairs | 3 | .33 | 5 | 1 | 1 |
| Looks cool | 5 | .33 | 7 | 1 | 1 |

$$\frac{5.112 + 5.568 + 5.122 + 5.487 + 5.476}{5} = 5.353$$

This is one way to approximate a mathematical quantity known as $\lambda_{max}$ (lambda max).

**Step 4:** The next part of the calculation is to compute the *consistency index* and then derive the *consistency ratio* in the final calculation.

The formula is as follows (where $n$ equals the number of criteria):

$$\frac{\lambda_{max} - n}{n - 1} = \frac{5.353 - 5}{4} = .088 \text{ (Consistency Index)}$$

**Figure 9.20**

| Criteria: (B▶) (A ▼) | Economy | Safety | Roominess | Low repairs | Looks cool | Average row sum |
|---|---|---|---|---|---|---|
| Economy | 0.081 | 0.151 | 0.143 | 0.060 | 0.037 | 0.094 |
| Safety | 0.243 | 0.457 | 0.238 | 0.542 | 0.562 | 0.408 |
| Roominess | 0.027 | 0.091 | 0.048 | 0.036 | 0.026 | 0.046 |
| Low repairs | 0.243 | 0.151 | 0.238 | 0.181 | 0.187 | 0.200 |
| Looks cool | 0.406 | 0.151 | 0.333 | 0.181 | 0.187 | 0.252 |

**Figure 9.21**

| Criteria: (B►)(A ▼) | Economy (.094) | Safety (.408) | Roominess (.046) | Low repairs (.200) | Looks cool (.252) | Row total |
|---|---|---|---|---|---|---|
| Economy | 1(.094)+ | .33(.408) + | 1(.046) + | .33(.200)+ | .20(.252) = | 0.482 |
| Safety | 3(.094) + | .1(.408) | 5(.046) + | 3(.200) + | 3(.252) = | 2.274 |
| Roominess | .33(.094) + | .20(.408) + | 1(.046) + | .20(.200) + | .14(.252) = | 0.234 |
| Low repairs | 3(.094) + | .33(.408) + | 5(.046) + | 1(.200) + | 1(.252) = | 1.098 |
| Looks cool | .33(.094) + | .33(.408) + | 7(.046) + | 1(.200) + | 1(.252) = | 1.377 |

**Step 5:** Using the *random consistency* table below (Figure 9.25), divide the calculated *consistency index* created in Step 4 by the random consistency for a 5 × 5 matrix thus:

$$\frac{0.088}{1.110} = 0.080 \quad \text{or} \quad 8\%$$

This is well within the 10% requirement of consistency for this grid.

It looks like the Smiths were very clear headed when they ranked the criteria that were important to them in choosing a family car! What this means is that you can state with better-than-average confidence that the rankings created in the decision criteria grid were made with a high degree of consistency and point to a general clarity in judgment. As the creator of the AHP, Thomas Saaty, lucidly stated, "It is better to be approximately right than precisely wrong."

Just to show the other side of the equation, let's see what happens when all the cars are ranked against a specific criterion in the Car AHP, and it comes out with *less* than the required consistency.

## An Inconsistent AHP Matrix

Here we have taken the *looks cool* criterion and applied the vehicle scores to a consistency ratio calculation.

**Step 1:**  Let's see what happens in Figures 9.22 and 9.23.

**Step 2:**  Using the *row sums* in the criteria scores grid, place the *average row sum* for each criterion in its matching column (shown in Figure 9.24), and multiply the *column average* by each selection from the decision criteria grid as shown in the figure.

**Step 3:**  Now take the column of *row totals* created in Step 2, divide each row total by its corresponding *criteria scores average row sum*, created in Step 1, and compute the average of the five numbers:

$$\frac{.364}{.07} = 5.175 \quad \frac{2.401}{.420} = 5.717 \quad \frac{.669}{.121} = 5.545 \quad \frac{1.223}{.202} = 6.053 \quad \frac{1.102}{.187} = 5.898$$

$$\frac{5.175 + 5.717 + 5.545 + 6.053 + 5.898}{5} = 5.678$$

**Step 4:**  The next part of the calculation is to compute the *consistency index* and then derive the *consistency ratio* in the final calculation.

The formula is as follows (where *n* equals the number of criteria):

$$\frac{\lambda_{max} - n}{n - 1} = \frac{5.678 - 5}{4} = .169 \quad \text{(Consistency Index)}$$

**Figure 9.22**

RANK—Looks Cool

| Criteria: (B▶) (A ▼) | Volvo | Toyota | Ford | Honda | Volkswagen |
|---|---|---|---|---|---|
| Volvo | 1 | .33 | .20 | .33 | .33 |
| Toyota | 3 | 1 | 5 | 3 | 3 |
| Ford | 5 | .20 | 1 | .25 | .33 |
| Honda | 3 | .33 | 4 | 1 | 1 |
| Volkswagen | 3 | .33 | 3 | 1 | 1 |

**Figure 9.23**

VEHICLE SCORES—Looks Cool

| Criteria: (B▶) (A ▼) | Volvo | Toyota | Ford | Honda | Volkswagen | Average |
|---|---|---|---|---|---|---|
| Volvo | 0.067 | 0.152 | 0.015 | 0.060 | 0.059 | 0.070 |
| Toyota | 0.200 | 0.455 | 0.379 | 0.537 | 0.529 | 0.420 |
| Ford | 0.333 | 0.091 | 0.076 | 0.045 | 0.059 | 0.121 |
| Honda | 0.200 | 0.152 | 0.303 | 0.179 | 0.176 | 0.202 |
| Volkswagen | 0.200 | 0.152 | 0.227 | 0.179 | 0.176 | 0.187 |

**Figure 9.24**

VEHICLE SCORES—Looks Cool

| Criteria: (B▶) (A ▼) | Volvo (.070) | Toyota (.420) | Ford (.121) | Honda (.202) | Volkswagen (.187) | Row total |
|---|---|---|---|---|---|---|
| Volvo | 1(.070) + | .33(.420) + | .2(.121) + | .33(.202) + | .33(.187) = | 0.364 |
| Toyota | 3(.070) + | 1(.420) + | 5(.121) + | 3(.202) + | 3(.187) = | 2.401 |
| Ford | 5(.070) + | .20(.420) + | 1(.121) + | .25(.202) + | .33(.187) = | 0.669 |
| Honda | 3(.070) + | .33(.420) + | 4(.121) + | 1(.202) + | 1(.187) = | 1.223 |
| Volkswagen | 3(.070) + | .33(.420) + | 3(.121) + | 1(.202) + | 1(.187) = | 1.102 |

**Step 5:** Using the *random consistency table* below (Figure 9.25), divide the calculated *consistency index* created in Step 4 by the *random consistency* for a 5 × 5 matrix to produce the *consistency ratio*, as shown in Figure 9.25 and in the following formula:

$$\frac{0.169}{110} = 0.153$$

This translates into 15.3%—in other words, we have exceeded the range of the consistency ratio for a 5 × 5 grid (10%) by over 5%. This indicates that the decision process used to determine the *looks cool* criterion was *inconsistent*.

**Figure 9.25**

| Matrix Size | Random Consistency |
|-------------|--------------------|
| 1 | 0.00 |
| 2 | 0.00 |
| 3 | 0.52 |
| 4 | 0.89 |
| 5 | 1.11 |
| 6 | 1.25 |
| 7 | 1.35 |
| 8 | 1.40 |
| 9 | 1.45 |
| 10 | 1.49 |

It looks like the Smiths, as a group, may have been struggling with the ranking process when they ranked the criteria that were important to them in determining what looks cool. When you see that there is inconsistency in a ranking process, several elements could be causing it:

1. There may have been some conflict within the group as to what really looks cool, and some of the decision makers may have been swayed by others in the group. The inconsistency in the decision can help to illuminate where further issues need to be aired and/or discussed at greater length.

2. The group may not have really thought through the process because a specific criterion may not have been as important to them as some of the other decision criteria. Therefore, they really didn't concentrate on the ranking process very carefully. You may want to examine this particular criterion and see if it might be better to replace it with another that is more important to the decision makers.

**3.** Some of the group members may be dissembling to deliberately skew the results and pursue their own agendas. Yes, it happens. Some individuals are not entirely forthright, for whatever reason. This is why the AHP is so resistant to tampering; the *consistency index* lets practitioners know when decisions are not being made consistently within the ranking process.

## A WORD ABOUT DATA MEASUREMENT AND ANALYSIS

There are a few things you need to know about measurement—specifically what is mathematically legal in performing a computation utilizing various scales of measure. In using the AHP, some have asked if the computations used in the process are mathematically legitimate or legal. In this case, an understanding of data types and what kinds of mathematical operations can be performed with each of those data types is in order.

*Data* can be broken down into three basic types:

**1.** Discrete

**2.** Continuous

**3.** Classified

*Measurement scales* can be broken down into four fundamental types:

**1.** Nominal

**2.** Ordinal

**3.** Interval

**4.** Ratio

Let's give examples of each data type using the illustration in Figure 9.26.

Here are the data types:

**Figure 9.26**

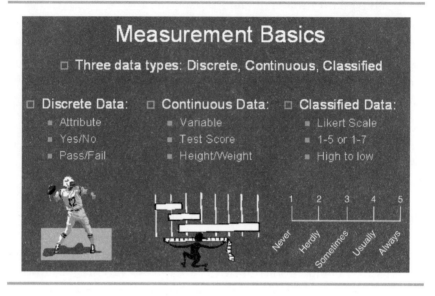

**Discrete Data:** Discrete data is attribute data—it does not contain an explicit measurement. It can be the number on a baseball jersey or the number of a bus route. It will answer questions like "Was the coin flip heads or tails?" (heads); or "Is the light on or off?" (on); or "Did you pass the test?" (yes or no). With the coin-flip example, you could perform a number of coin flips and then count the number of heads and tails to create a statistical distribution, but the coin flip itself does not embody a measurement.

**Continuous Data:** Continuous data is measurable: How many inches high is the refrigerator? What is your weight to the nearest Troy ounce? What is the shaft diameter of that electric motor to the nearest thousandth of an inch? Continuous data enables us to make histograms and statistical charts containing precise measurements.

**Classified Data:** Classified data is somewhere in between discrete and continuous data. Classified data scales are used when participants are asked how well they liked a particular training session or how they would rank how well they liked a product on a relative scale.

Let's look at the difference between the scale types. This is important because when the business asks for measurement metrics on specific business processes, you (the PM) must know what is being measured and what specific types of operations you can perform with your measurements!

**Nominal Scale:** This is essentially a label that identifies something such as a number on a football jersey or a route number for a bus. Nominal scale numbers are in the *discrete data* category. You can't perform arithmetic operations (addition, subtraction, multiplication, or division) on these numbers—the result would be meaningless. Train 107 subtracted from Train 198 is utter nonsense. However, it is possible to count the *number of times* that Train 107 runs in a week, a month, or a year and create a *frequency distribution* of the run based on time of day or year. This is the only way that an arithmetic operation can be performed on nominal data.

**Ordinal Scale:** An ordinal scale puts things in rank order as well as labeling them, as in nominal scale data. So if you are standing at 1 Maple Street and the houses are numbered from 1 to 300, you can be certain that the house at 105 Maple Street is further down the road than where you are standing now. The ranking can give the observer a relative sense of where the number lies on the scale. However, with ordinal scale data as with nominal scale data, arithmetic operations are meaningless. Ordinal scale data is considered *classified data* for the most part.

**Interval Scale:** As with ordinal scale data, the numbers serve as labels and are ranked, but with one critical difference: The interval spacing between the ranked numbers is of equal distance. A day consists of 24 equally spaced intervals called hours and a week is exactly seven days. The distance between this week and its neighbor is the same as it is between any other week and its neighbor. The caveat with interval scale data is that there is no Absolute Zero, or a real starting point. For example, the Fahrenheit and Celsius scales have zero points, but there are also points below zero on both scales. Our calendar is based on the Birth of Christ (the Year 1 A.D.), but there are years before that. The good news is, arithmetic operations can be performed on interval data using real numbers. Interval data is considered continuous data. The year 2000 divided by 2 is the year 1000. However, dividing the year 2000 by 2 does not result in a year that is half as long. Let's ask the question another way: 68°F divided by 2 does yield 34°F. However, does that make 34°F twice as cold as 68°F? No, it does *not*. And the reason it does not is due to the *ratio scale*.

**Ratio Scale:** Ratio scale data is identical to interval scale data, except that there is an Absolute Zero point from which measurement begins. A tape measure is a ratio scale—it starts at zero. Absolute Zero in temperature is measured in Kelvin or °K. Ask the temperature question again: Is 400°K twice as hot as 200°K? Without a doubt, it is. So back to our original question: Is 34°F twice as cold as 68°F? Not even close. The Fahrenheit measurements would have to be converted to Kelvin before the appropriate measurement could be made. Complex mathematical operations can be performed on ratio data. Ratio scale data is also considered to be *continuous data.*

The AHP is mathematically valid because its measurements have the characteristics of ratio scale, continuous data: The measurements are in *rank order* (ordinal), *equally spaced* (interval), and have an *Absolute Zero point* (ratio).

Keep this measurement exercise in mind, because it will pop up in later chapters of this book.

## Exercises

Here are some exercises that you can use to practice the concepts and process described in this chapter. Try working your way through the process by proceeding through the four steps as outlined above with the following.

Using the enclosed Excel grid—"Basic AHP Using 5 Criteria"— fill in the grid as follows:

**Basic AHP Exercises**

- Buying your dream house
- Selecting the best job from a variety of offers
- Selecting the best contractor for a software project
- Determining the best rock band in the United States
- Obtaining the best landscaping for your corporate headquarters

# REFERENCE

Saaty, Thomas L., *Decision Making for Leaders*, RWS Publications, 2001.

# FURTHER READINGS

Saaty, Thomas L., *Fundamentals of Decision Making Priority Theory*, RWS Publications, 2000.

Saaty, Thomas L., *The Analytic Network Process*, RWS Publications, 2001.

# Chapter
# 10

# Monte Carlo Analysis

"There are three kinds of lies: lies, damn lies and statistics."
—Benjamin Disraeli

T HE MONTE CARLO ANALYSIS is named for the famous casinos on the Mediterranean in the south of France. It is a statistical tool that helps decision makers create a somewhat accurate ballpark estimate—not just which ballpark you're in, but the size of the ballpark, where in the ballpark, and how much of the ballpark we're talking about. It is particularly useful when a decision has to be made that involves a fair level of uncertainty or in which there are multiple unknowns that have to be solved for your equation. (Contrary to what your high school math teacher told you, there is a way to solve for equations with multiple unknowns—it's called the *Monte Carlo analysis!*)

Here's the basic idea: In most games of chance, whether it be throwing dice or picking numbers on a roulette wheel, there are specific patterns that emerge based on the probability that certain numbers will turn up with any particular frequency.

For example, if you are gambling on a specific outcome if you roll a six-sided die, the probability that any number will be thrown, 1 through 6, is one out of six equally.

That is a fairly simple and obvious deduction to make. Things start to get complicated when you add a second die to the throw. Now you have results that can range from a low of 2 to a high of 12. What is the probability that you will throw any number between 2 and 12?

The grid in Figure 10.1 shows the die combinations compared side-by-side.

Because of the uncertainty of what will occur, a number of trials (throws of the dice) are run to see if there is any pattern in which throws are most likely to occur. Will the pattern that is generated be close to the mathematical probabilities shown in the grid above for one million throws of the dice? Running one million simulated throws

**Figure 10.1**

| Throw | Probability of Throw | Possible Combinations (2 Die) |
|---|---|---|
| 2 | 1 out of 36 | 1 and 1 |
| 3 | 2 out of 36 | 1 and 2,2 and 1 |
| 4 | 3 out of 36 | 1 and 3,3 and 1,2 and 2 |
| 5 | 4 out of 36 | 1 and 4,4 and 1,2 and 3,3 and 2 |
| 6 | 5 out of 36 | 1 and 5,5 and 1,4 and 2,2 and 4,3 and 3 |
| 7 | 6 out of 36 | 1 and 6,6 and 1,2 and 5,5 and 2,3 and 4,4 and 3 |
| 8 | 5 out of 36 | 2 and 6,6 and 2,3 and 5,5 and 3,4 and 4 |
| 9 | 4 out of 36 | 3 and 6,6 and 3,4 and 5,5 and 4 |
| 10 | 3 out of 36 | 4 and 6,6 and 4,5 and 5 |
| 11 | 2 out of 36 | 5 and 6,6 and 5 |
| 12 | 1 out of 36 | 6 and 6 |

**Figure 10.2**

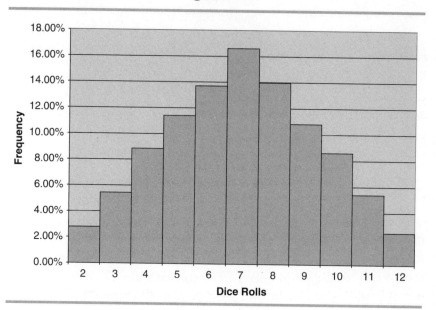

using a computerized random number generator enables the user to build the model shown in Figure 10.2.

As the reader can see from the histogram produced in the figure, one million simulated throws produces a frequency chart almost identical to the probability grid shown on the previous page. A dice roll of 7 will occur 6 times out of 36 throws or about 16.67% of the throws—a dice roll of 2 will occur 1 time out of 36 throws or approximately 2.77% of the throws, and so on. So, the model appears to be accurate; however, here's what the model does not tell you:

- While indicating average percentages over time and frequency of throws, it does not predict what specific throw will follow any other throw (the "crystal ball" effect). It can give you a probability, but not a certainty.

- The quality of the software random number generator used in the model may appear to be random, but may itself tend to "randomly" generate numbers skewed in a specific direction, or not generate numbers in a truly random fashion. It's really based on how well the software is written. How would you know? (If this subject interests you, please consult Bruce Schneier's *Applied Cryptography*, John Wiley & Sons, 1996, pp. 44–46, for a discussion on what constitutes a *real random number* sequence generator and why most commercial software such as Excel does not generate true random number sequences.)

- It is only a model. It does not consider real-world variables and the effects of those variables on actual results, such as:
  - □ The levelness of the dice table
  - □ The wear an tear of the felt on the table after 1 million throws
  - □ The wear and tear on the dice after one million throws—or—if the house replaces the dice after every 1,000 throws, inconsistencies in the manufacture between 1,000 sets of dice, which may skew results
  - □ The ambient temperature of the room (i.e., effects of expansion or contraction on the dice due to temperature changes)
  - □ Effects of vibration on the table while the dice are being thrown (i.e., from heavy equipment moving by the building, minor earth tremors, and so on)

However, the model provides something valuable and useful—it can give you a very good idea where the trends in the model may occur and it is a great improvement over the ubiquitous managerial "gut feeling" (i.e., reading tea leaves or animal entrails) utilized in making decisions. You may still have those gut feelings, but those feelings can now be backed up with some percentages that indicate how far on or off you may be.

The model can also shine light on the causes of variation and as a decision tool be useful in the following areas:

- Analyzing and mitigating risk potential on a project
- Financial modeling—the likelihood of an expected return on an investment
- Probability of a successful product launch—the potential of losing money on the launch

- Project schedule variation—identifying the potential that tasks will be completed by an expected date

- Quality variation with the manufacture of a product

Where is this helpful? Consider the following scenarios and give some thought as to whether you would rather simply go with your gut or spin up a Monte Carlo analysis to get a clearer idea of where you are:

- New product release—will it be successful? Sales could be high or low volume—this is an unknown. Unit price to produce the product is between $4.00 and $9.00—also an unknown; since the company has never made the unit before, they can only guess at the cost. What are the possibilities for success? Could you lose money—what is the probability? Could you make money and how much could you make? If your boss is expecting to make a $75,000 profit on the initial product release, how realistic is that demand? How would you know?

- You've got three critical tasks tracked on a project plan that are due to end at the same time. What is the probability that this will occur? In this case, you have three unknowns. The durations may be based on expert judgment (that is you've done something like the first path before and have a good idea how long it will take), or on varying degrees of information about the tasks on the second and third paths. What is the *merge bias* of the three concurrent paths (i.e., what is the real probability that all three tasks will complete at the same time)? How would you measure the potential variance as a percentage of your confidence level that the tasks would end by a specified date?

- You have defined seven critical risk elements for your project. Each risk element has been defined in a RAM (Risk Analysis Matrix—see Chapter 10) and quantified as to the impact of the risk on a scale of 0 to 1.00 and the probability of the risk occurring on a scale of 0 to 1.00. However, you are not sure that the probability figures are accurate. You determine that the probability ratings can be plus or minus 20% on either side.

Additionally, you want to combine all criteria evaluated for the entire project into an overall evaluation for all the risks combined—one big *impact and probability* number and a dollar amount attached to this risk. How would you compute this value? What is the probability that you would be correct in your assessment?

In each of the previous examples, a Monte Carlo analysis would go a long way to providing useful information that would, in all likelihood illuminate areas where risk could be mitigated or potentially eliminated. Keep in mind that these are models, not reality. As W. Edwards Deming said, "No model is accurate, but some models are useful." Why is this true? Because models are built on purely mathematical simulations; they are not subject to the inconsistencies and variation that occurs when performing a task in the real world.

## MONTE CARLO ANALYSIS EXAMPLE

Since many of the readers of this book may be project managers, let's focus our initial example on what happens when we have *multiple critical tasks* on a project. (That *never* happens, does it? For a refresher, review Chapter 3.) The PERT formula will play heavily into the development of the estimate, as we will see. We'll look at an example that has three critical paths and then see whether the Monte Carlo analysis helps us go back to management with a solid basis-of-estimate instead of the usual gut-feeling or reading-tea-leaves approach.

To show this picture, we will use a charting technique familiar to project managers everywhere—the Gantt chart. Figure 10.3 is a picture of a typical Gantt chart.

This particular Gantt was created using MS Project 2003. Notice there are two panels with which to view the tasks:

1. A task list in the left panel
2. A timeline in the right panel that shows the time duration of each task in a visual representation

**Figure 10.3**

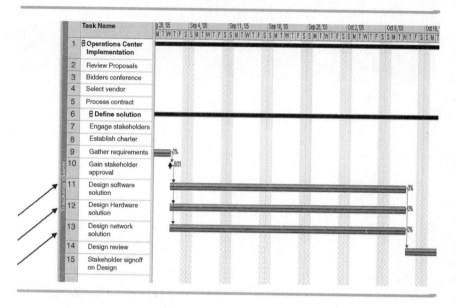

In the chart in Figure 10.3, notice that there are three tasks that occur simultaneously:

- Design software solution
- Design hardware solution
- Design network solution

Notice also there are some tasks represented with a black diamond shape (◆). This represents a milestone on the project plan or a point in time that shows the completion of some major deliverable on the project. The achievement of milestones on a project makes everyone happy, especially the project sponsor.

In order to help us develop the estimates used in the Monte Carlo analysis we also need a tool that will help us describe the potential variances in the project schedule. For this we utilize the PERT estimate that was described in Chapter 3.

The three tasks are scheduled to take 30 days each. In spinning up the PERT estimate, however, the people doing the estimates had

**Figure 10.4    PERT in Days**

| | Pessimistic | Most Likely | Optimistic | PERT Estimate: (P+ 4(ML)+O)/6 |
|---|---|---|---|---|
| Design software solution | 65 | 30 | 20 | 34.2 |
| Design hardware solution | 65 | 30 | 20 | 34.2 |
| Design network solution | 65 | 30 | 20 | 34.2 |
| Average of three estimates | | | | 34.2 |

differing opinions on the *pessimistic, most likely,* and *optimistic* durations for these tasks, as you will see in Figure 10.4.

The PERT chart in this case is a shorthand estimate. What it *doesn't* offer is: What is the realistic probability that the three tasks will be completed within the approximate average of the three estimates—32 days? In addition, the PERT estimate does *not* identify potential dependencies between the tasks that might show up on your timeline as "discovery" (i.e., an unanticipated interaction between tasks). This is where the Monte Carlo analysis is useful. We will compute the probability of a task completing by a by a certain time showing the percentage of confidence we have in the estimate at each point in time. We will then repeat the process for three tasks that are supposed to complete at the same time and see if the time estimate differs.

## THE SINGLE PATH ESTIMATE

Let's start with doing a simple estimate of only one of the *critical path* elements—the *design software solution* task.

For running the estimate, we will use Excel to graph the results. Here, we will estimate the probability that Line 11 in the Gantt chart in Figure 10.3, "Design Software Solution," will complete by the 30-day deadline shown for the task. The PERT estimate in Figure 10.4 shows that this task will, in all likelihood, take 34.2 days to complete.

We have input PERT estimates of 20 days Optimistic, 30 days Most Likely, and 65 days Pessimistic into a *triangular distribution* formula. (This is used in cases where the relationship between the variables is known but the data is scarce—which, in this case, is true because the task hasn't happened yet and there is no data at all.)

The chart in Figure 10.5 depicts *cumulative distribution* showing the percentage of total probability over time that the task will complete by the due date. The numbers from the PERT estimate of:

- 20 days optimistic
- 30 days most likely
- 65 days pessimistic

were fed into the Monte Carlo analysis engine and a trial of 10,000 iterations of the estimate were run. The graph in Figure 10.5 was produced.

**Figure 10.5**

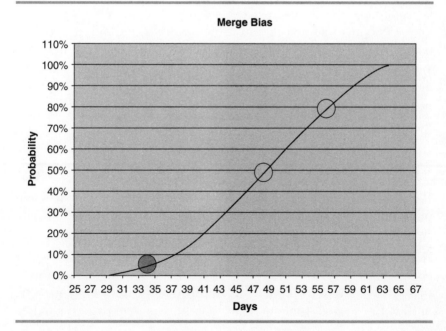

It should immediately become clear from viewing the cumulative chart that:

- There is only a 5–6% probability/confidence that the *design* task will complete in the estimated 34.2 days shown in the PERT estimate (shown by the red circle).

- There is a 50% probability that the task will complete in 43 days (shown by the yellow circle).

- If one is to reach an 80% confidence level that the job will complete, the task will actually take 56–57 days (shown by the green circle).

The previous simulation was run 10,000 times based on estimates from what we will call, for this example, *trusted sources;* that is, you have high confidence that the optimistic/pessimistic/most likely estimates you have received are reliable.

Given the potential variation in the estimates from trusted sources, what would be your confidence level if you were dealing with a vendor that continued to offer estimates that were a moving target? Considerably less, I imagine; yet businesses frequently hire consultants to do just that and those businesses put great faith in the estimates from the vendor. I have worked on over 100 projects and have yet to see a customer or a vendor make use of a Monte Carlo estimate, much less its less accurate second cousin, the PERT estimate. (If you need a refresher, reread the Introduction and the *CHAOS Report* numbers.)

## THE MULTIPLE CRITICAL PATH ESTIMATE

For the next example, we will show a Gantt with three concurrent paths that merge into a single path. All three tasks show that they are scheduled to begin and end on the same day. At first glance, one might think that the schedule variation as described in the *single path* approach shown above would be the same for three concurrent paths. However, in reality the probability that the three tasks will end at the prescribed time to feed into the merge path decreases

**Figure 10.6**

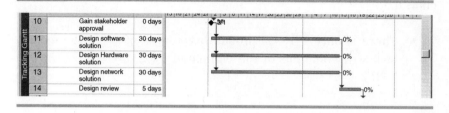

significantly. (Remember our example with the dice? What would the distribution look like if we threw three dice instead of two?)

The Gantt chart in Figure 10.6 again shows an example of the three concurrent tasks:

1. Design software solution
2. Design hardware solution
3. Design network solution

all merging into the task "design review."

Three tasks are executed simultaneously: Using the PERT estimate that was created for each task, we spin up our triangular distribution for each path, output the maximum value of the three estimates for our chart, and iterate 10,000 times.

Remember, the average of the three PERT estimates yielded an estimate of almost 33 days. The chart in Figure 10.7 indicates the probability that the three tasks will complete within 33 days.

Looking at this chart, the results are quite a shock! In computing the *merge bias* of three critical paths, notice the incredible difference in the probability that the three tasks will complete in their 33 day window: There is now only an 8% probability that the three tasks will complete within 33 days! To reach an 80% confidence level, the tasks will have to complete in 59 days—almost four weeks past their original due date.

While this is only a model, let us remember W. Edwards Deming's observation that no model is accurate but some models are useful. This model is definitely useful if for no other reason than to

**Figure 10.7**

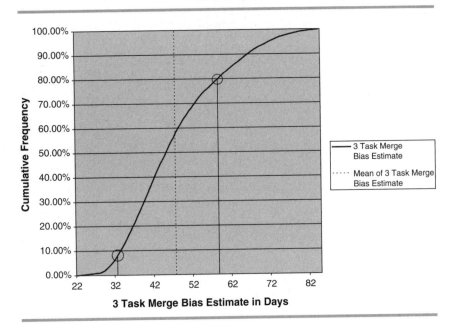

start conversation with the team and management about how to mitigate the probability of losing four weeks on the project. On most projects, this conversation never occurs.

In this case, the usefulness of the Monte Carlo analysis was critical in pointing out that the probability of one task completing on time (35%) versus three tasks completing on time (8%) changed by more than a factor of 4! Bringing this information back to management will go a long way to helping your team transform from the "Hair-on-Fire" squad to the "Data-and-Fact Doctors." The information presented with the help of the Monte Carlo analysis can focus a team as well as management on what needs to be done to identify the causes that contribute to making a task late, identify ways to mitigate or eliminate risks that might occur, and help the team and management make the decisions that will get them to the finish line, on time and on budget.

Try the following schedule exercise using the link to the "Triangular Distribution Formula" spreadsheet and follow these instructions:

1. Before you attempt to open the spreadsheet, change your macro setting to *medium* by accessing the following in the Excel "Tools" menu:

Tools → Macro → Security

2. The box in Figure 10.8 will appear. Select the radio button next to "Medium" and click "OK."

Excel will now ask you whether to *enable macros* whenever you open a spreadsheet containing macros. In this case, select the "Triangular Distribution Formula" spreadsheet and then click the "Enable Macros" button, as shown in Figure 10.9.

The table in Figure 10.10 will appear in the Excel spreadsheet.

**Figure 10.8**

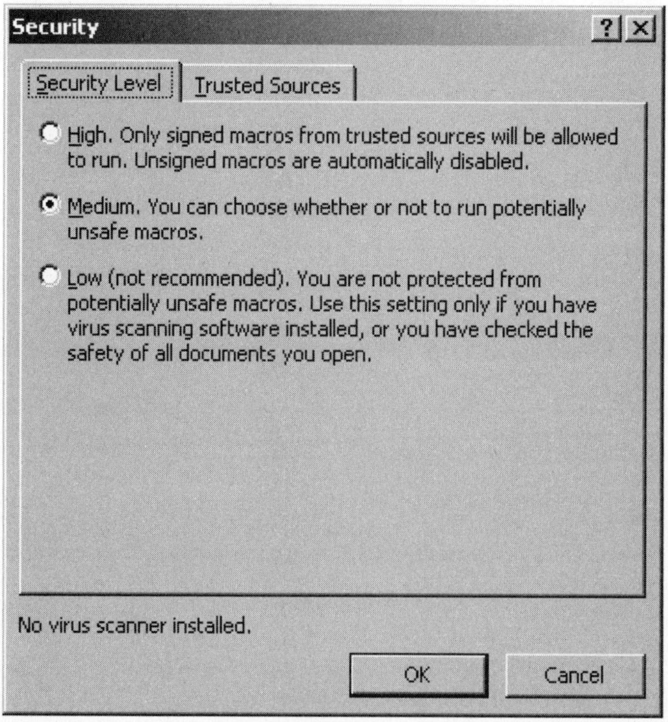

**Figure 10.9**

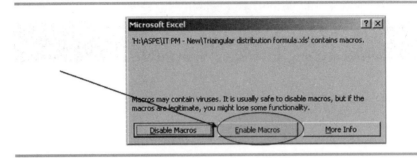

Suppose you are tracking three parallel paths for a project:

**1.** LAN/WAN network design

**2.** Application GUI design

**3.** Database design

Also suppose that you had set up these tasks in a serial sequence—the most likely completion schedule for each is seven weeks. Now, being a thrifty PM, you are looking for ways to shorten the project's critical path and question the heads of all three teams. You discover

**Figure 10.10**

| | Optimistic Min | Most Likely Mode | Pessimistic Max | PERT |
|---|---|---|---|---|
| Path 1 | | | | 0.0 |
| Path 2 | | | | 0.0 |
| Path 3 | | | | 0.0 |
| Path 4 | | | | 0.0 |
| Path 5 | | | | 0.0 |
| | | | | |
| | Run Simulation | | | |

**Figure 10.11**

|  | Optimistic Min | Most Likely Mode | Pessimistic Max | PERT |
|---|---|---|---|---|
| LAN/WAN | 4 | 7 | 14 | 7.7 |
| Database | 4 | 7 | 14 | 7.7 |
| Application | 4 | 7 | 14 | 7.7 |
| Path 4 |  |  |  | 0.0 |
| Path 5 |  |  |  | 0.0 |
|  |  |  |  |  |
|  | Run Simulation |  |  |  |

that the work for each can be done in parallel! Now, instead of 21 weeks you have shortened the design time to 7 weeks. But just to be sure, you set up a PERT estimate to get the team leads' *most likely, optimistic,* and *pessimistic* estimates for the project. The PERT shows that, after all the estimates have been averaged, you would see a parallel path of just over 7.7 weeks, as depicted in Figure 10.11.

You appear to have a significant time savings on all the design aspects and are leaping for joy at having thought of it—or so you think, until you run the Monte Carlo simulation and view the results as shown in Figure 10.12.

The simulation shows there is a just over a 6% chance of completing all three timelines within 7.7 weeks. To reach a 50% confidence factor, we are at about 10.6 weeks and to achieve an 80% confidence factor we are at 12 weeks.

While you did save time over the serial approach of three 7.7 weeks serial path with a total of 23.1 weeks, the time savings is not quite what you had anticipated. If you started your design efforts on October 23 thinking that in 7.7 weeks you would easily be done by December 15, in time to give your team a well-earned rest for the Christmas holidays, think again. Your team will be working through

**Figure 10.12**

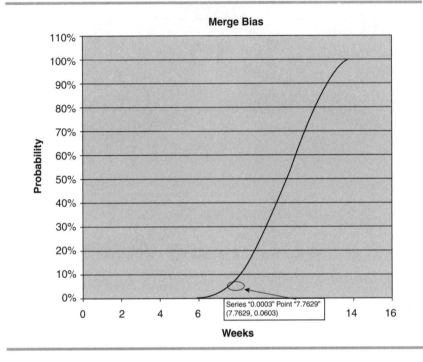

Christmas to complete the design and that is only at a 50% confidence level!

You can try this yourself with up to five parallel paths using the link to the spreadsheet. See what happens when you try different estimates with multiple parallel paths.

## REFERENCES

Savage, Sam, *Decision Making with Insight*, Thompson Learning, 2003.
Hulett, David, *Project Schedule Risk Analysis*, Primavera User Conference, 2002.

# Chapter
# 11

# Decision Tree Analysis

$D$ECISION TREE ANALYSIS is a useful tool for determining the *expected value* of an investment or any decision where there are multiple outcomes possible. For example, a company is looking to expand its business and has several possibilities for proceeding:

- Build a new facility.
- Renovate a current facility.
- Buy a facility from a competing company that is forced to sell due to an impending bankruptcy.
- Do nothing and maintain the status quo.

The decision tree is built with each possibility following a separate path in the tree with the final expected values at the end of the process. The drawing in Figure 11.1 is a highly simplified version of a decision tree chart.

The interesting aspect of this type of decision process is that there is always the option to do nothing in reference to the other options. If none of the options look like they will produce the desired result, it

**Figure 11.1**

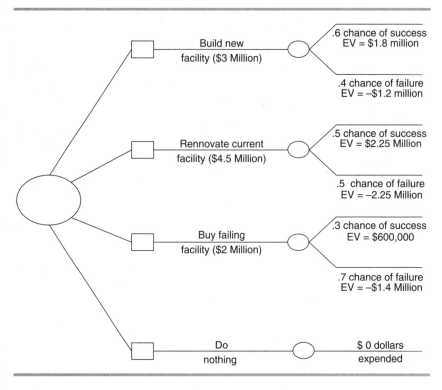

may be better to do nothing at all or rethink the problem from a different point of view.

One critical aspect of decision tree analysis is that *you are required to estimate the anticipated probability that an event will occur*—these estimates are represented by numbers next to each "chance of success" phrase on the diagram. How well you perform these estimates will render the decision tree analysis either accurate or flawed. This is why it may be necessary to spin up the analysis multiple times, to determine what range of estimates will deliver the expected values in the analysis and achieve your desired results.

Before we work an actual example, let's define some terms and basic concepts for the decision tree that will help you understand what is taking place in the diagram:

**Probability.** Outside of throwing dice or some other activity in which the probability of a certain outcome can be estimated/calculated with fair accuracy, the probability of any given event occurring depends on your own experience and beliefs. It is fundamentally a subjective exercise. When a product development decision needs to be made by executives on your project (develop it or not?) they rely on their own experience or the expert capability of subject-matter experts to guide their decision-making process. Yet the decision stills boils down to your own personal experience and beliefs.

**Utility.** This concept helps us compare unlike elements in a decision by using a common reference value that places a relative common value on the disparate elements (i.e., playing with your dog, buying a DVD, or mopping the kitchen floor might be commonly expressed in terms of time or dollars).

**Expected Value.** This is the result of the decision tree analysis, on average, if we repeat the analysis numerous times. Expected value (EV) is calculated as follows:

$$EV = [(\text{Probability of outcome } \#1) * (\text{Utility of outcome } \#1)]$$
$$+ [(\text{Probability of outcome } \#2) * (\text{Utility of outcome } \#2)]$$

**Decision Forks.** There are two types of forks created in a decision tree analysis. The first is a *decision fork*, which is used to present the various alternatives in the decision tree (i.e., we could make or buy the product). The *uncertainty fork* is used to compare the various uncertainties contained in the decision tree analysis (e.g., what is our anticipated profit if we make the product in the United States vs. Mexico?).

**Value of Information.** This quantifies the value of obtaining additional information for a decision analysis, even if the quality of the information is variable.

**Sensitivity Analysis.** Since the inputs to the decision tree are never known with absolute certainty, the sensitivity analysis can be used to bolster your confidence in your decision estimates.

**Conditional Probability.** This refers to the probability of one event occurring after we know that another event has occurred. If you live in a busy city, you might hear ambulance sirens randomly throughout the day. However, the probability that you will hear an ambulance siren is usually less than the probability that you will hear an ambulance siren after witnessing a five-car collision at a busy intersection.

**State Variables.** These allow the user to construct complex decision tree utility functions in which there are numerous inputs. More on this later.

## DECISIONS AND OUTCOMES

Decisions are only as good as your ability to effectively execute them. U.S. General George Patton, considered by the Third Reich to be the best general in the U.S. military, was quoted as saying: "Good tactics can save even the worst strategy. Bad tactics will destroy even the best strategy." In other words, your ability to execute may even be more important than the decision you make—however, making the best decision and executing well may render the best outcome.

You could execute a decision tree analysis on the best car to buy based on performance, luxury, comfort, and eye appeal and decide on buying a BMW 750i. However, buying this particular automobile doesn't make you a good driver and will not guarantee you won't get into an accident. *Good decisions do not necessarily lead to positive outcomes*. The decision tree analysis does not offer a guarantee, only the ability to analyze the possibilities with the hope of making an informed decision. How well you execute is up to you.

Let's try the following example and see what benefits the decision tree offers for the decision maker.

## BASIC DECISION TREE

You are the portfolio manager for a company that is making a decision on what projects will be of the strongest strategic value to the company. The criteria included elements such as:

1. Selecting projects with the largest financial returns

2. Selecting projects with major implications for helping the company succeed five to ten years out

3. Selecting projects that consider elements 1 and 2 with the additional benefit of having a positive impact on the public and society at large, thus improving the perception of your company as a good corporate citizen, which has benefits that translate into more business and your company's ability to attract the best human capital resources in the business (is this measurable?)

You have picked three large projects that satisfy the above criteria and decide to perform a decision tree analysis on each of the three projects. The decision tree for the first project appears in Figure 11.2. We need to quantify the project for the immediate future and assign a dollar value to its successful completion. Don't forget, there is also a downside to this exercise—the company may not execute well and some of these projects could cost the company money. Each node/leaf on the decision tree will represent a different state of the world depending on the probability of the events. The chart in Figure 11.2 represents our possibilities and values for each.

Given the above scenario, we will construct a decision tree that contains the following forks:

—Build ERP system   —Project moves forward   —Project succeeds
—Project has limited success   —Project fails   —Reject project

The resulting decision tree graph appears in Figure 11.3.

**Figure 11.2    State of the Possibilities**

| Projects | Value in $ |
|---|---|
| Global ERP system implementation is successful | $300 million |
| Global ERP system is implemented with severely limited success | $30 million |
| Global ERP system fails and is abandoned | −$20 million |
| Project is rejected by management; no loss or gain | $0 |

**Figure 11.3**

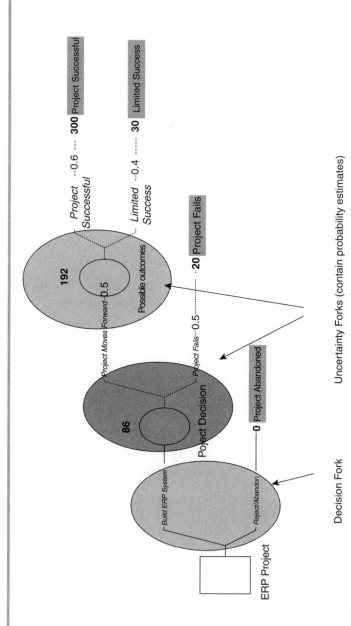

Decision Fork      Uncertainty Forks (contain probability estimates)

Notice that the decision tree shows:

- *Probabilities* (in purple print) at each uncertainty node
- *Utilities* (in black print)
- *Expected values* (in red print) at each converged uncertainty node (at the "project moves forward" node and the "build ERP system" node)

In this example, the expected value at the convergence point of "project successful" and "limited success" is $192M—more than one-third less than the euphoric estimate of $300M for a completely successful project. Taken back to the original uncertainty fork of "project moves forward" and "project fails," notice that the expected value here is $86M, or only 29% of the estimate for the successful project.

The probabilities shown in the chart are simply best guesses. Depending on whom you ask in the company, you might get wide-ranging opinions: The CEO might think there is a 75% chance that the project will move forward and an 80% chance of success, while the CFO might tell you there is only a 35% chance that the project will move forward and a 40% chance of success. You can spin up the decision tree with both (or more) sets of estimates. The benefit of performing the decision tree is that you can derive a range of estimates that pinpoint when the project is worth initiating. A portfolio manager performing this type of estimate on a series of potential projects can identify the project or projects that have the greatest chance of success and provide the highest returns for the company.

Now that you have the basics of how to perform a decision tree analysis, let's peel away another layer to dig more deeply into the process.

## CONDITIONAL PROBABILITY, BAYES' THEOREM, SENSITIVITY ANALYSIS

It terms of the example we just completed in decision tree analysis, *conditional probability* can play a role in determining what the probability of a specific outcome may be. Therefore, the computation of conditional probability becomes important in setting probabilities at the uncertainty nodes in the decision tree forks. Conditional probability refers to the probability of Event A occurring given that Event B has just occurred. In other words, conditional probability states that there is a causal relationship between Event A and Event B. If the occurrence of Event A does not affect the probability of the occurrence of Event B, the two events are said to be *independent*.

**Example:** The probability that you will hear an ambulance or police car siren while you are walking down the street in a busy city is generally less than the probability that you will hear an ambulance/police car siren given that you just witnessed a five-car collision at a busy intersection, and there are bodies strewn on the road.

However, determining conditional probability is not always so obvious, and it is easy to commit the logical fallacy of inferring a connection between two events through a casual observation without performing the needed analysis, as evidenced in the following scenario:

> *Mr. X was convicted of selling marijuana. The judge, having observed that 95% of heroin addicts start on marijuana, declared: "You are in effect a heroin pusher," and gave the fellow a thirty-year sentence. It was fortunate that Mr. X did not deliver milk because 100% of the heroin addicts started on milk.*

The logical fallacy is that the judge was assuming the conditional probability of heroin use given the use of marijuana was higher than the probability of heroin use alone. While this may or may not be the case, it cannot be simply inferred based on the judge's initial observation. In terms of logic, this error is most closely associated with the "questionable cause" fallacy, which takes the general form:

- A and B are associated on a regular basis.
- Therefore, A is the cause of B.

**Example:** The following is a potential real-life scenario in which the concept of conditional probability is demonstrated.

Imagine that a test for business aptitude is given to all business school applicants as a determinant for whether the student is capable of handling graduate studies at college. Based on previous scores, it has been determined that 95% of the college graduate population who are interested in attending business school are qualified to enter business school—only 5% are considered not qualified for graduate school business studies. The test results go on the student's permanent record and are the primary deciding factor in whether the student will be recommended for further educational studies. Students are told that all U.S. colleges subscribe to this test and follow its recommendations. There is a predetermined cutoff score on the test—any student scoring below this cutoff score will not be recommended for business school.

For those who score above or below the cutoff line, the test is 90% effective—that is, it is accurate 90% of the time (student is qualified or unqualified) and inaccurate 10% of the time (i.e., a qualified student tests *unqualified,* or an unqualified student tests *qualified*).

Now, imagine that a student selected at random tested as *unqualified*—did not pass the cutoff—on the college business aptitude test. What is the probability that the student was *actually* unqualified, given that he *tested* as unqualified? The probability that someone drawn at random is *actually unqualified* for business school given that he or she *tested unqualified* for business school is (take your best guess):

**a.** 99%

**b.** 98%

**c.** 58%

**d.** 30%

**e.** 23%

**f.** 14%

**g.** 10%

For the purposes of this example:

■ "True Unqualified" indicates that students who are unqualified are correctly identified as unqualified.

- "True Qualified" indicates that qualified students are correctly identified as qualified.

- "False Unqualified" indicates that a student who tested as unqualified is actually qualified.

- "False Qualified" indicates that a student who tested as qualified is actually unqualified.

The population can be subdivided into the four categories shown in Figure 11.4, based on 5% of the population determined to be unqualified for college study.

Based on the percentages listed in (a) through (f) above, some simple multiplication will yield some startling results.

## True Qualified

Given that 95% of college students are qualified for business school and the test is 90% accurate, the percentage of students who are actually qualified is:

$$95\% \text{ of } 90\% = 85.5\%$$

## True Unqualified

Given that 5% of students are unqualified for business school and the test is 90% accurate, the percentage of students who are actually unqualified is:

**Figure 11.4**

| False qualified | 10% of unqualified college students test as qualified or above the cutoff score. |
|---|---|
| True unqualified | 90% of unqualified college students test as unqualified or below the cutoff scores. |
| False unqualified | 10% of qualified college students test as unqualified or below the cutoff scores. |
| True qualified | 90% of qualified college students test as qualified or above the cutoff score. |

$$90\% \text{ of } 5\% = 4.5\%$$

## False Unqualified

Given that 95% of college students are qualified for business school and the test has a 10% margin of error, the percentage of students who test as unqualified but are actually *qualified* is:

$$10\% \text{ of } 95\% = 9.5\%$$

## False Qualified

Given that 5% of college students are unqualified for business school and the test has a 10% margin of error, the percentage of students who test as qualified but are actually *unqualified* is:

$$10\% \text{ of } 5\% = 0.50\%$$

What percentage of the student population tested as unqualified? Add the False Unqualified percentage to the True Unqualified percentage:

$$9.5\% + 4.50\% = 15\%$$

Finally, what percentage of the student population who tested as unqualified actually was unqualified? Divide the True Unqualified by the total who tested as unqualified:

$$\frac{4.5\%}{15\%} = 30\%$$

So, the probability that someone drawn at random is *actually* unqualified for college given that he or she *tested unqualified* for college is answer (d): approximately 30%.

*More than 70% of the people who tested as unqualified are actually qualified.*

Suppose there are 2 million graduating college students who want to go to business school. This test would indicate not only that 100,000 graduating college seniors (5%) were unqualified for an MBA but that the test got it wrong for 70% of them! So, 70,000 qualified students would be told that they were unqualified and had missed the cutoff for business school. Also notice that the chance of the test delivering a false positive—accepting a student who is actually unqualified—is only one-half of one percent! This is why evaluating students simply on the basis of a single national test without considering the whole person is generally considered a bad idea, even without the lawsuit potential.

Don't feel too badly if you didn't get this off the bat—consider the following statistics:

- One percent of the population has some disease.
- There is a test for this disease that is correct 99% of the time.
- What is the probability that you actually have the disease given that you test positive for the disease?

When asking MDs this question, 85% of doctors get the answer wrong and there are numerous empirical studies to back this up. The key to understanding conditional probability is that the answer is never the obvious choice. Digging into the real numbers requires a different kind of thinking and a different approach. The graduate business school example is a simplification of computing conditional probability. The real deal is shown below—it is called *Bayes' Theorem*.

## BAYES' THEOREM

Reverend Thomas Bayes, an eighteenth-century (1702–1762) mathematician and minister, established a mathematical theory for probability inference. He set down his findings on probability in a document entitled "Essay Towards Solving a Problem in the Doctrine of Chances" (1763), which was published posthumously in the *Philosophical Transactions of the Royal Society of London*. The fundamental theorem is stated in Figure 11.5.

**Figure 11.5**

$$P(A|B) = \frac{P(B|A)P(A)}{P(B)}$$

## Figure 11.6    Bayes' Theorem

| | Probabilities | |
|---|---|---|
| $P_{(A)}$ = Probability of being + | **0.95** | Qualified for business school |
| $P_{(\sim A)}$ = Probability of being − | 0.05 | Unqualified for business school |
| $P_{(B\|A)}$ = Probability you test + if you are really + | **0.9** | Test qualified— really qualified |
| $P_{(\sim B\|A)}$ = Probability you test − but are really + | 0.1 | Tested unqualified— really qualified** |
| $P_{(B\|\sim A)}$ = Probability you test + but are really − | **0.1** | Tested qualified— really unqualified |
| $P_{(\sim B\|\sim A)}$ = Probability you test − if you are really − | 0.9 | Tested unqualified— really unqualified |

$P_{(B)} = [P_{(B|A)} \times P_{(A)}] + [P_{(B|\sim A)} \times P_{(\sim A)}]$
(Probability that you test positive)        0.8600

$P_{(\sim B)} = [P_{(\sim B|A)} \times P_{(A)}] + [P_{(\sim B|\sim A)} \times P_{(\sim A)}]$
(Probability that you test negative)        0.14

$P_{(A|B)} = [P_{(B|A)} \times P_{(A)}]/P_{(B)}$
(i.e., probability you are really        0.9942
+ and test +)

$P_{(\sim A|B)} = [P_{(B|\sim A)} \times P_{(\sim A)}]/P_{(B)}$

FALSE POSITIVE
(i.e., the probability you are really        0.0058
− but test +)

$P_{(\sim A|\sim B)} = [P_{(\sim B|\sim A)} \times P_{(\sim A)}]/P_{(\sim B)}$
(i.e., probability you are really        0.32143
− and test −)

$P_{(A|\sim B)} = [P_{(\sim B|A)} \times P_{(A)}]/P_{(\sim B)}$

FALSE NEGATIVE
(i.e., probability you are        **0.67857****
+ but test − )

**We are most interested in this result!

In plain English (if that is possible), if we use our previous graduate school example, it sounds something like this:

*The probability you are qualified for business school (A) given that you tested as qualified (B) = the probability that you tested as qualified and are qualified (B|A), times the probability that you are qualified (A), divided by the probability that you tested qualified for biz school (B).*

The vertical bar in the formula "|" is mathspeak for the word *given*.

To perform a detailed calculation, the basic formula can be expanded to include a host of relationships. A full-blown example is shown in Figure 11.6. (Note: The tilde "~" is mathspeak for *not*.)

If we plug the same numbers into the grid (entering data only in the bold outlined cells), we get what is shown in Figure 11.6.

In this case, " + "means *qualified* and "−" means *unqualified*. Notice that the more complex and more precise formula still yields a result that is close to the approximation we performed above. In this case, there was a 67.857% chance that the test would show a *false negative* (i.e., the student *tested as unqualified* but was really *qualified*).

If the result you need has to be very accurate, use the grid in Figure 11.6—otherwise, use the shorthand method. The only numbers you have to fill in are the numbers in the Probabilities column that are indicated by the bold outlines around the box. The spreadsheet will compute the rest.

For a different and an engagingly humorous look at Bayesian mathematics, please consult E. Yudkowsky's enlightening treatise, "An Intuitive Explanation of Bayesian Reasoning," at http://yudkowsky.net/bayes/bayes.html.

# REFERENCES

Yudkowsky, Eliezer, "An Intuitive Explanation of Bayesian Reasoning," http://yudkowsky.net/bayes/bayes.html.

Savage, Sam, *Decision Making with Insight*, Thompson Learning, 2003.

Winkler, Robert L. *An Introduction to Bayesian Inference and Decision*, Probabilistic Publishing, 2003.

# Chapter
# 12

# The Seven Ishikawa Quality Tools

$I$N HIS *GUIDE TO QUALITY CONTROL*, originally published by JUSE (Union of Japanese Scientists and Engineers) in 1968, Kaoru Ishikawa described seven quality tools that could be easily learned by employees in manufacturing.

Ishikawa maintained that if workers knew how to correctly apply these seven tools, 95% of all defects, variation, and inconsistency could be eliminated from any process. The seven tools are:

1. Histogram
2. Scatter diagram
3. Pareto chart (a specific type of histogram)
4. Ishikawa diagram (cause-and-effect or *fishbone* diagram)
5. Statistical process chart
6. Flowchart
7. Checksheet

# HISTOGRAM

The histogram is a vertical (or horizontal) bar chart that is used to show how data is distributed in a given set. It's like a snapshot—it shows data distribution or frequency of data at a given moment in time. Figure 12.1 is a histogram of ticket sales at a movie theater for one week.

Here is your snapshot in time, in this case called a *frequency histogram* because it shows you (1) the spread of the measurements and (2) how many of each measurement there are.

Why is the chart important to the business? What if you were investing in a movie theater chain and wanted to see how well the theater was doing—would you base your investment decision on one day's worth of ticket sales, Saturday's for example, or would you want to see how well the business did (1) on different days of the week, (2) at different times of the year, (3) with blockbuster first-run films, and (4) with film festivals featuring the work of specific genres, famous directors, or actors? Chances are you would want to collect data for a variety of situations to see if the investment was viable. The histogram is a data chart that helps the user make this decision.

**Figure 12.1**

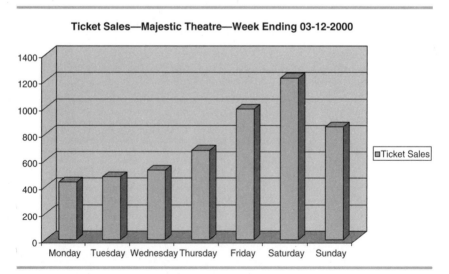

Ticket Sales—Majestic Theatre—Week Ending 03-12-2000

**Figure 12.2**

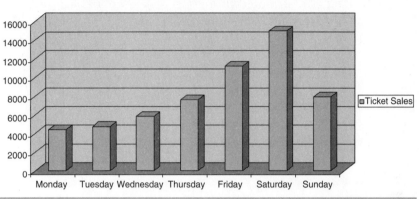

Ticket Sales—Majestic Chain—Week Ending 03-14-1999

Notice that the diagram is not cluttered with lots of different information (i.e., ticket sales from 10 theaters all jammed onto the same page)—that picture might be a bit confusing to read, much less understand. The chart in Figure 12.1 is simple and direct and clearly answers the question, "How many tickets did the Majestic sell each day for the week ending 3-12-2000?" Should the user want to see the combined sales from 10 theaters, the chart would look very much like the one in Figure 12.1, only the ticket quantities would be much larger, as shown in Figure 12.2.

## SCATTER DIAGRAM

This is another quality tool that is used to help solve quality problems. It is fundamentally different from the histogram in that the scatter diagram is used to show how one variable relates to another variable.

**Example:** You want to see if GMAT scores of students admitted into your school's MBA program have any relationship to how much they are earning five years after graduation. So you take a sample of 100 students from the program and create a scatter diagram that shows the data points as given in Figure 12.3.

**Figure 12.3**

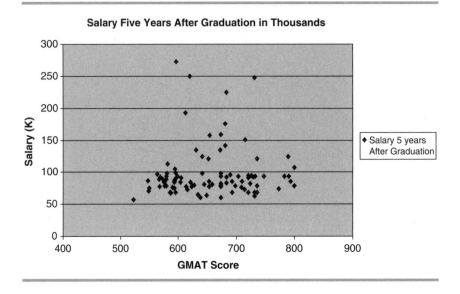

**Salary Five Years After Graduation in Thousands**

## Interpretation

Notice in this example there doesn't appear to be any correlation between GMAT score and salary. However, there are actually five possible outcomes in the scatter diagramming process:

1. No correlation between the two variables
2. A possible positive correlation between the variables
3. A strong positive correlation between the variables
4. A possible negative correlation between the variables
5. A strong negative correlation between the variables

Let's look at what a possible weak correlation between the variables would look like. In the example in Figure 12.4, as the GMAT scores increase, the salary increases somewhat, but there could be other variables affecting salary that would make the salary not directly comparable to the GMAT scores.

**Figure 12.4**

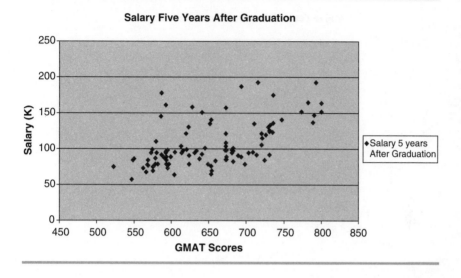

The chart in Figure 12.5 shows a strong correlation between the GMAT score and salary five years after graduation.

What if the opposite were true? What if there were a strong negative correlation between scores on the GMAT and salary five

**Figure 12.5**

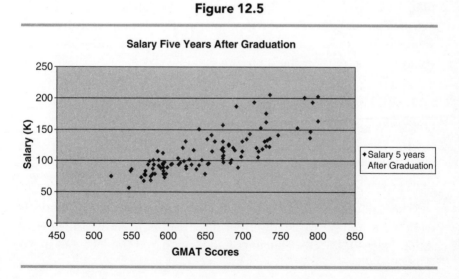

**Figure 12.6**

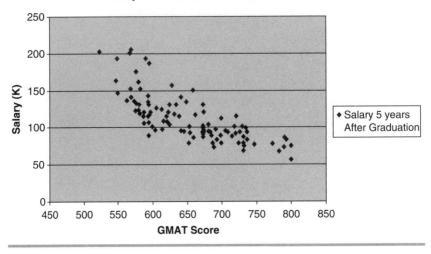

**Salary Five Years After Graduation**

years after graduation? The chart might look something like Figure 12.6.

This would mean that the higher the GMAT score, the less likely the student would be doing well financially five years after graduation! Not a good scenario for your MBA program, is it? This is why you will probably never see such a correlation done at a business school relating test scores to future financial success unless the result showed a positive correlation between the two!

Finally, Figure 12.7 is a scatter diagram that shows a weak negative correlation between GMAT scores and salary five years after graduation.

The chart appears to trend slightly lower and be more spread out as the GMAT score increases, but there could be other factors at work that are not obvious by simply viewing the data in the chart.

The usefulness in this exercise is that viewing data in this way can direct the user to ask different questions, especially if the correlation between the two elements being compared produces an unexpected result.

**Figure 12.7**

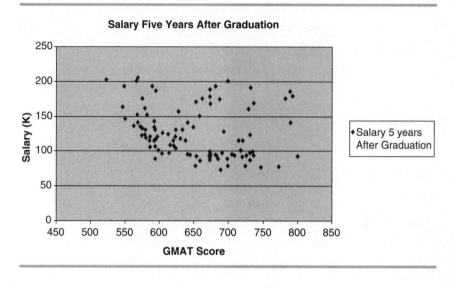

**Salary Five Years After Graduation**

PARETO CHART
==

The Pareto chart is named for Italian economist Vilfredo Pareto (1848–1923), and is probably the most misinterpreted and misunderstood of the quality tools. Pareto created a mathematical formula to describe the unequal distribution of wealth in his country, observing that 20% of the people owned 80% of the wealth. While it may be misnamed, *Pareto's Principle*, or *Pareto's Law*, as it is sometimes called, can be an excellent tool to help you manage problems effectively (from *SPC Simplified: Practical Steps to Quality*, Amsden, Butler, Amsden, Productivity, Inc., 1998; also: http://deming.eng.clemson.edu).

After Pareto made his observation and created his formula, many others observed similar phenomena in their own areas of expertise. In the late 1940s, Dr. Joseph M. Juran inaccurately attributed the 80/20 rule to Pareto, calling it Pareto's Principle. Working in the United States in the 1930s and 1940s, Juran recognized a universal principle he called the "vital few and trivial many," and reduced it to writing. In an early work, a lack of precision on Juran's part made it appear that he was applying Pareto's observations about economics to a broader body of work. (The name *Pareto's Principle* stuck, probably because it sounded better than *Juran's Principle*.)

As a result, Dr. Juran's observation of the "vital few and trivial many," the principle that 20% of something always is responsible for 80% of the results, became known as *Pareto's Principle* or the *80/20 rule*. You can read his own description of the events in the "Appendix to Chapter 3—The Non-Pareto Principle: Mea Culpa," from Juran's book, *Juran on Quality by Design* (The Free Press, 1992).

## The 80/20 Rule Explained

The *80/20 rule* means that in anything a few (20%) are vital and many (80%) are trivial. In Pareto's case, it meant that 20% of the people owned 80% of the wealth. In Juran's initial work, he identified 20% of the defects causing 80% of the problems. Project managers know that 20% of the work (the first 10% and the last 10%) consume 80% of your time and resources. You can apply the 80/20 rule to almost anything, from the science of management to the physical world. Within a few percentage points either way, it is an observation that has withstood the test of time.

You know 20% of your stock takes up 80% of your warehouse space and that 80% of your stock comes from 20% of your suppliers. Also, 80% of your sales will come from 20% of your sales staff, 80% of your business will come from 20% of your customers, 20% of your staff will cause 80% of your problems, but another 20% of your staff will provide 80% of your production. It works both ways.[1]

At some point, a light bulb usually goes off in the reader's head when he or she realizes that, based on this observation, if one could only eliminate the 20% of the issues causing 80% of the problems, life would be grand. However, human nature being what it is, our own internal barometer is readjusted once the new level of performance is achieved, and then other matters causing the remaining 20% of the problems (that were only trivial issues before) now loom much larger—in effect *they* become the new 20% of your issues causing 80% of the problems! And so it goes in a constant, cosmic game of management Whack-a-Mole. (When I worked in telecom, the same idea was expressed by management, embodied in the concept of gathering low-hanging fruit when problems needed to be resolved. The low-hanging fruit represented the 20% of the issues causing 80% of the problems.)

Here's an example of how a Pareto chart can be used to identify the 20% of your issues that are causing 80% of your problems. Let's say you manage a large apartment complex and you decide to hold your first "ask-the-landlord" soirée—you have invited the residents to a town hall meeting to address any concerns they may have with the management of the property. Boy, do you get an earful! After the meeting, you ask the secretary to compile a list of all the issues discussed to see what the problems are and which are most prevalent. The table in Figure 12.8 is created.

Fortunately, the landlord's daughter has read *this* book and has quickly spun up a Pareto diagram to highlight the major areas of concern and put together an action plan to resolve the issues (Figure 12.9).

Notice that the top five issues based on the highest number of complaints constitute over 70% of the problems confronting the building management team—fairly close to the 80/20 distribution. The top seven issues constitute just over 80% of the problems. Interestingly enough, when these first five issues were addressed, they also had a positive impact on some of the other issues as well (there were some issue dependencies that we did not discuss). Once the front door security issue was addressed and a higher police presence almost eliminated the vagrancy problem, the broken mailboxes, parking space squatters, and excessive noise issues also were almost eliminated as well.

The Pareto analysis can help focus efforts to correct problems; it gives the user the ability to manage issues with data and facts instead of the usual hair-on-fire approach.

## ISHIKAWA DIAGRAM (CAUSE-AND-EFFECT OR *FISHBONE* DIAGRAM)

Yes, when you complete the diagram, it actually *does* look something like a fishbone, but what's the point? Why not just *list* the issues? The advantage to using the Ishikawa diagram is that the user can

## Figure 12.8

| Issues | Number of Complaints | Percentage of Total |
|---|---|---|
| Major cockroach infestation. | 335 | 12.87% |
| Poor lighting in the common areas—internally and externally in courtyard areas. | 117 | 4.50% |
| The grounds are poorly kept— garbage on the ground near receptacles. | 385 | 14.80% |
| Landscaped sections are dying and not cared for. | 35 | 1.35% |
| Washing machines broken over 50% of the time. | 421 | 16.18% |
| Laundry room is not well maintained or cleaned. | 63 | 2.42% |
| Elevators are *very* slow and unresponsive. | 75 | 2.88% |
| All mailboxes do not lock— broken locks are not fixed for months. | 34 | 1.31% |
| Front-door security is practically nonexistent. Several people have been mugged. | 459 | 17.64% |
| Assigned parking spaces taken up by nonresidents. No enforcement is used to remove the cars in violation. | 53 | 2.04% |
| Excessive noise after 10 P.M. disturbs residents who have to rise early for work. | 33 | 1.27% |
| No area to post building notices to announce services or events. | 25 | 0.96% |

**Figure 12.8 Continued**

| | | |
|---|---|---|
| Sidewalks are not cleared after major snowstorms quickly—this is dangerous for the older residents. | 109 | 4.19% |
| Courtyard areas around the buildings are heavy with vagrants-several residents have been threatened. | 255 | 9.80% |
| Heat in the winter is intermittent and extreme—it is either cold or too hot. | 121 | 4.65% |
| Leaking roof on several of the buildings has damaged some upper-floor apartments and residents' furnishings. | 23 | 0.88% |
| Appliances in some of the rental units are nonfunctional and in dire need of repair. | 16 | 0.61% |
| Emergency fire doors are not secured from the inside—they are a building security risk. | 22 | 0.85% |
| Front-door intercom is nonfunctional. | 21 | 0.081% |

visualize cause-and-effect relationships clearly—it becomes easy to see how a series of events or deficiencies can cascade into an overall problem or failure. Ishikawa wrote in his classic *Guide to Quality Control* (JUSE Press Ltd., 1968) that there are several ways in which cause-and-effect diagrams are useful:

- Preparing a cause-and-effect diagram is educational in itself.
- A cause-and-effect diagram is a guide for discussion.
- The causes of variation are actively sought.

**Figure 12.9**

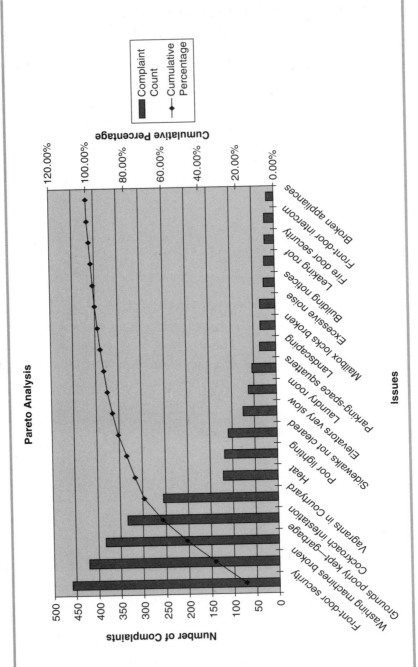

- Data are collected within the cause-and-effect diagram.
- The cause-and-effect diagram shows the level of technology.
- The cause-and-effect diagram can be used for any problem—it is a guide to concrete action.

The Ishikawa diagram typically addresses the following.

**The Four *Ms* + *E*:**
- Methods
- Machinery
- Manpower (people)
- Materials
- Environment

Ishikawa referred to the elements in the cause-and-effect chart as *quality dispersion*—the entire process may appear to be functioning uniformly but, on closer examination, there are differences within the individual parts and how they perform. Figure 12.10 is a high-level picture of the Ishikawa diagram.

**Figure 12.10**

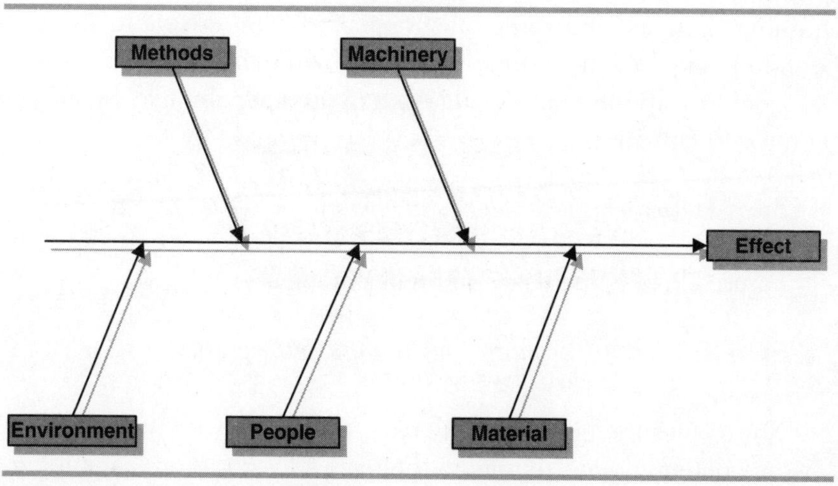

It may not be necessary to use all five generic categories each time the diagram is drawn, and there may be other categories that can be used in the diagram depending on what is being analyzed (e.g., "Schedule," "Financing,"etc.).

There are five steps in creating the Ishikawa diagram:

1. Identify the problem or the objective in the diagram (i.e., the *effect*), and draw the effect box and the centerline.
2. Identify the primary contributors to the problem or objective (i.e., the *categories*), and connect the category boxes to the main spine.
3. Identify causes that contribute to the main categories and add sub-branches for each contributing cause. This is where the process can create a chain of interrelated causes.
4. Continue to add detail until all identifiable causes have been diagrammed.
5. Analyze the diagram for elements requiring further study or investigation.

For example, suppose the coach of the volleyball team came to you with a problem: He's got six strong players on the team, and the team should be clobbering all opponents. The reality is, the team is in fifth place and demoralized and the coach is unsure how fix the problem. He's tried different rotations, motivational activities, longer training sessions, and so on, all to no avail. You decide to sit down with him and do a brainstorming session using the Ishikawa diagram as a tool to help illuminate issues that up to this point may be unseen or not quite obvious.

**Step 1:** *Define  the problem statement or objective.*

Figure 12.11 is the basic problem statement.

**Step 2:** *Identify  primary contributors to the problem.*

Now comes the brainstorming part—you meet with the coach and discuss potential contributors to the team's losses. (For example, are

**Figure 12.11**

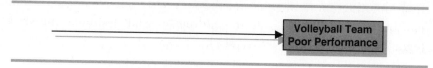

the players not supporting their teammates? Has the competition gotten much stronger? Are the strategies on the playing court outmoded?)

In the discussion, the following four elements come to the forefront as the major contributors to the problem:

1. Play execution
2. Player usage
3. Training
4. Play strategy

The Ishikawa now looks like Figure 12.12.

**Figure 12.12**

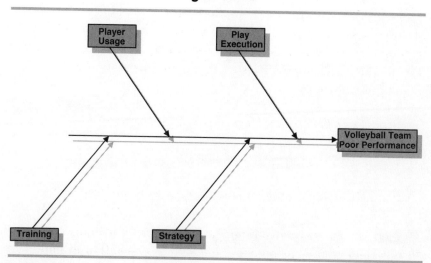

**Step 3:** *Identify the major causes contributing to the effects.*

As the discussion continues and various questions are asked not only of the coach but the players, the issues shown in Figure 12.13 come to light.

**Step 4:** *Continue adding details on causes contributing to the effects.*

One can continue to add details to the chart in Figure 12.14; however, be aware of some pitfalls:

- If the diagram turns out to be too complex, it may indicate that your knowledge of the process is too shallow or that the diagram is too generalized.
- If the diagram is too simplistic and contains only five or six generalized causes, it is probably inadequate.

## Figure 12.13

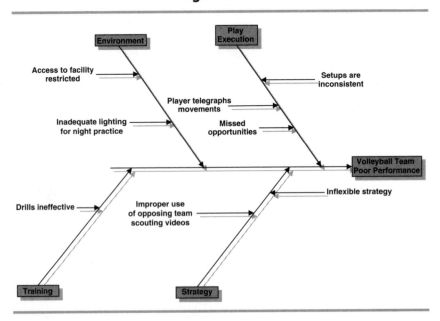

**Figure 12.14**

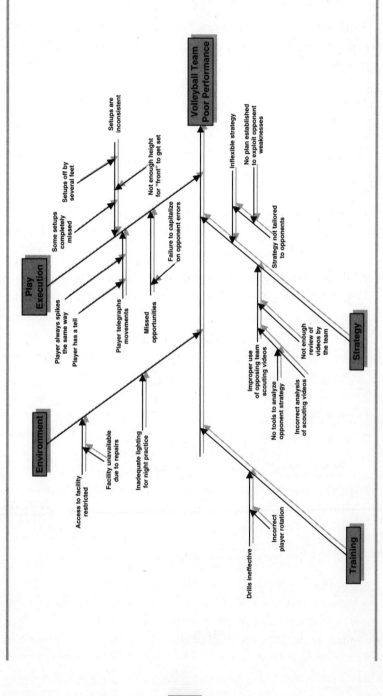

# STATISTICAL PROCESS CHART (SPC) OR CONTROL CHART

The SPC chart is one of the most useful tools in the project manager's quality tool kit—and it can be used in a wide variety of situations. A simplified example of the SPC control chart was demonstrated in the Quality Pioneers section in Chapter 2 describing Dr. Walter Shewhart's contributions to the developing the foundations of quality processes that exist to this day.

There are a number of different types of control charts that can be created, but in reality, they can be boiled down to two distinct types of charts:

1. *The variable control chart.* This type of chart is used to measure *variations* in your predicted output—whatever it is. You could be measuring the variance in motor drive-shaft end-play, the outside diameters of valve fittings, or how many minutes (or seconds) it takes your helpdesk dispatchers to respond to an emergency call. These types of measurements are called *variable data,* and we will shortly examine the different type of charts that can be used to measure variable data.

2. *The attribute control chart.* The attribute control chart is used in a situation where you are dealing with some characteristic of your product or process that you need to control, but it is very difficult or impossible to measure. Yet, being able to measure and/or control the characteristic is very important to the customer. For example, a painted surface may have dings in it, the grade of paper used in a book may be generally consistent but may have distracting surface blemishes that detract from readability, panes of glass used to replace broken windows at a large facility have surface irregularities that may subtly distort what one sees through the glass (i.e., things that are very difficult to measure, but that to the customer may be okay or *not* okay upon final inspection). These characteristics are called *attributes* and they provide *attribute* or *counting data.*

Before we dive into the creation and graphing of the SPC chart, let's look at the components of an SPC chart, what they mean, how to read the chart, and how to interpret the information contained in the chart:

- *Average:* The computed average of all measurements in the sample.

- *Standard deviation:* The square root of the variance of the sample average represented by the Greek symbol: $\sigma$ (sigma).

- *Upper control limit (UCL):* Three standard deviations above the measurement average.

- *Lower control limit (LCL):* Three standard deviations below the measurement average.

- *Upper specification limit (USL):* The customer's requirement for the process or product; may be above or below the UCL.

- *Lower specification limit (LSL):* The customer's requirement for the process or product; may be above or below the LCL.

- *Attributable cause:* Any data point landing above the UCL or below the LCL. Attributable causes are errors that can be corrected by line workers or properly trained people who are close to the process being measured. Processes that show attributable causes are generally considered *out of control*.

- *Common causes:* The process is considered *in control*; however, it also means that any data point inside the UCL and LCL limits represents potential opportunities for process improvement. Reduction in process variation, which in turn would produce a reduction in the UCL or the LCL, can be resolved only by management.

- *The "rule of seven":* A series of at least seven data points that continuously trend in either an ascending or descending direction or that continuously alternate above and below the average. Data points that do so are considered *attributable causes*.

In reviewing the examples in Figures 12.15 and 12.16, you will notice that control charts showing a trend of more than seven data points in one direction constitute an attributable cause.

**Figure 12.15**

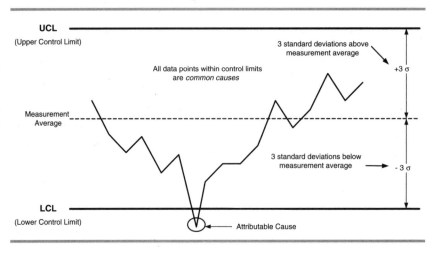

If you were to look at a *normal distribution* created from the SPC charts in the previous two figures, it might look something like Figure 12.7.

You will notice on the chart in the figure that each vertical division represents *1 σ* of deviation. There are two measurements of

**Figure 12.16**

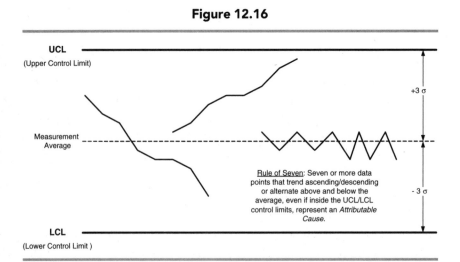

**Figure 12.17**

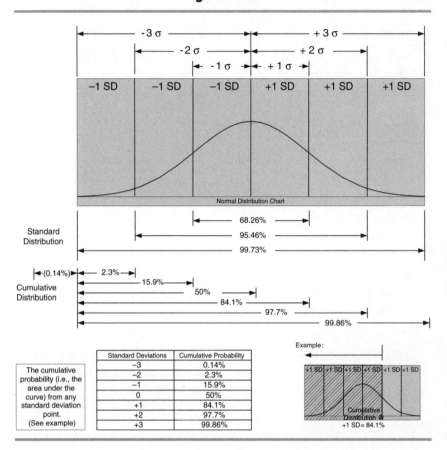

deviation shown on the chart. The first is the *standard distribution*, which shows how much of the sample lies within the −1 and +1 sigma range (one standard deviation above and below the average) or 68.26%; how much lies within −2 and +2 sigma or 95.46%; and how much lies within −3 and +3 sigma or 99.73%.

The *cumulative distribution* shows how much of the sample lies under the curve at any given point. So for any data point at −3 sigma or under, this represents 0.14% of the total sample. Any data occurring up to −2 sigma represents 2.3% of the total sample, and so on. In the example in Figure 12.17, the small graph shows the cumulative percentage of up to $+1$ sigma on the chart (shaded area) or 84.1% of the total sample.

In the following example, however, we will be using the control chart for a different and somewhat novel purpose. In this case, you will see that showing a trend may have a positive impact on the ultimately desired result.

## Variable Control Chart

The most commonly used variable control chart is the $\overline{X}-R$ ("X bar R"), or the *average* and *range* charts. What these terms mean is this:

- *Averaging* takes the total of all the measurements and divides them by the number of measurements to get the average measurement.

- *Range checking* is simply taking the difference between the highest and lowest measurements.

For example, let's say you want to measure your distance driving ability on the golf course. You go to the driving range and you hit 10 tee shots a day for 10 days to see if your distance driving ability improves. The data shown in Figure 12.18 is collected.

The simplest way to set up SPC charts to check range and average is to set up a simple measurement chart in Excel and let the program do the calculations for you. Excel can easily perform the *averaging* function by selecting the AVERAGE function and selecting the range of cells to average. For example, the function AVERAGE(B5:B14) will give you the average of the numbers in all the cells from B5 through B14.

Setting up the formula for the range check is slightly more complex, but easily workable. Excel provides two functions out of the box that you can easily combine: the MAXA function and the MIN function. Within the same range of numbers described in the preceding paragraph, use the MAXA function to find the largest number in the column, then use the MIN function to find the smallest number in the column. To calculate the *range* in the column, set up the formula

**Figure 12.18    Tee Shots in Yards**

| Day1 | Day2 | Day3 | Day4 | Day5 | Day6 | Day7 | Day8 | Day9 | Day10 |
|------|------|------|------|------|------|------|------|------|-------|
| 275 | 234 | 284 | 229 | 324 | 303 | 294 | 276 | 298 | 313 |
| 231 | 342 | 296 | 298 | 296 | 294 | 301 | 291 | 286 | 320 |
| 321 | 319 | 315 | 264 | 256 | 286 | 287 | 341 | 324 | 346 |
| 285 | 295 | 324 | 314 | 284 | 272 | 334 | 328 | 329 | 329 |
| 290 | 287 | 303 | 285 | 278 | 293 | 302 | 316 | 348 | 302 |
| 246 | 267 | 296 | 279 | 319 | 323 | 293 | 324 | 322 | 346 |
| 325 | 259 | 284 | 321 | 302 | 305 | 318 | 347 | 309 | 355 |
| 283 | 295 | 257 | 303 | 287 | 298 | 317 | 306 | 356 | 327 |
| 271 | 304 | 307 | 296 | 292 | 351 | 328 | 319 | 312 | 319 |
| 268 | 312 | 286 | 268 | 265 | 326 | 336 | 327 | 299 | 304 |
| 94 | 108 | 40 | 92 | 68 | 65 | 49 | 65 | 70 | 53 |
| 279.5 | 291.4 | 295.2 | 285.7 | 290.3 | 305.1 | 311 | 317.5 | 318.3 | 326.1 |

Red = longest drive
Yellow = shortest drive

thus: = MAXA(B5:B14)−MIN(B5:B14). (This takes the largest number in the column and subtracts the smallest number in the column, leaving the result: the *range*.)

Now that we have computed the *average* and the *range* of the data, we can now create a statistical process control (SPC) chart that shows us whether our tee shots are within the statistical control limits, thus showing that the ball is being hit with consistency—or whether the tee shots are outside the statistical control limits, thus showing the measurements outside the control limits that may warrant correction. (Granted in almost all situations, exceeding your average tee shot by 50 to 100 yards would normally be a good thing. However, for the hole that is 275 yards from tee to flag, hitting a 320-yard tee shot would place you well beyond the green and potentially to the tee of the next hole!)

Creating the SPC chart requires the following four elements:

1. A graph of daily average measurements
2. A graph of the average (mean) of all the measurements for all 10 days

3. A graph of the upper control limit (UCL), which is 3 standard deviations above the 10-day average

4. A graph of the lower control limit, which is 3 standard deviations below the 10-day average

Using the "Tee Shots" chart in Figure 12.18, you can use the following Excel functions to compute the *range average* for 10 days, the *standard deviation* of the range, and three times the standard deviation, and then set up the chart as in the grid shown in Figure 12.19.

The *10-day range average* was computed using the Excel function AVERAGE. The numbers in the "Range" row were averaged: AVERAGE(B21:K21). The result, 75.1, was placed in cell B18. Then, the value from cell B18 was copied into cells B20 through K20.

The standard deviation was computed using the Excel STDEV function. Once again, the numbers in the "Range" row were used: STDEV(B21:K21). The result, 18.47, was placed in cell C18. Three times the standard deviation, 55.40, was placed in cell D18.

The UCL was created by taking the 10-day range average (75.1) and adding the value for three standard deviations (55.40). The result, 130.5, is copied into cells B19 through K19.

The LCL was created by taking the 10-day range average (75.1) and subtracting the value for three standard deviations (55.40). The result, 19.70, is copied into cells B22 through K22.

**Figure 12.19**

| | B | C | D | E | F | G | H | I | J | K |
|---|---|---|---|---|---|---|---|---|---|---|
| | 75.1 | 18.47 | 55.40 | | | | | | | |
| UCL | 130.50 | 130.50 | 130.50 | 130.50 | 130.50 | 130.50 | 130.50 | 130.50 | 130.50 | 130.50 |
| rangee | 75.1 | 75.1 | 75.1 | 75.1 | 75.1 | 75.1 | 75.1 | 75.1 | 75.1 | 75.1 |
| | 94 | 108 | 67 | 92 | 68 | 79 | 49 | 71 | 70 | 53 |
| LCL | 19.70 | 19.70 | 19.70 | 19.70 | 19.70 | 19.70 | 19.70 | 19.70 | 19.70 | 19.70 |

**Figure 12.20**

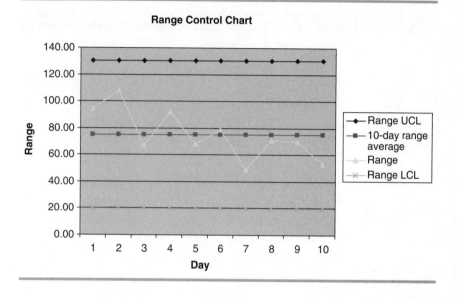

For the *range chart*, we will take the measurements for all 10 days and combine them into a single chart: one for *average* and one for *range*. The results are shown in Figure 12.20.

The reason for repeating the numbers for the UCL, LCL, and 10-day range average 10 times can be seen in the chart in Figure 12.20—they are shown as constant values so that the actual daily ranges can be easily compared to constants.

The same process was used to create the tee shot grid in Figure 12.21.

- The average tee shot for the 10 days was 302.01 yards.
- The standard deviation of the daily averages was 26.997 (cell C25).
- Three times the standard deviation is 80.99 (cell D25).
- The UCL is the average tee shot over 10 days + 3*(standard deviation): 302.01 + 80.99 = 383.
- The LCL is the average tee shot over 10 days − 3*(standard deviation): 302.01 − 80.99 = 221.02.

**Figure 12.21**

| | B | C | D | E | F | G | H | I | J | K |
|---|---|---|---|---|---|---|---|---|---|---|
| 25 | 302.01 | 26.997 | 80.99 | | | | | | | |
| 26 Average UCL 10 day yardage | 383.00 | 383.00 | 383.00 | 383.00 | 383.00 | 383.00 | 383.00 | 383.00 | 383.00 | 383.00 |
| 27 average | 302.01 | 302.01 | 302.01 | 302.01 | 302.01 | 302.01 | 302.01 | 302.01 | 302.01 | 302.01 |
| 28 Averages | 279.5 | 291.4 | 295.2 | 285.7 | 290.3 | 305.1 | 311 | 317.5 | 318.3 | 326.1 |
| 29 Average LCL | 221.02 | 221.02 | 221.02 | 221.02 | 221.02 | 221.02 | 221.02 | 221.02 | 221.02 | 221.02 |

The resulting *average chart* is shown in Figure 12.22.

From the two charts, one can make some observations:

- The *range chart* clearly shows that the variance in the difference between the longest ball hit and the shortest ball hit looks to be diminishing; in other words, the shots are less rangy and more consistent.

- The rule of seven in this case may be showing a desired result instead of an attributable cause. The *average chart* shows that the average distance for tee shots is gradually increasing—

**Figure 12.22**

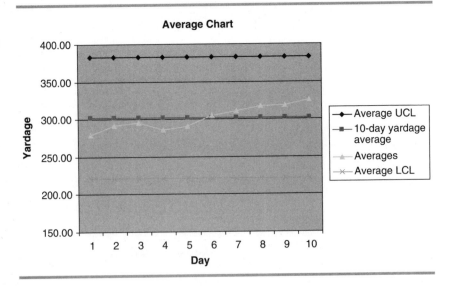

*trending up* as they say in the stat biz. This may be considered a positive result if the desired goal is to increase your drive distance.

What is the value in making these measurements, and what would it mean if you found numbers that were outside the measurement UCL or LCL limits? For measuring golf tee shots, here are some possibilities:

- For golf tee shots that had a *range* above the UCL on a given day, it might indicate an alarming inconsistency in the tee shots. You might need to consult a professional golf trainer to work on how to produce a less rangy and more consistent result.

- For golf tee shots that had a *range* below the LCL on a given day, it might indicate an extraordinary consistency in the tee shots. You might want to examine what you did to make the shots so consistent on that day and try to repeat the process!

- For golf tee shots that had an *average* above the UCL on a given day, you would want to examine what you did differently to consistently exceed the UCL distance so you could repeat the process!

- For golf tee shots that had an *average* below the LCL on a given day, it might indicate a failure in executing proper technique in the tee shots. You might need to consult a professional golf trainer to work on how to produce a more consistent result.

## Customer Specification Limit

This is usually where the vendor finds outs whether his process, which has been determined to be in statistical control, actually meets the needs of the customer. We will now define a chart containing the USL (upper specification limit) and the LSL (lower specification limit) and compare it to our SPC chart containing the UCL and LCL range.

**Figure 12.23**

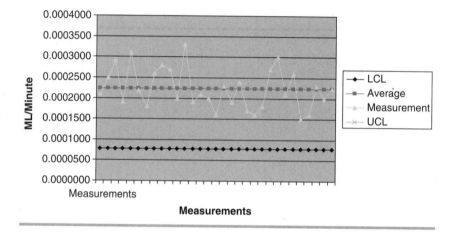

**Example:** Your company manufactures valves that control high pressure (up to 10,000 psi) and your values typically have a very low leak ratio of 0.0002 ml/minute (or $6.76 \times 10^{-6}$ fluid ounces) over a maximum period of five minutes. You check a batch of 30 valves and collect the data shown in Figure 12.23.

The data in the figure appears to show that you have a high-quality process in which only minute amounts of unwanted material get through at 10,000 psi. This might be okay if you're controlling water leakage—unfortunately, the customer needs the valves to control the flow of highly volatile liquid oxygen going through the system. When the valve shuts off—*it had better shut off*.

The customer specification chart looks like Figure 12.24.

The customer specification clearly shows that the USL is 0.0001 ml/minute and that the LSL is zero (i.e., leakproof)! Notice that USL shown by the arrow in the diagram in Figure 12.24 is at a lower level than any of the measurements taken. In other words, the process may be in control, but the process does not at all meet the customer specification.

**Figure 12.24**

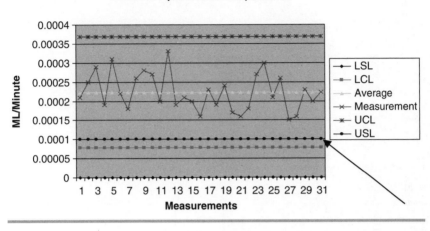

Therefore, management addresses the common causes of the variation and improves the process. After the process improvement is implemented, the leakage assessments of another 30 valves are measured, with the results shown in Figure 12.25.

There are two observations that should be obvious from looking at the chart in Figure 12.25:

**1.** We have two measurements that fall outside the upper control limit, indicating that we have some special causes to address in our process.

**2.** However, *all* the measurements fall below the upper specification limit (the customer's requirement) and we have met and exceed the requirements, even though the process still needs a little tuning due to the two special cases in item 1. Six of the leakage measurements were exactly zero. All in all, it is a better place to be than where we were before.

Please note that in the examples above, we have combined UCL/ LCL charts and USL/LSL charts in a single graphic. To avoid confusion

**Figure 12.25**

it is always better to construct two charts; one is an SPC chart that indicates the statistical control of your process, and a second one shows how your process meets customer requirements specifications.

## Attribute Control Chart

There are four types of attribute control charts that are commonly used for attribute measurements:

1. The p chart measures the percent defective in a sample of parts (think *p* for *percent*).

2. The np chart measures the number of defective parts in a sample of parts.

3. The c chart measures the number of defects *per part* in a sample of parts. This is slightly different from the np-chart measurement, which measures the number of defective parts regardless of the number of defects each part may contain.

**4.** The u chart determines the stability of counted data when the sample size varies.

Let's run an example of each type of attribute chart using the same sample. Let's say you are opening a chain of tournament pocket-billiard parlors nationwide and need a reliable source for high-quality billiard balls. You have just gone on a field trip to a company that makes premier billiard balls, Roll With It Baby, Inc., to check out their product. The operations manager shows you the latest measurements taken from the last batch of billiard balls created at the facility and you see the report shown in Figure 12.26.

Setting up the same format for the Billiard Unit Defect Report as we did for the *variable* control chart, we create the attribute *p* and *np* charts (Figures 12.27 and 12.28).

With the *c* chart, you will be measuring the number of defects, *per inspected unit*. See if you can put the *c* chart together yourself based on what we have demonstrated on the variation and other attribute charts. Figure 12.29 is the table of defect data with the number and the type of defect for each part—in this case, a completed seat

**Figure 12.26**

| Billiard Unit Defect Report—7 Days | | | | | | | |
|---|---|---|---|---|---|---|---|
| Date | 12-Jul-03 | 13-Jul-03 | 14-Jul-03 | 15-Jul-03 | 16-Jul-03 | 17-Jul-03 | 18-Jul-03 |
| Sample size | 15750 | 23500 | 40000 | 50000 | 50000 | 50000 | 50000 |
| Defect count | 17 | 22 | 28 | 26 | 31 | 35 | 24 |
| Percent defective | 0.11% | 0.09% | 0.07% | 0.05% | 0.06% | 0.07% | 0.05% |
| **Defect type:** | | | | | | | |
| Cracked | 3 | 6 | 8 | 7 | 9 | 7 | 6 |
| Scratched | | 3 | 1 | 2 | | 8 | 2 |
| Pitted | 4 | 2 | 6 | 5 | 5 | 5 | 4 |
| Finish worn | 5 | 3 | 5 | 4 | 7 | 4 | 6 |
| Blemished | 2 | 4 | 6 | 5 | 5 | 7 | 4 |
| Other | 3 | 4 | 2 | 3 | 5 | 4 | 2 |

**Figure 12.27**

| | | | | | | | |
|---|---|---|---|---|---|---|---|
| p UCL | 0.137% | 0.137% | 0.137% | 0.137% | 0.137% | 0.137% | 0.137% |
| p average | 0.072% | 0.072% | 0.072% | 0.072% | 0.072% | 0.072% | 0.072% |
| p measurements | 0.108% | 0.094% | 0.070% | 0.052% | 0.062% | 0.070% | 0.048% |
| p LCL | 0.007% | 0.007% | 0.007% | 0.007% | 0.007% | 0.007% | 0.007% |

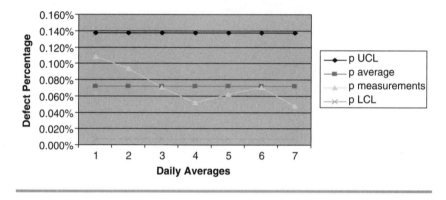

**p Chart—Billiard Defect Percentage**

assembly for a child's swing-set. Use the formulas and the functions defined in the previous example to apply to the *c* chart.

# FLOWCHART

Most people have seen a flowchart in one form or another. The flowchart allows great flexibility to the user because there are a number of ways it can be implemented:

- A *process flowchart*, showing how a manufacturing process progresses step-by-step, how a project management process is executed, or how to structure a telephone sales call.

- A *data flowchart*, showing how information moves through a computer system.

- A *logic flow diagram*, showing how a computer program progresses through a series of logical steps (i.e., loops, conditional

## Figure 12.28

| np UCL | 43.93 | 43.93 | 43.93 | 43.93 | 43.93 | 43.93 | 43.93 |
|---|---|---|---|---|---|---|---|
| np average | 26.14 | 26.14 | 26.14 | 26.14 | 26.14 | 26.14 | 26.14 |
| np measurements | 17 | 22 | 28 | 26 | 31 | 35 | 24 |
| np LCL | 8.36 | 8.36 | 8.36 | 8.36 | 8.36 | 8.36 | 8.36 |

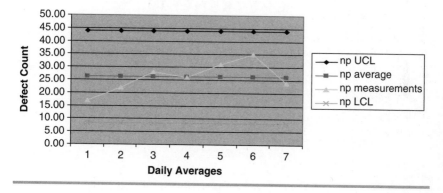

np Chart Billiard Defect Count

## Figure 12.29

| Swing Seat Unit Defect Report—1 Day | | | | | | | | | | | | | | |
|---|---|---|---|---|---|---|---|---|---|---|---|---|---|---|
| Date | 12-Jul-03 | | | | | | | | | | | | | |
| Part name | Swing Seat | | | | | | | | | | | | | |
| Defect count | 27 | 22 | 18 | 23 | 34 | 31 | 22 | 15 | 33 | 26 | 14 | 30 | 33 | 26 | 30 |

**Defect type:**

| | | | | | | | | | | | | | | | |
|---|---|---|---|---|---|---|---|---|---|---|---|---|---|---|---|
| Cracked | 3 | 6 | | 7 | 9 | 7 | 6 | | 12 | 8 | 5 | 17 | 13 | | 9 |
| Scratched | 8 | 6 | 3 | 7 | 12 | 11 | | 3 | 7 | 2 | | 5 | 8 | 5 | 5 |
| Pitted | 6 | 3 | 7 | | 8 | 2 | 6 | 2 | | 6 | 3 | 2 | 7 | 4 | 3 |
| Finish worn | 5 | 3 | | 4 | | 4 | 6 | 9 | 11 | 8 | 5 | | | 12 | 7 |
| Blemished | 2 | 4 | 6 | 5 | 5 | 7 | 4 | | 3 | 2 | 1 | 4 | 5 | 5 | 2 |
| Other | 3 | | 2 | | | | 1 | | | | | 2 | | | 4 |

branching, etc.). Logic flows can also be used to map a trouble-shooting process (e.g., for a faulty computer program or failed mechanical assembly).

A classic example of a flowchart is the *process flow*. The flow in Figure 12.30 shows a high-level process for a company that sells custom garage and deck kits.

## CHECKSHEET

The checksheet has several useful functions that have statistical application as well as use in a project management context:

- Production distribution checks
- Defective item checks
- Defective location checks
- Defective cause checks
- Checkup confirmation—(checking for all required parts in a kit or to verify all required steps in a process have been followed)

The production distribution checksheet in Figure 12.31 is from the *Guide to Quality Control*, by Kaoru Ishikawa (JUSE Press Ltd., 1968).

A standard histogram could have been created to represent the data shown in the checksheet; however, to collect the data necessary to prepare a histogram and then create a frequency distribution (normal distribution chart) may seem to be an unnecessary duplication of effort. With the chart in Figure 12.31, it is easier to collect and sort the data as it is collected. The resulting checksheet almost looks like a two-peaked distribution chart.

Similar charts can be made for listing the number of defective items, for the location of defects on a part or assembly, or for identifying the cause of a defect. However, the checkup confirmation checksheet is one that is most familiar to project managers. Here the user

**Figure 12.30**

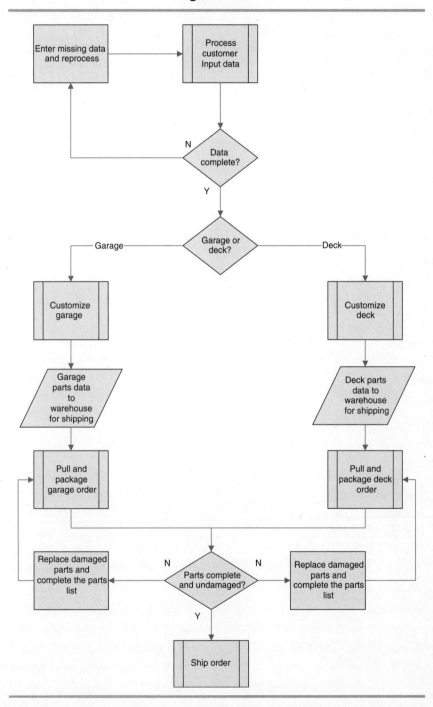

**Figure 12.31**

| (Continuous data use) | | No. _____ |
| --- | --- | --- |
| | Check Sheet | |

| | |
| --- | --- |
| Product name _____ | Date _____ |
| Usage _____ | Factory name _____ |
| Specification _____ | Section name _____ |
| No. of inspections _____ | Data collector _____ |
| Total number _____ | Group name _____ |
| Lot number _____ | Remarks _____ |

Dimensions: 1.5 1.6 1.7 1.8 1.9 2.0 2.1 2.2 2.3 2.4 2.5 2.6 2.7 2.8 2.9 3.0 3.1 3.2

| Total frequency | 1 | 2 | 6 | 13 | 10 | 16 | 19 | 17 | 12 | 16 | 20 | 17 | 13 | 8 | 5 | 6 | 2 | 1 |
| --- | --- | --- | --- | --- | --- | --- | --- | --- | --- | --- | --- | --- | --- | --- | --- | --- | --- | --- |

reviews a listing of all the elements needed to satisfy the checkup. It can be a list of parts for a kit, the steps in a test procedure, or a sequenced list of tasks that need to be completed for construction of a structure or software component. A partial example is provided in Figure 12.32.

**Figure 12.32**

| Project Plan Review Criteria | Done? Y/N | Comments |
|---|---|---|
| **1.** Has the project plan passed the pre-bid checklist and any outstanding issues been addressed and corrections made? | | |
| **2.** Have all required sections of the PMP been completed either by reference to other documents (which *Must* exist in final form), by justification of absence, or waiver? | | |
| **3.** Has the Introduction section been revised to reflect reality? | | |
| **4.** Have the necessary waivers been completed (personnel, document formats, development kernels/processes, etc.)? | | |
| **5.** Does the Project Description section contain the final project description, via a complete SOW? | | |
| **6.** Do the revised assumptions reflect reality? | | |
| **7.** Do detailed requirements describe the method to be used to refine or acquire the requirements? | | |
| **8.** Reasonable, measurable acceptance criteria defined? | | |
| **9.** Identified products and deliverables? | | |
| **10.** Timely, periodic status analysis activities, tools, and reports? | | |

# NOTE

1. Edited from John Reh Management Guide: www.PeopleAreCapital.com.

# REFERENCES

Ishikawa, Kaoru, *Guide to Quality Control*, JUSE Press Ltd., 1968.

Deming, W. Edwards, *Out of the Crisis*, MIT Center for Advanced Engineering Study, 1986.

Amsden, Robert T., Davida M. Amsden, and Howard E. Butler, *SPC Simplified*, Productivity Inc., 1998.

# Chapter
# 13

# Quality Function Deployment

*Q*UALITY FUNCTION DEPLOYMENT *(QFD)* is a structured approach for product/project planning and development that focuses on the "voice of the customer" as the key element in the design and development process. It is also one of the cornerstones of the Six Sigma process. Many businesses think that constructing a high-quality product, by their own standards, defines product or process quality. Nothing could be further from the truth. America's foremost business philosopher and writer, Peter Drucker, said it succinctly:

> *Quality in a product or service is not what the supplier puts in. It is what the customer gets out and is willing to pay for. A product is not quality because it is hard to make and costs a lot of money, as manufacturers typically believe. This is incompetence. Customers pay only for what is of use to them and gives them value. Nothing else constitutes quality.*[1]

The QFD process recognizes this fact and places the customer's needs *first* in the process and then determines how the technical qualifications and competing products meet that need so that the business can do a better job of meeting the customer's needs. Developed by Dr. Shigeru Mizuno and Dr. Yoji Akao in the mid-1960s, the first reported case study of QFD was originally utilized at Bridgestone Tire in Japan in 1966. Further implementations occurred at Matsushita Corporation in the late 1960s and at Mitsubishi's Kobe shipyards in Japan in 1972. Since that time it has been widely used in Japanese industry and was more recently brought to American industry in 1983. The most recent implementation of modern QFD is entitled "QFD II" by the QFD Institute (www.qfdi.org).

The traditional view of QFD is what has historically been called the *house of quality (HOQ)*. The matrix, as shown in the last section of this chapter, while very useful, is really used as one of the seven *management process (MP) tools* in the deployment phase of a project. There are a number of steps needed prior to the construction of a "house of quality" and it is only one of several specialized matrixes that can be used in the deployment phase of a project, if it is needed at all.

In this chapter we run through the parts and pieces of modern QFD and then apply the steps to the creation of a QFD for a video product, so that you can get a high-level view of how the process works, and describe the benefits of implementing QFD for products, processes, or services.

One of the most important aspects of QFD is its ability to capture the requirements of the product or process in great depth. Most traditional requirements-gathering approaches capture at best 80% of the requirements actually needed for the project. This is because the people from the technical team are asking for requirements from business users who usually:

1. Are too busy to do a thorough job of describing the requirements
2. Don't really know what a requirement is
3. Have received no training in how to elaborate requirements

If you don't believe it, try this the next time you need to obtain requirements from business users: Ask the Sales Director, CFO, Business Manager, or VP if their job description states that they must be able to deliver precise, accurate, and lucid requirements to the technical side of the business. Then ask if any of them have ever been trained on how to create effective business requirements. The responses will likely be in the low-single-digit percentages.

Customers don't create requirements; the technical team does. It is the customer's job to define *what* the needs of the business are; but it is the technical team that creates the requirements and defines *how* the needs of the business will be accomplished. You will find that when compared to other methods of gathering project requirements the QFD process is, hands down, the most complete method yet devised for effectively and accurately elaborating project requirements.

First, let's review the seven management planning tools used in modern QFD. For those who have studied Six Sigma, you will note that most of these tools are also part of the Six Sigma toolset:

1. Affinity diagram
2. Analytic Hierarchy Process
3. Failure mode effects analysis (FMEA)
4. Relationship or data flow diagram (DFD)
5. Decision tree diagram
6. Matrix diagram (HOQ is a matrix diagram)
7. Precedence diagram (critical chain project management)

The basic steps in modern QFD take the following path:

1. Define the key project goal (Ishikawa diagram).
2. Identify key customer segments (customer segment table).
3. Gather voice-of-the-customer data and enter it in the *customer voice table* (gemba visit).
4. Identify and structure customer needs (affinity diagram).
5. Prioritize customer needs (AHP).
6. Display the prioritized customer needs in a maximum value table.
7. Implement the deployment utilizing any of the seven management planning tools (one of which is the traditional "house of quality").

# DEFINE THE PROJECT GOAL

There are many kinds of goals an organization may wish to accomplish. Some are tied to overall organizational goals such as profit, market share, and so on. Other goals may focus on product innovation or improvements, while still other goals may focus on timely project execution and delivering on budget and within the defined scope.

As a project manager, you may be focused on the project management goals, but understand that the overarching reason for this focus ties back to organizational or product goals. Remember: Every supply chain starts with a customer. You can use a simple matrix to list your goals and objectives for the project; however, sometimes the Ishikawa diagram can be useful in this situation. This diagram is not only used to identify contributors to issues but can also be used in the exact opposite way: to elaborate contributors to an overall organizational goal.

While you may have a number of goals for your project, pare them down to one key goal and identify the following for this goal:

- The current process state
- The desired future state
- The timeline to achieve the future state
- The target value of the future state (how you know when you are done)

Usually the reason a project is implemented is because there is a positive customer impact that will occur, which in turn will help to make your organization more successful. If your organization has a number of customers, which customers are the most important to your organization's success? To understand this, the organization needs to define its customers, identify the potential customer segments, and then create a plan for how to study its key customers.

# DEFINE THE CUSTOMER SEGMENT

What kinds of customers are important to your organization's business? How do customers use your products to satisfy their needs? Are your products being used in ways you never considered? Would this use constitute a new opportunity or a key to expanding and improving your product or service?

The *customer segments table* can be used to identify the 5 *W*s + *H* in the format given in Figure 13.1.

## GATHER THE VOICE OF THE CUSTOMER

In Japan, this is called "going to gemba," which literally means going to where the work is done. The idea is to actually see how the customers perform their tasks and observe (1) what they are trying to do, (2) what satisfies or disturbs them, (3) what tasks they perform, (4) problems in the current mode of operation. You must actually see what happens while the customers are tackling their own issues as well as *their customers' issues* to gain a complete picture of the day-to-day operations, problems, and potential opportunities.

The process is usually composed of three steps:

1. **Plan the visit.** Once again, you use the same approach a journalist uses in tracking down a story—the 5 *W*s + *H*: *who, what, where, when, why,* and *how*:
   a. Who is doing the job?
   b. What do they do, specifically?
   c. Where is it done?
   d. When in the entire process is the task (or tasks) done?
   e. Why do they do it?
   f. How is it accomplished?

Creating a workflow diagram or process model is a key element in helping the gemba team understand what the customer does. The process model should be reviewed with the customer for accuracy and with as much supporting detail as possible.

2. **Execute the plan—conduct the visit.** You must then conduct the gemba visit according to the plan established. Document your observations and the customer's words, behaviors, and attitudes (positive or negative), and identify the wants and needs of the customer.

**Figure 13.1  Customer Segments Table**

| Goals | Who uses the product? | What is product used for? | Where is the product used? | When is product used? | Why is the product used? | How is the product used? |
|---|---|---|---|---|---|---|
| Build energy-efficient house | Single persons or families | Dwelling | Anywhere where ample light or wind exists | 7 x 25 | Makes the house energy efficient through the use of solar | Sleeping, exercise, entertainment, recreation, study |
| Use environmentally friendly materials | | | | | | |
| Easy to maintain | | | | | | |

3. **Document the result.** Create a log of what you did, whom you spoke with, what processes you observed, behaviors observed, customer statements, and particularly your impressions (seen, heard, and felt) while on the gemba visit. Frequently, what is *not* said is as important as what you heard. In all cases, put yourself in the customer's shoes and see things from their point of view.

The results of the visit are generally compiled in a table that generically resembles the one in Figure 13.2. You can add your own specific columns of information as needed.

## IDENTIFY AND STRUCTURE CUSTOMER NEEDS

What is a customer need? If we think of the reasons why a customer implements a project, we can understand most of the customer's needs as well. Projects are undertaken:

- Because of a regulatory requirement
- Due to a customer or market demand
- To deliver a competitive advantage for the organization via a product or process improvement or innovation
- Because of technical necessity
- To improve goodwill toward the organization
- To expand market share or enter a new market

The gemba visit helps us to understand the customer's need by way of interviews, observations, focus groups, and so on. A goal of the gemba visit is to have the customer describe the issues they face as well as the benefits they wish to realize. From your observations and analysis of the gemba visit, you may see issues facing the organization that are not evident to the customer or to which the customer may be blind. These issues may not be evident as the result of a single interview or gemba visit. It might be necessary to plan several gemba visits under different circumstances to gain a clear picture of

**Figure 13.2**

| Gemba Log | | | | | | | |
|---|---|---|---|---|---|---|---|
| Project Title | | | | | | | |
| Highest Priority Project Goal: | | | | | | | |
| Customer Segment: | | | | | | | |
| Location | Customer Contacts | Date | Duration | Team Members | Observations | Next Steps? | Lessons Learned | Follow-up Date |
| | | | | | | | |
| | | | | | | | |
| | | | | | | | |

354

the unidentified or unseen needs that will have impact on the organization if not addressed.

When addressing customer needs make sure you help the customer understand the difference between a need and a solution! Too frequently, the customer will begin designing the solution before the real needs are adequately understood. Needs must be clearly defined so that you can identify and discuss *solution options*.

What is the difference between a need and a requirement? It may help to think about it in these terms: The needs represent *what benefits* the customer is seeking, while the requirements specify *how* the benefits can be realized. There may be a number of solution options that can be pursued to satisfy the need depending on the cost, timeline to develop, priority, or convenience of the solution.

The perennial issue with traditional requirements-gathering methods is that some percentage of requirements are excluded—some studies suggest that only 80% of the customer's requirements are ever verbalized. This harks back to the ISO definition of quality, in which quality is defined by the stated as well as the implied needs of the product, process, or system. What can we do to address the implied needs? One of the tools used to structure customer needs so that implied needs can be surfaced is called the *affinity diagram*.

The "KJ Method^TM" was developed by cultural anthropologist Dr. Jiro Kawakita as a method for identifying how people think about the systems they work upon, or put in another way, how customers think abut their needs. The KJ Method is the process used to create the affinity diagram. For example, if you wanted to gain an understanding of how a construction crew views their work, you might do something like the following:

- List a number of specific tasks, one task to a 3″ × 5″ index card. (See the task list in Figure 13.3.)
- Ask the exercise participants to arrange the cards into logical groups.
- Have the team discuss and write a *header* for each group defining what the name means.

**Figure 13.3    Task List**

| Electrical: wiring and panel | Windows and doors | Insulation |
|---|---|---|
| Plumbing: kitchen/bathroom | Framing | Hookup to electric company |
| Sheetrock/wallboard | Painting | Flooring |
| Roofing | Driveway paving | Kitchen/bathroom cabinetry |
| Bathroom fixtures | Appliance installation | Sewer and water hookup |
| Landscaping | Catch basin | HVAC: central heat/air |
| Sump pump | | |

The grouping created reflects the point of view of the exercise participants. This is not a prioritized listing; it is simply a tool to show how the customers conceptualize their work.

The affinity diagram for a construction project at a high level might look something like Figure 13.4.

In this case, the crew looked at the card elements and arranged them according to how they viewed the fundamental breakdown of the work. Depending on how the work was to be accomplished, the affinity diagram might look very different if, for example, there are prefabricated elements in the construction. In this instance, notice that anything that has to do with plumbing, sewage, kitchen, or bathroom hookups is grouped under the heading of "Water," indicating that there are specific controls and devices designed around the handling of water (either for drinking, showering, or waste) within a dwelling. Also notice that the sump pump has a "Water" as well as an "Electrical" component and was included in both categories.

Once the affinity diagram is created, a hierarchical structure of the work can be assembled that gives the users the ability to more

**Figure 13.4**

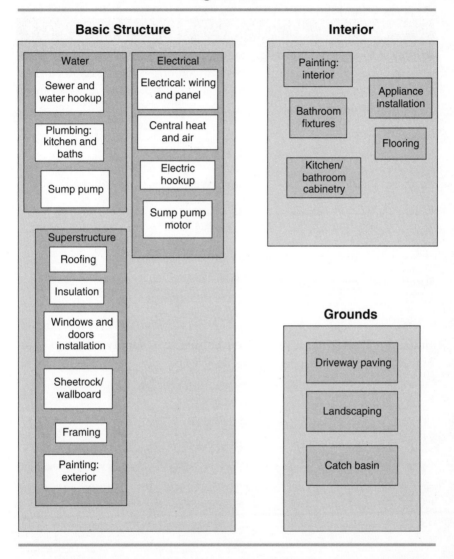

deeply analyze the needs they have identified. It is with the hierarchy matrix that you can begin to surface the elusive "implied needs" on the process or product. The hierarchy can be created by basically turning the affinity diagram on its side so that a suitable drilldown can be performed to elaborate details on the higher levels. An example is shown in Figure 13.5.

Notice that some of the drilldown is displayed in the "Interior" section to further disambiguate some of the hierarchy elements, such as with flooring, bathroom fixtures, and sheetrock/wallboard. Further drilldown can be applied to uncover some of the implied needs until a detailed hierarchy can be elaborated.

**Figure 13.5**

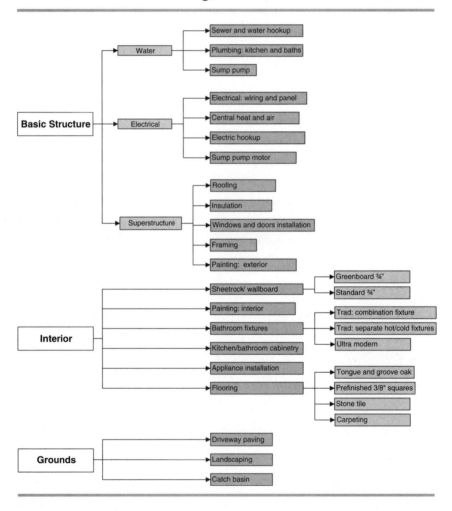

## PRIORITIZE CUSTOMER NEEDS

Remember the *Analytic Hierarchy Process (AHP)* from Chapter 6? This is exactly the tool that is used to take the hierarchy of needs and prioritize them according to which needs are most important to the customer. How would we use the AHP on the diagram in Figure 13.5, for example?

Separate AHP grids can be set up to prioritize which bathroom fixtures and flooring types would be most desirable to the customer. An example of how the *flooring* AHP grid would be set up is shown in Figure 13.6. In this case, the customer showed that the oak floor had the highest value, followed by a preference for prefinished wood squares.

## MAXIMUM VALUE TABLE

The *maximum value table (MVT)* is used to elaborate exactly what we will do to deliver the needs and benefits to the customer in the form of *functional requirements*. It shows which elements in the design or development effort are of highest importance to the customer. At the project level, the maximum value table can constitute the *action plan* to deliver the service or product.

A key element in the table is that it is used as a traceability matrix so that specific elements of the design, functional requirements, or the solution can be traced back to a customer benefit or business need. An example of the table is shown in Figure 13.7.

Once the MVT is created, you may want to go into more detail on any aspect of the project. For instance, you may want to better understand the relationship between customer benefits and the design of the solution or between customer needs and requirements. For that elaboration, any of the seven MP tools can be used depending on the focus of the elaboration. However, the best known of these tools is the QFD matrix called the *HOQ* ("house of quality").

## HOUSE OF QUALITY

First we will explore some high-level descriptions and a basic picture of a QFD diagram. Each of the lettered sections appearing below represents a high-level structured definition of a product or process that

**Figure 13.6**

| Decision Criteria | Oak | "3/8" squares | Stone Tile | Carpet | Weighted Criteria | | | | | | Sum | % |
|---|---|---|---|---|---|---|---|---|---|---|---|---|
| Oak | 1.00 | 3.00 | 5.00 | 7.00 | 0.597 | | 0.662 | 0.536 | 0.438 | | 2.232 | 0.558 |
| 3/8" squares | 0.33 | 1.00 | 3.00 | 5.00 | 0.199 | | 0.221 | 0.321 | 0.313 | | 1.053 | 0.263 |
| Stone tile | 0.20 | 0.33 | 1.00 | 1.00 | 0.119 | | 0.074 | 0.107 | 0.188 | | 0.487 | 0.122 |
| Carpet | 0.14 | 0.20 | 0.33 | 1.00 | 0.085 | | 0.044 | 0.036 | 0.063 | | 0.228 | 0.057 |
| | 1.68 | 4.53 | 9.33 | 16.00 | | | | | | | 4.000 | 1.000 |

# Figure 13.7

## Maximum Value table

| | Customer Benefits | | | | | | | Product Features | | | | | | |
|---|---|---|---|---|---|---|---|---|---|---|---|---|---|---|
| | Customer | | | | Solutions | | | | Design | | | | Project | |
| Characteristics | segment characteristics | problems | needs | characteristics & capabilities | functions | processes (service) | solution technology | Availability | reliability | maintainability | usability | suportability | Schedule | Tasks |
| Looking for home with low cost maintenance | Typically family of four + pets | most houses have old inefficent appliances and high energy costs | Cheap electricity, heating and cooling | Availbility of numerous energy efficient options | solar roof shingles | Solar electric power | | Systems always online | systems downtime and maintenance  maintenance window is 01% | Readily available components | simple, user-friendly interfaces | phone | Complete by July 2005 | 1. Mfg 2.Purchase 3.Install 4. Configure 5. UAT |
| | | | | | Wind Turbines | wind generated power | | | | | | Web based | | |
| | | | | | Energy converting insualted windows | heating and cooling | | | | | | | | |

documents the development team's understanding of the overall planning process for the product, service, or process. Let's review each section and generically describe what goes into it:

**A.** *Customer wants and needs.* This is a listing of the customer's wants and needs for the product, service, or process.

**B.** *Planning matrix.* This section contains three fundamental areas of information:
  i. Quantitative market data that expresses the customer's satisfaction with its own organization versus the competition's current offerings
  ii. Strategic goals for the new product or service
  iii. Ranking customer wants and needs in prioritized importance

**C.** *High-level description of product or service.* This is usually constructed in response to the customer wants and needs described in Section A.

**D.** *Development team evaluation of the strength of the correlation between a customer's wants and needs and the technical response.* The grid created here is at the heart of the QFD. This is where the correlation and interrelationships between the customer's wants and needs and the elements of the technical solution are visually displayed in a prioritized graphical format.

**E.** *Technical correlations.* This identifies the strength of the interrelationships among the elements in the technical solution.

**F.** *Technical matrix.* Three areas are identified here:
  i. The rank of the technical responses based on the elements defined in customer wants and needs (Section A)
  ii. Information on the performance of a competitor's product or service
  iii. Technical performance targets

A picture of this representation appears in Figure 13.8.

**Figure 13.8**

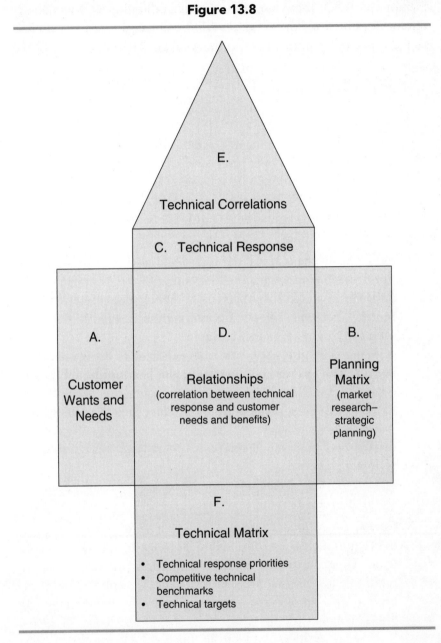

Essentially, we break down the picture in Figure 13.8 into a series of *whats* and *hows*—that is, *what* do we do and *how* do we do it?

From Figure 13.8, Section A describes one of the *whats: customer wants and needs*, or as it is called in QFD, the "voice of the customer." Sections B, C, D, E, and F describe the *hows*.

The general order in filling in the matrix proceeds as follows:

1. *Section A—customer wants and needs.* This is usually performed though customer interviews. It is critical that the development team understand customer needs well—failure to maximize customer involvement at this stage can lead to misunderstanding, confusion, and ultimately project failure.

2. *Section B—planning matrix.* This is usually the second section to be constructed. Here, the high-level goals are set based on the development team's understanding of the customer's want and needs, marketing data, or other necessary input to the process. Some of the specific information entered in the planning matrix covers elements such as:
   a. What is the prioritized rank of each need to the customer?
   b. How well is the need now being met in a similar product or service?
   c. How well does a competitor's product meet the customer's needs?
   d. How well does the development team want to meet the customer's needs?
   e. Can meeting a customer need be used as a sales point for the business?

3. *Section C—technical response.* This is a set of process or product requirements stated in technical terms by the development team. This can include high-level metrics, product or service requirements, or product features. Whatever approach or combination of approaches is chosen here, the names given to these elements are the *substitute quality characteristics (SQCs)*. If there is considerable detail in this area, a hierarchy of characteristics can be displayed in *tree diagram* format in this section of the HOQ (more on this shortly).

4. *Section D—relationships section.* This is the largest section of the matrix and is constructed using a method called the *prioritization matrix method* to develop the relationships between customer wants and needs and the SQCs. It is the heart of the QFD process and shows the SQCs with the greatest overall impact on customer satisfaction.

5. *Section F—technical matrix.* Particularly the line items entitled "Competitive Benchmarks" and "Targets" represent the fifth and sixth steps in completing the HOQ.

6. *Section E—technical correlations matrix.* This is usually the last step in constructing the HOQ. It is a matrix designed to show how the SQCs either support or impede each other. This can be a great aid in discovering design or communication bottlenecks in the process.

Now that we have described the basics of the QFD, let's take a short road test to see how an HOQ is actually assembled.

**Example:** The customer wants to implement a video security system on their network utilizing the latest IP cameras and the latest digital video (DV) recording software. The current video security system is an out-of-date analog system that offers the users minimal control of cameras and unresponsive video control software, and requires constant maintenance. The system is also proprietary, which means they are tied to their current vendor.

First, collect the inputs that represent the *voice of the customer (VOC)* and sort these into major categories. The resulting *customer wants and needs* (Section A) is based on two MP tools we defined and used previously: the *affinity diagram* and the *hierarchy diagram*.

1. *Affinity diagram.* This is a tool that organizes *qualitative* information in a hierarchical structure, built from the bottom up. This is the place where the customer can express their ideas to define the wants and needs from the product, process, or service. Ideas for the affinity diagram can be created *internally* in the form of a brainstorming activity, if the team is attempting to

define the problem with little data at hand, or *externally*, based on facts the team has acquired to address the problem.

2. *Tree diagram.* This is similar to the affinity diagram, but it is constructed from the top down rather than from the bottom up. It also represents the customer wants and needs in a more abstract manner than the affinity diagram: The customer states what they want but in generally nontechnical terms.

For our purposes, we will use the *hierarchy diagram*—it will look something like this in outline form:

- The cameras are easy to use:
  □ All the cameras pan, tilt, and zoom.
    - The zoom feature is very powerful (100 ×), allowing users to read the license plate on a car from 100 yards away (or similar capability)
    - Pan-and-tilt features can be controlled by a user or can be set on automated, user-defined sweep patterns.
  □ They are easy to install—no special skill required.

- The cameras are rugged and highly impact resistant, and can withstand harsh winter weather (to −50°F), high heat (to + 147°F), and humidity.

- The DV software is easy to use:
  □ Users can group up to 16 images on a single screen.
  □ Customized views can be created—the users are not limited to viewing a single area but can create views from multiple areas.
  □ Software is very responsive—when camera controls are engaged, the cameras respond quickly.

- The DV software allows for secured archiving, copying, and forwarding:
  □ The video frame is encrypted and cannot be altered or tampered with.
  □ The archived video will stand up as evidence in a court of law.
  □ Standard MPEG or .avi video clip copies can be created from the archived originals.

□ Video clip copies can be created, stored, and forwarded as e-mail attachments to management.

(Due to the basic selection of IP cameras and "open" DV software products, the customer is automatically freed from being tied to a single vendor; thus, this was not stated as a "need" in the QFD—it was a *given*.)

We will now transfer this outline to Section A of the HOQ grid in *tree diagram* format.

The diagram in Figure 13.9 is, of course, a simplification of the actual process. There may be far greater detail in the customer wants and needs section. The collection of user information may necessitate the creation of submatrixes to handle the detail as we drill down into

**Figure 13.9**

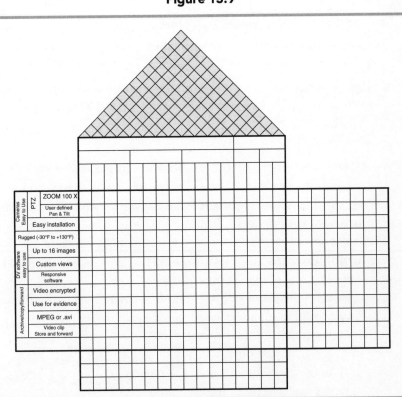

the process. The idea here is to simply give the reader an outline of how to proceed.

Next, we tackle the daunting task of establishing the *planning matrix*—Section B. This section usually takes a bit longer than the others, because this is where the strategic planning for the product, process, or service occurs, and it represents the *quantitative* data about each of the customer's wants and needs.

Below is the textbook standard for this section, which constitutes seven columns of data completed by a normalized weighting of the criteria in the eighth column. The seven areas are typically subject to customization—there can be more or fewer than seven columns depending on what is being developed. The seven areas (plus one) are generically:

1. Importance to the customer
2. Customer satisfaction performance
3. Competitive satisfaction performance
4. Goal
5. Improvement ratio
6. Sales point
7. Raw weight
8. Normalized raw weight (an extension of item #7, raw weight)

Let's look at each area to identify and quantify what is important to the customer (see Figure 13.10):

1. **Importance to the customer.** This area is usually represented by one of three types of data:
   a. *Absolute importance.* For example, on a 1–5 scale the importance ranking may proceed as follows:
   (1) Not important to the customer
   (2) Minor importance to the customer
   (3) Moderately important to the customer
   (4) Very important to the customer
   (5) Highest order of importance to the customer

**Figure 13.10**

| Case | Current Satisfaction Performance | Goal | Improvement Ratio |
|------|----------------------------------|------|-------------------|
| 1 | 2 | 4 | 2 |
| 2 | 1 | 3 | 3 |
| 3 | 3 | 5 | 1.67 |
| 4 | 4 | 6 | 1.5 |
| 5 | 2 | 2 | 1 |

(Please note that customers will frequently rank *every-thing* as a number 5, meaning everything is of highest importance. This indicates an inability on the customer's part to prioritize. If everything is of the highest importance, then *nothing* is important. Priorities can be logically determined once the wants and needs are clearly identified. The customer may need some guidance in this area.)

b. *Relative importance.* The relative importance scale is best established through the use of an *Analytic Hierarchy Process.* (See Chapter 2.) Here, a scale of 1–9 is generally used. If need A is twice as important as need B, and need B is three times as important as need C, the score for A will be double that of B and six times more than C. In numbers, this might be represented as A = 6, B = 3, C = 1. We will use the 9-point scale in the QFD and rank each element on its importance on a scale of 1–9. *This is the recommended approach.*

c. *Ordinal importance.* This is similar to relative importance, except that there is no quantitative measure between elements that are less or more important. The elements are simply ranked on a numerical scale. So Element A could be ranked a *10* and Element B ranked a *9*, but there would be no way to determine if a ranking of *10* was slightly more important, twice as important, or three times as important as a ranking of *9*. Since arithmetic operations cannot be performed using the ordinal scale (mathematically, that is an *illegal* operation), this approach will not be considered.

2. **Customer satisfaction performance.** This measurement represents the customer's perception of how well the *current product or service* is meeting the customer's requirements. If the purpose of the QFD is to best determine how to automate a currently *manual* process, then the current process may not be meeting the customer's needs very well at all. This element is generally estimated by conducting customer interviews to determine how well each customer want and need has been met by the current process. *Once again, use the AHP to determine their rankings.*

3. **Competitive satisfaction performance.** The project development team must understand how well the product, service, or process they will build (or evaluate) stacks up against the competition. Some information on competitors can be found in trade journals or from companies that supply business intelligence for a fee. However, sometimes the best way to find out how well your product or the competition's product is doing is by asking your own and the competition's customers! This can be done in the form of a mailed survey or by purchasing information on product satisfaction from a company such as the Gallup organization or IRI. From performing this analysis, your development team can decide where best to focus their efforts to make or select the product, service, or process in specific key areas that will make your customers more satisfied than the competition can. Another option here is that if the company has already outsourced the work you may want to compare the solutions of other vendors to that of the incumbent. *(This is also shown on a scale of 1–5 or 1–10.)*

4. **Goal.** Here the development team decides what level of performance they want to achieve in meeting the customer's wants and needs. Once again, as in other sections of this grid, the goals need to be prioritized. Given a project in which time, scope, dollars, and resources are not available on an unlimited basis, prioritization and setting performance levels of goals are critical to project success. This measurement is usually combined with the next element on the list: the *improvement ratio.*

5.  **Improvement ratio.** The improvement ratio is determined by combining the *current rating* (customer satisfaction performance) with the *goal*, utilizing the following formula:

$$\frac{\text{Goal}}{\text{Current satisfaction}} = \text{Improvement ratio}$$

The more the *goal* exceeds the *current satisfaction performance*, the more opportunity there is for improvement in the product, service, or process—however, these ratios do not indicate the relative difficulty in achieving the stated goals. In making a decision about what to improve, use of the Pareto histogram in evaluating which goals would be the simplest to achieve might be helpful in evaluating where the development team can provide the most bang-for-the-buck:

1. **Sales point.** This information ranks the ability of the organization to sell the product, service, or process based on the degree to which each customer need is met. The typical values assigned to this area are:
   a. No sales point
   b. Moderate sales point
   c. Strong sales point

   Use the AHP to set up a $3 \times 3$ grid to rank the importance of the sales promotion. This aspect of the planning matrix may not carry the same weight as some of the other aspects for the following reason: If customer wants and needs are met to a high degree, the product will be much easier to sell.

2. **Raw weight.** This is a score that shows the overall importance of each customer want and need to the development team. It is computed by multiplying:

Raw weight = (Importance to customer) * (Improvement ratio) * (Sales point)

   The higher the raw weight score, the more important is the customer want and need to the development team. This score represents the importance of an overall strategic business objective of the customer needs to the overall success of the project.

**3. Normalized weight.** This field is calculated by dividing the *raw weight score* for a customer need by the *raw weight total score* for *all* the customer needs in column seven:

$$\text{Normalized raw weight} = \frac{\text{Raw weight of customer need (Col 7)}}{\text{Raw weight total (all Col 7 rows summed)}}$$

Be advised that the scores created above are determined by computing the average of the inputs for each criterion from all participants in the QFD.

Based on this input, we have set up the next step in the HOQ grid to include numbers for the elements described above. The results can be seen in Figure 13.11.

The next step in the process is to set up the *substitute quality characteristics (SQCs)* or the *technical response* in Section C of the HOQ. To be more precise, the *quality characteristics* are the customer's wants and needs stated in nontechnical language, whereas the *substitute* quality characteristics are the customer's wants and needs translated into technical language the development team can use to create the product, process, or service. The HOQ in Figure 13.12 shows the technical response section filled in according to (1) where the technical elements reside in the solution and (2) the extent, when applicable, to which the technical solution meets (or hopefully exceeds) customer wants and needs.

Notice that the technical responses include specific technical capabilities of the cameras, the digital video recording software, and also the network on which these elements are required to operate. The *network* elements may not mean anything to the customer; however, in terms of fulfilling the technical solution the development team included this information to identify whether the environment would support the customer's needs. It is an important part of the technical response.

Now that the initial sections of the HOQ are filled in, we come to the heart of the process—Section D: *relationships*. Before we begin the setup of the grid, it will help to understand how we will be expressing relationships between the customer's wants and needs

**Figure 13.11**

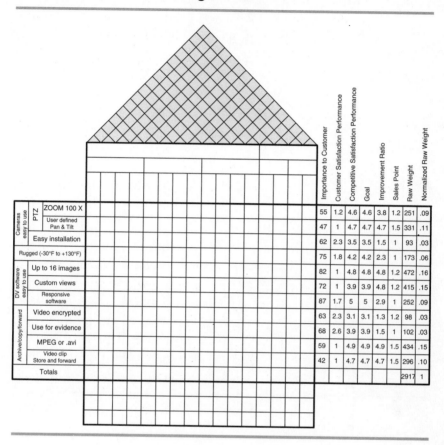

| | | | Importance to Customer | Customer Satisfaction Performance | Competitive Satisfaction Performance | Goal | Improvement Ratio | Sales Point | Raw Weight | Normalized Raw Weight |
|---|---|---|---|---|---|---|---|---|---|---|
| Cameras easy to use | PTZ | ZOOM 100 X | 55 | 1.2 | 4.6 | 4.6 | 3.8 | 1.2 | 251 | .09 |
| | | User defined Pan & Tilt | 47 | 1 | 4.7 | 4.7 | 4.7 | 1.5 | 331 | .11 |
| | | Easy installation | 62 | 2.3 | 3.5 | 3.5 | 1.5 | 1 | 93 | .03 |
| | Rugged (-30°F to +130°F) | | 75 | 1.8 | 4.2 | 4.2 | 2.3 | 1 | 173 | .06 |
| DV software easy to use | | Up to 16 images | 82 | 1 | 4.8 | 4.8 | 4.8 | 1.2 | 472 | .16 |
| | | Custom views | 72 | 1 | 3.9 | 3.9 | 4.8 | 1.2 | 415 | .15 |
| | | Responsive software | 87 | 1.7 | 5 | 5 | 2.9 | 1 | 252 | .09 |
| Archive/copy/forward | | Video encrypted | 63 | 2.3 | 3.1 | 3.1 | 1.3 | 1.2 | 98 | .03 |
| | | Use for evidence | 68 | 2.6 | 3.9 | 3.9 | 1.5 | 1 | 102 | .03 |
| | | MPEG or .avi | 59 | 1 | 4.9 | 4.9 | 4.9 | 1.5 | 434 | .15 |
| | | Video clip Store and forward | 42 | 1 | 4.7 | 4.7 | 4.7 | 1.5 | 296 | .10 |
| | | Totals | | | | | | | 2917 | 1 |

(Section A) and the technical response SQCs (Section C). The table and the grid in Figure 13.13 demonstrate how this works. We first show the "impact symbols"—the measure of how closely the wants and needs map to the technical response—and then show these symbols on the HOQ grid.

When these symbols are placed on the HOQ grid, the resulting correlations are shown in Figure 13.14 between each need and its technical response.

We can now fill in the *relationships* section of the HOQ—Section D—with which of the customer's needs are strongly, moderately,

## Figure 13.12

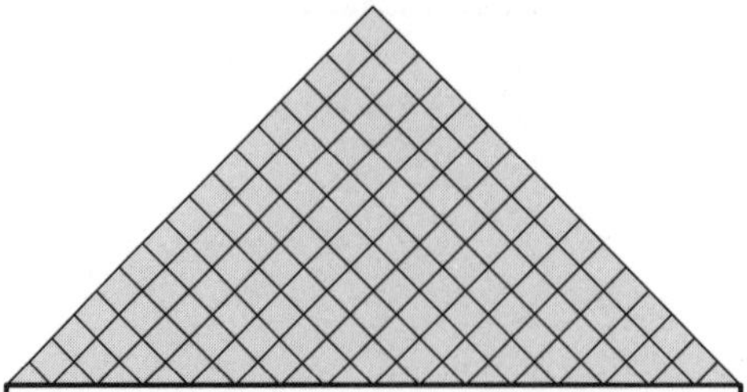

House of Quality matrix with the following row labels and competitive assessment data (the relationship matrix cells for Camera Features, DV Features, and Network are blank):

| | Importance to Customer | Customer Satisfaction Performance | Competitive Satisfaction Performance | Goal | Improvement Ratio | Sales Point | Raw Weight | Normalized Raw Weight |
|---|---|---|---|---|---|---|---|---|
| ZOOM 100 X (Cameras easy to use / PTZ) | 55 | 1.2 | 4.6 | 4.6 | 3.8 | 1.2 | 251 | .09 |
| User defined Pan & Tilt | 47 | 1 | 4.7 | 4.7 | 4.7 | 1.5 | 331 | .11 |
| Easy installation | 62 | 2.3 | 3.5 | 3.5 | 1.5 | 1 | 93 | .03 |
| Rugged | 75 | 1.8 | 4.2 | 4.2 | 2.3 | 1 | 173 | .06 |
| Up to 16 images (DV software easy to use) | 82 | 1 | 4.8 | 4.8 | 4.8 | 1.2 | 472 | .16 |
| Custom views | 72 | 1 | 3.9 | 3.9 | 4.8 | 1.2 | 415 | .15 |
| Responsive software | 87 | 1.7 | 5 | 5 | 2.9 | 1 | 252 | .09 |
| Video encrypted (Archive/copy/forward) | 63 | 2.3 | 3.1 | 3.1 | 1.3 | 1.2 | 98 | .03 |
| Use for evidence | 68 | 2.6 | 3.9 | 3.9 | 1.5 | 1 | 102 | .03 |
| MPEG or .avi | 59 | 1 | 4.9 | 4.9 | 4.9 | 1.5 | 434 | .15 |
| Video clip Store and forward | 42 | 1 | 4.7 | 4.7 | 4.7 | 1.5 | 296 | .10 |
| Totals | | | | | | | 2917 | 1 |

Column groups across the top: Camera Features (360° pan 180° tilt, IP cameras, -50°F thru +147°F, Zoom to 100X, Bullet-proof housing, Handles MPEG -4), DV Features (Up to 25 filed images, Encrypts at source, Saves MPEG or .avi format, Advanced clip editing, Customizeable views, Video time-stamp & watermark), Network (All IP based, Windows™ based, Low bandwidth/camera (36KB), OC-3 fiber backbone).

## Figure 13.13

| Symbol | Meaning | Numerical Value (AHP) |
|---|---|---|
| <blank> | Not linked | Usually 0 |
| △ | Weakly linked | 1 |
| ◯ | Moderately linked | 3–5 |
| ◎ | Strongly linked | 7–9 |

**Figure 13.14**

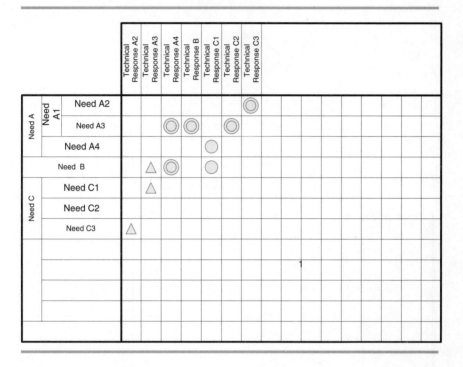

weakly, or not-at-all linked to the technical responses in the technical response section of the HOQ. The filled-in grid appears in Figure 13.15.

From the filled-in relationships grid in the figure, you can see which user needs and technical responses are strongly linked, moderately linked, weakly linked, or have no correlation. For example:

- Notice how the user need "easy installation" is moderately linked with the technical responses "all IP based" and "Windows based." Both of these technical responses, while not directly addressing the need "easy installation," do show a connection in this case because the network is using a common and unified protocol (IP) as well as a standard operating environment (Windows).

**Figure 13.15**

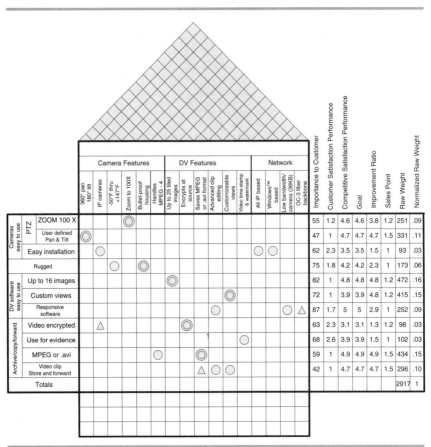

- Notice how the user need "rugged" shows a high correlation with the technical response "bullet-proof housing" and a moderate response to the temperature range of $-50°$ through $+147°F$.

There are more examples shown in the grid, showing the remaining correlations as strong, moderate, or weak.

We now start to put together the results of all the comparisons and calculations we have performed so far. This is done in Section F: the *technical matrix*.

The technical matrix usually consists of the following rows at the bottom of the HOQ:

- Contributions
- Competitive benchmarks
- Company's performance
- Targets

## Priorities

Once the relationships part of the grid is filled in and we have determined the impacts and linkages between the customer needs and the SQCs/technical responses, we need to determine the overall impact of the SQCs on the customer's total satisfaction. Some simple math is done here to ascertain these values: Multiply the numeric value for the strong, moderate, or weak correlation by the *normalized raw weight* score. The resulting number is called the *relationship* of the technical response to the customer need.

In this case we will set the weights of the impact symbols to the values shown in Figure 13.16.

The results of the multiplication of (Normalized raw weight * Impact symbol value) are shown in the grid in Figure 13.17, with the relationship value shown in the upper diagonal of the cell.

The numeric outputs shown in the contributions section of Figure 13.17 give the customer and the technical team a picture of which of

### Figure 13.16

| Symbol | Meaning | Numerical Value (AHP) |
|--------|---------|-----------------------|
| <blank> | Not linked | Usually 0 |
| △ | Weakly linked | 1 |
| ○ | Moderately linked | 5 |
| ◎ | Strongly linked | 9 |

**Figure 13.17**

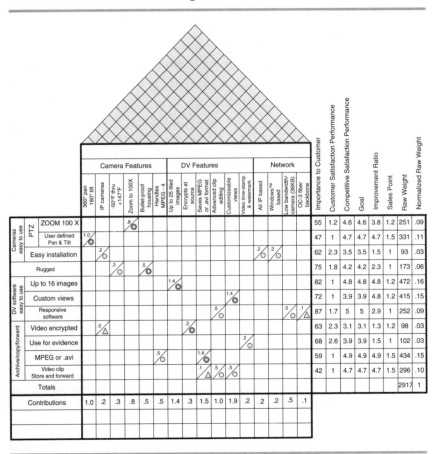

the SQCs bear most significantly on the customer's wants and needs; the larger the contribution, the more impact that each SQC has on the *customer satisfaction* performance, and thus the more important it is in order for the product/service to do well.

## Technical Correlations

We need to add one more section to the QFD picture before we complete the diagram with our *technical benchmarks* and the *targets*. The last section in the QFD diagram is the "roof," or the *technical correlations*. This section maps interrelationships between the SQC responses—in other words, we need to see if the development of one specific quality characteristic has a positive or negative effect on the implementation of another quality characteristic. This can help identify bottlenecks in design or impacts on the development effort. It can also identify where design or development synergies may exist.

For example, as seen in the diagram in Figure 13.17, there may be some potential conflicting technical correlations that need to be addressed, such as:

- Will the 360° pan and 180° tilt capability be impacted by the required operating temperature range of −50°F to + 147°F? What are the implications of the effects of extreme temperatures on the motor drive(s) that control pan and tilt?

- Will the possible number of viewed tiled images (25) have an impact on to what extent the views can be customized? Twenty-five simultaneous images presented on a computer screen may create enormous complexities in terms of being able to create customized views from widely disparate locations.

- Does the low bandwidth of the captured image have an impact on the quality of the stored image whether it is an MPEG or .avi image?

SQC generally uses a technical scale that denotes five degrees of impact of one SQC on another, as in the diagram in Figure 13.18.

The type of question that can be answered using the technical correlation is, for example, "Does moving SQC #1 toward improvement have a positive or negative impact on other SQCs?" See the technical correlations in Figure 13.19 for an example.

In this instance, notice that there are strong positive correlations between:

- Camera features of "360° pan 180° tilt" and "zoom to 100 ×" and the DV feature of "customizable views"

- Camera feature "IP camera" and network "all IP based"

**Figure 13.18**

| | |
|---|---|
| √√ | Strong positive impact |
| √ | Moderate positive impact |
| <blank> | No impact |
| x | Moderate negative impact |
| xx | Strong negative impact |

**Figure 13.19**

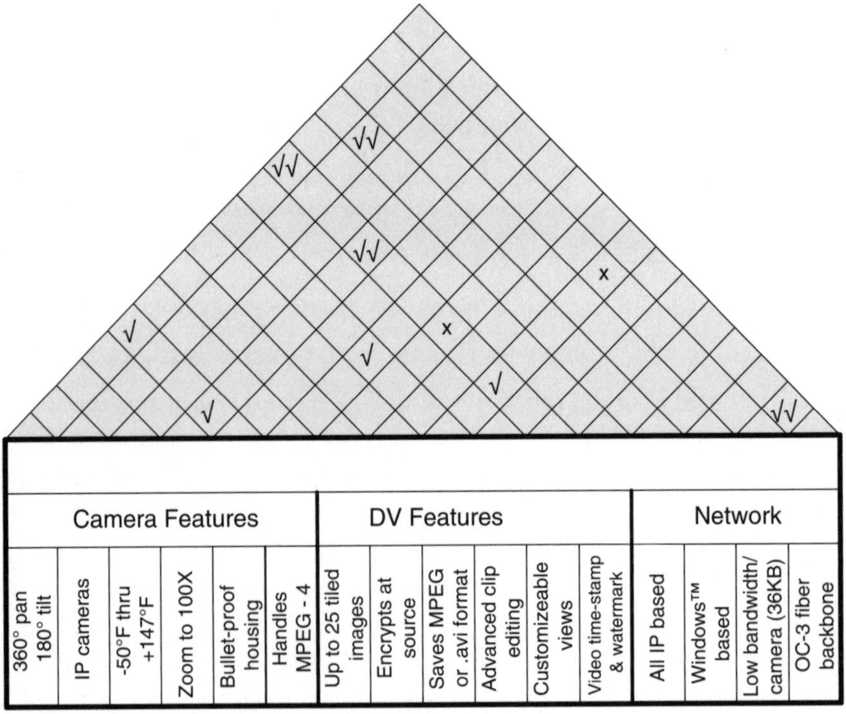

Notice also that there are moderate negative correlations between:

- DV features "up to 25 tiled images" and "customizable views"
- DV features "saves MPEG or .avi format" and "low-bandwidth/camera (36 Kb)"

From elaborating the technical correlations the technical team can determine where concentrated efforts need to be applied in implementing the technical solution to satisfy customer needs.

With the technical correlations identified, we can now proceed to the final steps in the QFD design: the technical benchmarks and the targets.

## Technical Benchmarks

The purpose of the *technical* or *competitive benchmark* is to determine how the developed or selected product, process, or service compares to competing products, processes, or services. In some cases, the benchmarking activity may compare several external vendors and their abilities to satisfy the customer's needs. In other cases, the benchmarking activity may compare an internally developed product, process, or service to the competing products, processes, or services of external vendors.

As in the case of our video security system, the only internally developed aspect of the solution is the network infrastructure defined in the "network" SQCs. However, regarding the "camera features" and "DV features," the customer would look at the various competing products and determine which solution would best satisfy the defined customer needs.

An example of the technical benchmark grid shows on a scale of 1–5 (*1* being the lowest correlation and 5 being the highest correlation) how various solutions would satisfy the SQCs. In this case, the customer is comparing a unified video/digital recording software solution to a componentized solution utilizing video camera hardware from one source and digital video editing software from a second

**Figure 13.20**

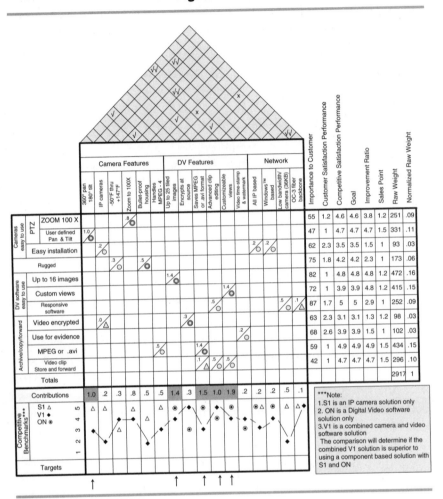

source. The ratings for the combined solution are connected by a line, so the difference in the solutions can be easily identified.

Notice that for the SQCs with the highest contribution levels, the solution favoring the individual components appears to provide a higher customer satisfaction rating on four of the five top SQCs than the combined solution provides. See the diagram in Figure 13.20.

You will notice that most significant contribution levels in this instance are best addressed by the component-based solution (S1 + ON) that achieved the highest scores in four out of the five top contributions. (You will also notice that the contributions in most of the other areas are best addressed by the component-based solution that scored higher in 11 out of the 16 total contribution points!)

## Targets

In this final section of the QFD, we examine the process of determining the targets we wish to achieve for key SQCs. What do the targets mean? In setting any target, the customer has to balance the quality, availability, and cost of the potential solution against customer needs. In the above scenario we can define targets that represent the top world-class solutions for the video security system. For example:

- Is the customer willing to pay for the top world-class solution?
- Do the customer's needs require that the technical team assemble the best solution available anywhere?
- Do we rank the current best solution against a world-class solution and determine if the current benchmark levels meet the customer's objectives?

For those areas that are considered customer "delighters," the team must decide how aggressive it needs to be in terms of setting the target value. For those areas that would be considered customer "dissatisfiers," the team must deliver nothing less than what the customer demands—anything less results in customer dissatisfaction.

There are two basic approaches to setting the targets:

1. Numeric mathematical modeling approach
2. Nonnumeric approach, utilizing the *continuum model* or *subfeature model*

## Numeric Target Modeling

If we look at the *customer satisfaction performance* as a function of the *technical performance measure*, the formula would look like this:

Customer satisfaction performance$_A$ = $f$(Technical performance measure$_X$)

This mathematical approach basically uses the basic point/slope algebraic formula that most of us learned in high school algebra and geometry:

$$Y = mx + b$$

In this example, if the customer is looking for SQCs that indicate how the target, world-class, and team performance relate, there are three elements in the formula:

**1.** Target performance (what the customer wants)

**2.** World-class product (performance of "best in the world")

**3.** Team's product

Following this concept, the formula would be set up as follows:

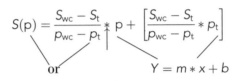

$$S(p) = \frac{S_{wc} - S_t}{p_{wc} - p_t} * p + \left[ \frac{S_{wc} - S_t}{p_{wc} - p_t} * p_t \right]$$

or $\qquad Y = m * x + b$

Where:

$S(p) =$ Customer satisfaction performance of a customer need shown as a function of a substitute quality characteristic (SQC) of type $p$

$s_{wc} =$ Customer satisfaction performance with the top world-class product

$s_t =$ Customer satisfaction performance with development team's solution

$p_{wc} =$ Technical performance of an SQC with a top world-class product

$p_t =$ Technical performance of an SQC with development team's solution

$p =$ Technical performance of an SQC

You can see where the numeric modeling approach follows the point/slope formula. There are other numeric approaches that can be used that are generally more complex and beyond the scope of this treatment, but this will give the reader an idea of what is involved in performing a numeric modeling target determination.

## Nonnumeric Modeling

If the numeric modeling approach seems a bit daunting and the user is looking for more of a qualitative comparison, the *continuum/subfeature* approach may serve the purpose. In this case, an ordinal scale combined with a grid of subfeatures can graphically give the user an immediate grasp of the three key elements shown in Figure 13.21.

**Figure 13.21**

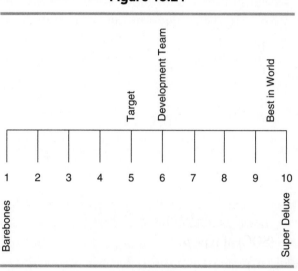

**Figure 13.22**

| Subfeature | Team | Best in World | Target |
|---|---|---|---|
|  | 6 | 9 | 7 |
|  | 8 |  | 6 |
|  |  | 8 |  |
|  | 6 |  | 4 |
|  |  | 7 | 5 |
|  | 7 | 8 |  |
|  | 4 |  | 7 |

From here, the big picture can be broken down into the specific subfeatures so a comparison can be drawn with each possible feature available for the product (Figure 13.22).

Notice that there are some features that may not have been included in the target for the product. This can be because the specific needs of the customer may not include certain features that are available in best-in-world products. Conversely, there are also some features that are not in the best-in-world product but are considered in the target and development team performance. This may indicate that new features have been requested/developed that do not yet exist in current best-in-world products—possibly a sign of product innovation!

## NOTE

1. Peter F. Drucker, *Innovation and Entrepreneurship*, Harper & Row, 1985.

## REFERENCES

Cohen, Lou, *Quality Function Deployment: How to Make FD Work for You*, Addison Wesley/Longman, 1995.

Akao, Yoji, *Quality Function Deployment: Integrating Customer Requirements into Product Design*, Productivity Press, 1990.

The QFD Institute: http://www.qfdi.org/.

# Chapter
## 14

# Financial Management and Risk Tools

## The Real PV-NPV-IRR Calculations

## FINANCIAL TOOLS

The *PMBOK* describes finances from the point of view of performing cost estimating, cost budgeting, and controlling costs on a specific project. To this end, the tools used to estimate costs on a project vary from ballpark estimates (analogous estimates) that utilize expert opinions and past experience to very exacting estimates (bottom-up estimating, parametric estimating) that use mathematical models. *Earned value (EV) management* is typically used to control costs on a project (see Chapter 6). But how did we decide on the project in the first place? How do we know if the project makes financial sense? Moreover, what risks will we face on the project that may increase the project's costs, push out the project's deadline, or impact the project's quality and deliverables? The tool we use to make such a decision is called *net present value (NPV)*.

Net present value is a capital budgeting tool that is used in the investment decision process to determine which investment yields the highest return for the investor. In a project the NPV can help decision makers choose which of the projects presented to them has the greatest potential for yielding the highest return. This return can be in dollars returned, dollars saved, and improved efficiencies that drive higher sales or generate more business.

NPV looks at a project's projected *cash flow* (the expected return on the investment) and the *opportunity cost of capital* (what you could have earned in a fixed security—also known as the *discount rate*).

The formula for the NPV calculation looks like Figure 14.1.

where:

$Cf$ = Future cash flows
$t$ = Years in the investment
$i$ = Discount rate
IO = Initial investment

**Explanation:**

$Cf$: The *future cash flow* amount is what you expect the investment to return on a yearly basis. The yearly amount can change based on whether the cash flows will remain steady, decrease, increase, or fluctuate over the term of the investment.

$t$: Years in the investment.

$i$: The discount rate can be a combination of elements that can include:
   □ The anticipated yearly rate of inflation.
   □ The interest rate paid on money borrowed to finance the project.
   □ The *opportunity cost of capital (OCC)*—the return rate based on some other investment; that is, if you took the

**Figure 14.1**

$$NPV = \sum_{t=1}^{N} \frac{Cf_t}{(1+i)^t} - IO$$

dollars and invested the money in a fixed annuity or bond, what would be the rate of return expressed as a percentage?

IO: The initial investment, or what it will cost you to implement the project. This is usually deducted at the beginning of the project and not as it shows in the formula.

**Example:** Company X wants to invest in a new client/server system for order processing. The new system will reduce order errors by 97% and will electronically process orders instantaneously instead of with the 6-hour delay now experienced. It is estimated that after the initial year's expense to build and deploy the solution, sales will increase by approximately 10% ($5.5M) the first year, 14% ($7.5M) the second year, 19% ($9.5M) the third year, 24% ($12M) the fourth year, and the costs of order processing will be reduced by $3M per year for all four years of the investment. The cost reduction is rolled into each of the yearly cash flow increases, effectively bumping up the cash flow for each year by $3M. Thus $5.5M in the first year yields an increase of $8.5M, and so on.

Here are the significant numbers:

IO: $17.5M

$t$: 4 years

$i$: 15% (broken out into 3.5% inflation rate plus 11.5% OCC guaranteed return on a fixed investment)

The formula would be drawn out as shown below:

$$NPV = -17.5M + \frac{\$8.5M}{(1+.15)^1} + \frac{\$10.5M}{(1+.15)^2} + \frac{\$12.5M}{(1+.15)^3} + \frac{\$15M}{(1+.15)^4}$$

Notice that the exponent for $t$ grows by one for each year of the investment. If the term were six years, the final-year $t$ exponent would be 6.

The NPV for a $17.5M investment with a 15% discount rate and combined cash flows and cost savings as shown in the formula above will yield after four years:

$$\$12,718,316.91$$

Notice how much the *time value of money* eats into the NPV. If we were to simply take all the projected cash flows + savings or $46.5M and subtract the initial investment of $17.5M, the result would appear to be an overall return of $29M. However, in four years the time value of money ate up $16,281,683.09! In the long run, the business still comes out way ahead in terms of what the company would have made in a passive investment versus the investment in improving their internal process.

Demonstrated above was the *basic* NPV calculation. In the world of finance there are actually three ways of computing net present value:

- Adjusted present value (APV)
- Flows to equity (FTE)
- Weighted average cost of capital (WACC)

The new element that is added in each of the three calculations that is not addressed in the pure NPV calculation is the effect of the *tax rate* or *tax shield* on the profitability of the project or investment.

With the addition of the three additional NPV calculations we are getting a clearer view that demonstrates how financing decisions and investment decisions can interact.

Theoretically, the three approaches are supposed to yield the identical result; however, in real life, the results are seldom identical. After all, why would you bother to figure out three ways to compute a result if the result would always be the same? Let's see what the differences are and what the different formulas mean in terms of computing NPV.

For the purposes of these examples we will be looking at each potential project investment as though it were the sole project in a one-project company (i.e., the business will stand or fall based on the investment/financing decisions for this solo project). In the real world, a business that is examining a portfolio of projects would take a more synergistic approach to choosing projects; suboptimizing the business for the sake of the profitability of one project might be a bad idea. Big-picture thinking must prevail in these situations.

Let us begin. In order to better understand how to apply the various NPV types we need to understand a basic concept: What is *leverage?*

If you remember back to your high school physics class, the concept of physical leverage was introduced. For example, how do you lift a 300-pound weight one foot in the air when you are only strong enough to lift a dead weight of 100 pounds? The answer is *leverage.* The picture of the simple fulcrum in Figure 14.2 should bring back memories.

Financial leverage uses a similar concept. The term *LBO (leveraged buyout)* was popularized in the 1980s to describe the hostile takeover of a business (e.g., in the film *Wall Street* with Michael Douglas).

In simple terms, an LBO is a takeover in which 70–90% of the money used to buy the acquiring stock is *borrowed.* The acquired company's assets are used as security for the loans taken out by the takeover firm. The takeover firm then repays the debt out of the free cash flow from the acquired company, which may also include the sale of assets of the acquired firm. This technique minimizes the acquisition price paid by the acquiring company at the time of the takeover.

In a similar vein, for the purposes of tracking a project we will discuss companies that are *levered* or *unlevered:*

**Figure 14.2**

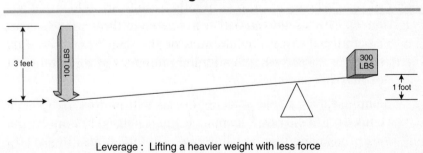

Leverage :  Lifting a heavier weight with less force

- A firm that has borrowed money from debtholders to fund a project is called a *levered* firm.

- A firm that uses its equity (has the money sitting around or issues stock) to fund a project is called an *unlevered* firm.

Some readers will look at this idea and wonder why anyone would borrow money to fund a project. If the business knows how to accurately evaluate risk, the concept of *leverage* is a very powerful investment tool. Consider the following:

You have $100K to invest in a housing project in which you have one year to turn around the investment. You have carefully researched the properties, neighborhoods, and the trend in property values in many areas. You are faced with the following two possibilities:

1. Invest the $100K in one property selling for $100K with the following possibilities for return:
   □ 10% chance the value will drop 10%
   □ 20% chance the value will not change
   □ 40% chance the value will go up 20%
   □ 20% chance the value will go up 35%
   □ 10% chance the value will go up 50%

2. Invest $10K each in 10 properties with the same possibilities of return.

Experienced property turnover specialists would clearly make the second choice without hesitation—all things being equal.

Example #1 uses *unlevered* equity to make the property purchase. Assuming that the probable return is in the 20% range—the return on the investment after the property was sold at the end of the year would be *$20K*.

Example #2 uses *levered* debt (i.e., money borrowed from the bank(s)) to take out 10 mortgages and find 10 renters for one year. Assuming the probable rate of return is also in the 20% range—the return on the investment after each property was sold at the end of the year would be $20K *per house* or *$200K*. (Sounds a little like an LBO, doesn't it?) If you want to get a sense of the probability of the actual return, run a Monte Carlo analysis using the estimates above.

Same investment—but a *huge* difference in the return. For the company that is levered and funding a project, there are also tax shield advantages that can increase the actual return on the project. Let's look at our three NPV valuation methods and see what the differences are.

## WEIGHTED AVERAGE COST OF CAPITAL

A fundamental of the *weighted average cost of capital (WACC)* model is that it computes the *opportunity cost* of capital; that is, given that you could invest in something else that will give you a guaranteed return, what are you giving up (based on that return) to pursue some other investment? We will label the opportunity cost of capital $r$. This is the amount of money that investors would expect as a return if the company carried no debt at all. The idea is that once you have determined the correct discount rate using the WACC approach, you can plug that discount rate into the NPV formula. All the variables in the formula are applied to the business as a whole; therefore, this approach works for an average project for the company where the project is no safer or riskier than the average of the company's current assets. The basic formula looks like this:

$$r = r_D \frac{D}{V} + r_E \frac{E}{V}$$

Where:

$r_D$ = Expected rate of return on the cost of debt

$r_E$ = Expected rate of return on the cost of equity

D = Debt

E = Equity

V = Sum of all debt and equity or the total market value of the firm

What this formula forgets to show you is the effect of the tax shield on your project. The interest a business pays on debt is tax deductible. Therefore, in order to figure in the amount of money you will save in taxes, we have to compute the after-tax weighted average cost of capital. That formula looks something like this:

$$\text{WACC} = r_D(1 - T_C)\frac{D}{V} + r_E\frac{E}{V}$$

The additional figure, $T_C$, represents the marginal corporate tax rate.

For example, the XYZ Corporation shows the following numbers for its huge project—*Project X:*

- Cost of debt ($r_D$), that is, the interest rate charged for debt, is .10.
- Cost of equity ($r_E$), that is, the expected rate of return demanded by investors, is .14.
- $T_C$, that is, marginal tax rate, is .35.
- D/V ratio, that is, debt to value, is .4.
- E/V ratio, that is, equity to value, is .7.

The formula would play out as follows:

$$\text{WACC} = [.1(1 - .35) \times .4] + [.14 \times .7] = .026 + .098$$

$$\text{WACC} = 12.4\%$$

Project X was undertaken to design a giant earthmover. The initial investment in the project was $25M. Based on customer interest and orders placed, the anticipated cash flows for the next five years are:

*Year 1:* $3.75M

*Year 2:* $9.5M

*Year 3:* $12.4M

*Year 4:* $15.8M

*Year 5:* $18.3M

Given that the discount rate of 12.4% was just calculated using the WACC approach, what is the NPV of this project? If the business had to show a positive NPV at the end of the third year in the project, would you accept or reject the project? Where does the business break even on its investment? Use the NPV formula above to manually compute the actual return or plug the numbers into Excel using the format shown in Figure 14.3 for the NPV calculation.

- The discount rate is entered in the rate filed as a decimal (12.4% = .124).

- Value 1 is the dollar amount of initial investment expressed as a *negative* (after all, the $25 million is paid out before you start seeing a return on the investment).

- Value 2 is the return expected after the first year.

- Value 3 is the return expected after the second year.

- Value 4 is the return expected after the third year.

**Figure 14.3**

| Function Arguments | | ? X |
|---|---|---|
| NPV | | |
| Rate | .124 | = 0.124 |
| Value1 | -25000000 | = -25000000 |
| Value2 | 3750000 | = 3750000 |
| Value3 | 9500000 | = 9500000 |
| Value4 | 12400000 | = 12400000 |

= -4814932.97

Returns the net present value of an investment based on a discount rate and a series of future payments (negative values) and income (positive values).

**Value4:** value1,value2,... are 1 to 29 payments and income, equally spaced in time and occurring at the end of each period.

Formula result =           -4814932.97

Help on this function                              OK              Cancel

**Figure 14.4**

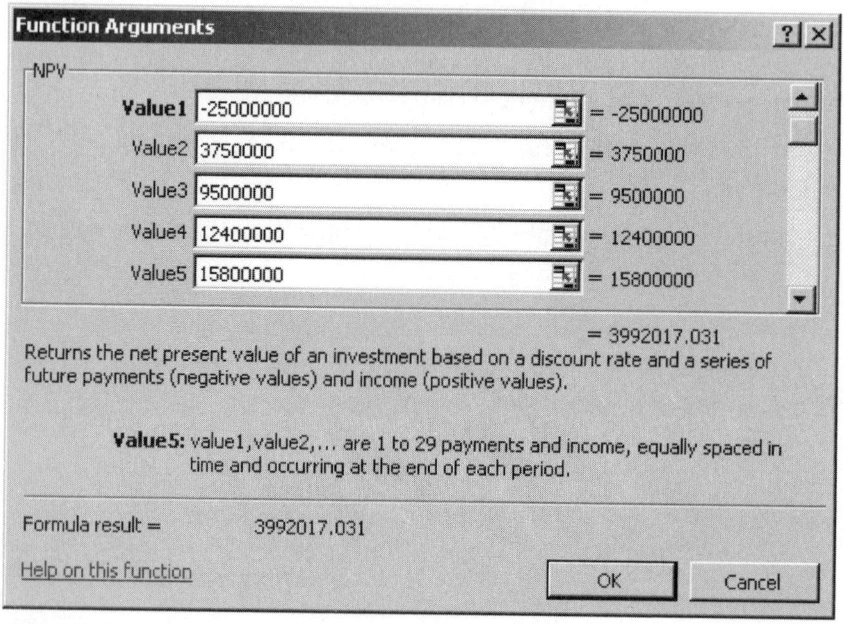

Notice the running formula result appears at the bottom of the dialog box so that you can see at which point the company breaks even and begins to see a return on the investment. After the third year, the company has still not yet recouped almost $5 million of its investment. With the computation of the anticipated return in the fourth year, we see that the company turns the corner and begins to make a profit—almost $4 million (Figure 14.4).

## FLOW TO EQUITY

Another approach to valuing a project or a company is the *flow-to-equity* method. While the WACC approach is used as the *discount rate* to evaluate the viability of an investment (i.e., a project), the flow-to-equity method is used to evaluate the *equity* in the company and is used primarily where the funds for the project are levered.

Here we discount the cash flow from the project to the equity holders (investors) of the levered firm at the levered cost of equity capital, $rS$. There are three steps in this process:

**Step One:** Calculate the levered cash flows.

**Step Two:** Calculate $rS$ (i.e., the discount rate for the NPV equation).

**Step Three:** Compute the value of the levered cash flows at $rS$.

**Example:** The company wants to invest in a project with an initial outlay of \$1M. The after-tax cash flows over a four-year period are:

*Year 1:* \$175K

*Year 2:* \$250K

*Year 3:* \$375K

*Year 4:* \$550K

Also:

- Unlevered cost of equity is 10% or $r_0$.
- Interest paid on debt is at 8% or $r_B$.
- Tax rate is 40% or $T_C$.

Let's say the company finances the project with \$600K of debt (borrowed funds), which means the shareholders only have to come up with \$400K of unlevered equity.

For each period, the equity holders must pay an interest expense on the \$600K of debt, which is calculated as Debt * Interest rate * (1 − Tax rate) or:

$$\$600K * .08 * (1 - 0.4) = \$28.8K$$

The tax rate offers a "shield" on the interest and lowers the interest rate from \$48K to \$28.8K.

**Step 1:** Calculate the levered cash flows.

This is a simple calculation with the interest expense deducted from the cash flows, or:

Initial Investment: –$400K
Cash Flow 1: $175K – $28.8K = $146.2K
Cash Flow 2: $250K – $28.8K = $221.2K
Cash Flow 3: $375K – $28.8K = $346.2K
Cash Flow 4: $550K – $28.8K – 600 = –$78.8K

(Don't forget, we have to subtract the $600K of borrowed funds.)

**Step 2:** Calculate the discount rate for the NPV equation.

The formula for computing the discount rate is as follows:

$$r_S = r_0 + \frac{B}{S}(1 - T_C)(r_0 - r_B)$$

Where:

$r_s$ = Discount rate
$r_0$ = Unlevered cost of equity expressed as a percentage
$r_B$ = Interest rate paid on debt
$B$ = Amount of debt
$S$ = Amount of equity
$T_C$ = Tax rate

The formula yields the following:

$$r_s = .10 + \frac{600}{400}(1 - .40)(.10 - .08) = 11.8\%$$

**Step 3:** Compute the NPV.

We can now compute the NPV for flow to equity by plugging in the discount rate into the NPV formula:

$$NPV = -400,000 + \frac{146,200}{(1.118)} + \frac{221,200}{(1.118)^2} + \frac{346,200}{(1.118)^3} - \frac{78,800}{(1.118)^4}$$

$$NPV = -400,000 + 130,769 + 177,101 + 247,816 - 50,448$$

$$NPV = \$206,134$$

# ADJUSTED PRESENT VALUE

In the case of WACC, it is assumed that any new projects or capital expenditures are financed at a constant debt-to-equity ratio. The flow-to-equity method, while allowing for variation in the long-term debt-to-equity ratio, assumes that the discount rate for equity is the cost of levered equity (i.e., borrowed money). However, the *APV (adjusted present value)* method allows for a *varying* debt-to-equity ratio over the course of a long-term project and is useful in a situation where the initial debt financing is paid down over time, causing a change in the debt-to-equity ratio.

The APV approach first values the company as if it were an all-equity firm (a firm carrying no debt). This is called the *base case NPV*. Then it adds the tax advantage from *leverage* (i.e., tax shields the business receives in the form of interest payments on borrowed funds), called the *NPV of the financing decisions*. Or, somewhat more graphically:

Project APV = Base case NPV
+ Sum of present values and side effects of financing

Let's look at an example:[1]

**Example:** A project to produce solar heaters requires a $10 million investment. If the project is financed on an all-equity basis, the after-tax cash flows are $1.8 million for 10 years. The cost of unlevered equity for such a solar heater project is 12% (i.e., the opportunity costs). The firm wants to raise an additional $5 million in debt financing that will be repaid in equal installments in 10 years. The interest rate on the debt is 8%. Is the project worthwhile?

The installment payment of the debt will result in variations in the debt-to-equity ratio over the 10 years of the project. In this case, the APV method is preferable to the WACC or the flow-to-equity method.

**Figure 14.5**

| Year | 0 | 1 | 2 | 3 | 4 | 5 | 6 | 7 | 8 | 9 | 10 |
|------|---|---|---|---|---|---|---|---|---|---|----|
| Cash flow | −10 | 1.8 | 1.8 | 1.8 | 1.8 | 1.8 | 1.8 | 1.8 | 1.8 | 1.8 | 1.8 |

First, let's look at a graph of the investment and the cash flows over a 10-year period, shown in Figure 14.5.

**Step 1:** Base case NPV.

Compute the value of the "all-equity project," or the base case NPV. To do this we use the NPV formula with the following values:

$t = 10$

$I = .12$

Initial investment $= -\$10$ million

$$\text{Base case NPV} = -10 + \sum_{t-1}^{10} \frac{1.8}{1.12^t} = 0.17 \text{ million or } \$170,000$$

**Step 2:** NPV for F.

Now, what are the side effects of financing? Here is where we look at the $5 million that was borrowed to help fund the project:

The marginal tax rate is 46%.

The interest rate on the loan is 8%.

The tax shield (money that the business gets to keep due to a reduction in tax because of interest payments on the loan) = Tax rate * Interest * Principal at the start of the year.

Let's look at the grid in Figure 14.6 to see how this works out.

For the first year, the formula is:

$$.08 * \$5,000,000 * .46 = \$400,000 * .46 = \$184,000$$

**Figure 14.6**

| Year | 1 | 2 | 3 | 4 | 5 | 6 | 7 | 8 | 9 | 10 |
|---|---|---|---|---|---|---|---|---|---|---|
| Principal at the start of the year (in $M) | 5 | 4.5 | 4 | 3.5 | 3 | 2.5 | 2 | 1.5 | 1 | 0.5 |
| Interest (in $M) | .4 | .36 | .32 | .28 | .24 | .20 | .16 | .12 | .08 | .04 |
| Tax shields (in $M) | .184 | .166 | .147 | .129 | .110 | .092 | .074 | .055 | .037 | .018 |

All of the succeeding years are computed in the same way. Adding up the tax shields over a 10-year period gives us a grand total of the NPV of the *financing decision* of $757,000. Thus, NPV + NPV for FD = $170K + $757K, or an APV of $927,000.

As you can see, performing the base NPV calculation showed that the company would make money on the investment with a positive NPV of $170K—but that's not the whole story. Computing the tax shield for the project added an additional $757K of value.

**Exercise:** Would the result have been better if the company had not used any of its equity to fund the project? What if the company had borrowed $15M to fund the solar heater project at the same 8% interest rate? Would the results be better or worse? (Don't forget that the base case NPV changes as well.)

## IRR

Finally, let's talk about *internal rate of return (IRR)*. The internal rate of return on a project is, very simply, the interest earned on an investment on a yearly basis. If you spend $10K on a bond that guarantees a 12% return yearly for 10 years, your rate of return is 12%. If you are evaluating projects looking to select which one you will initiate using only IRR as the selection criterion, obviously the project you would pick would have the highest IRR you could get. It seems very simple, but in reality there are pitfalls with the IRR process.

The first difficulty is the process of actually determining the IRR. Here is the technical definition of IRR:

*The IRR is the interest rate (discount rate) that the project will return to the investor when the NPV = 0.*

Think about that for a moment. In order to figure out how to get the NPV to equal zero, you would have to try a few guesses on the discount rate to move the NPV as close to zero as possible. This is fundamentally a hit-or-miss process.

For example, Figure 14.7 depicts a project with an initial investment and a five-year payback. We take a few *discount rate guesses* to see where the NPV lands and then zero in on the IRR.

**Guess #1:** See Figure 14.8.

**Guess #2:** Looks like Guess #2 is fairly close to an NPV of zero. After playing with the discount rate, we finally land on Figure 14.9.

So the IRR for this project with a five-year payback is 43.395%. The chart in Figure 14.10a graphs all percentages from 1% to 100% and shows the IRR percentage when the NPV is zero.

This looks to be an outstanding return on your project, until the unthinkable happens—your project loses money in one of the years.

**Figure 14.7**

| | | Discount rate: | 0.25 | | | | | | | |
|---|---|---|---|---|---|---|---|---|---|---|
| Year | 0 | 1 | 2 | 3 | 4 | 5 | 6 | 7 | |
| Income | −500 | 200 | 200 | 400 | 400 | 200 | 0 | 0 | NPV |
| Discounted | −500 | 160.00 | 128.00 | 204.80 | 163.84 | 65.54 | 0.00 | 0.00 | 222.18 |

**Figure 14.8**

| IRR with Positive Cash Flow | | | | | | | | | |
|---|---|---|---|---|---|---|---|---|---|
| | Discount rate: | 0.45 | | | | | | | |
| Year | 0 | 1 | 2 | 3 | 4 | 5 | 6 | 7 | |
| Income | −500 | 200 | 200 | 400 | 400 | 200 | 0 | 0 | NPV |
| Discounted | −500 | 137.93 | 95.12 | 131.21 | 90.49 | 31.20 | 0.00 | 0.00 | −14.05 |

In Figure 14.10b we have an example of a project with a six-year payout but with a loss of $900K in the last year. (All amounts are in the hundreds of thousands.)

With a 15% discount rate the project makes money—but what is the IRR? Actually there are two points at which the NPV can equal zero to show two distinct IRRs! Figure 14.11 is the same chart but with the NPV values for all percentages from 1% through 100%.

Notice that the IRR is at 7.685% with an NPV of zero *and* at 34.488% with an NPV of zero—they both can't be correct. In fact, *neither* is correct. When projects show negative cash flows in any year

**Figure 14.9**

| IRR with Positive Cash Flow | | | | | | | | | |
|---|---|---|---|---|---|---|---|---|---|
| | Discount rate: | 0.43395 | | | | | | | |
| Year | 0 | 1 | 2 | 3 | 4 | 5 | 6 | 7 | |
| Income | −500 | 200 | 200 | 400 | 400 | 200 | 0 | 0.00 | NPV |
| Discounted | −500 | 139.47 | 97.27 | 135.66 | 94.61 | 32.99 | 0.00 | 0.00 | 0.00 |

**Figure 14.10a**

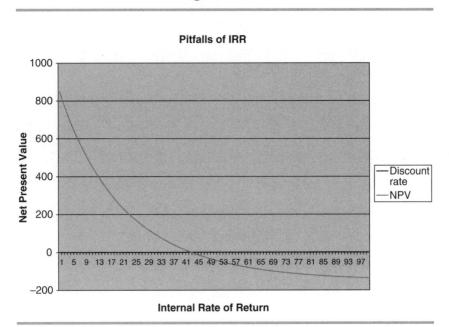

Pitfalls of IRR

of the payback cycle, IRR can produce conflicting and inaccurate results.

Here's another aspect of IRR you may not have considered: Would you rather obtain an IRR of 50% on a $100K investment or an IRR of 5% on a $10M investment? The IRR is higher on the first

**Figure 14.10b**

| IRR with Negative Cash Flow | | | | | | | | | |
|---|---|---|---|---|---|---|---|---|---|
| | | Discount rate: | 0.15 | | | | | | |
| Year | 0 | 1 | 2 | 3 | 4 | 5 | 6 | 7 | |
| Income | −500 | 400 | 300 | 200 | 200 | 200 | −900 | 0 | NPV |
| Discounted | −500 | 347.83 | 226.84 | 131.5 | 114.35 | 99.44 | −389.09 | 0 | 30.86 |

**Figure 14.11**

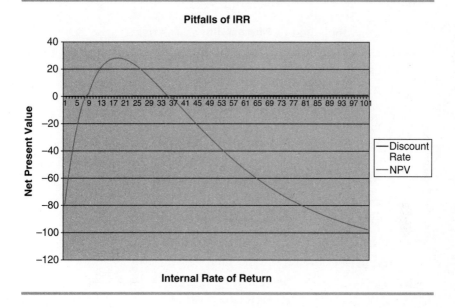

Pitfalls of IRR

project, but the ROI of the second project is 10 times that of the first! In conclusion, *IRR is only useful when evaluating investments of equal value over the same term of investment*; otherwise, it is generally better to use net present value as the best way of determining the ultimate monetary value of the project.

A URL at the end of the book points to an Excel spreadsheet with the grid readouts and charts as shown earlier. By changing the numbers in the *discount rate* cell and the cells on the "Income" row, you can try out your own NPV/IRR experiments.

See what happens when negative cash flows occur at the beginning, middle, or end of the investment cycle.

## MANAGING RISK ON A PROJECT

Up to this point, we have seen how a Monte Carlo analysis can help to illuminate the risk probabilities that a project timeline will actually meet expectation. In fact, most, if not all, of the tools shown up to this point are useful in helping to manage risk on a project. For example:

- Quality tools that can be used to assess risk:
  - □ Ishikawa diagram: for examining all factors leading to the effect of key resources not being available on your project when needed
  - □ Scatter diagram: for comparing two risk elements to see if one has an effect on the other
  - □ Histogram: for listing and counting of risk probabilities
  - □ Pareto chart: for ranking and sorting of risk probabilities
  - □ Flowcharts: for identifying risk response paths graphically
  - □ SPC: for listing prior risks and their dollar impact—Is our risk response in statistical control?

- AHP can be used to rank risks if there is disagreement on which risks are most important.

- Decision tree analysis can be used to evaluate risks based on percentage of probability and dollars incurred as a result.

But how do we go about identifying risks in the first place?

In returning to our quality examples from Chapter 3, the most pressing risk issues tend to center around the lack of adequate quality in the delivered product or process to the customer. Deming always spoke about products in terms of their "fitness for use" by the customer. A product that is low in quality and does not meet the customer expectation can be thought of as being unfit for use by the customer. In other words, the product/process does not meet the customer's stated or implied needs.

Risk on a project can be broken down into two major areas:

1. *Project risks:* The totality of factors inherent in the project that will cause the project to fail

2. *Business risks:* The business exposures inherent in undertaking the project[2]

For example, thanks to our friends at Enron, Global Crossing, and WorldCom, the *Sarbanes-Oxley (SOX)* Act was passed and went into effect in November 2004. SOX imposes a higher standard of proof on businesses when auditing their finances and overall business management practices.

If your company needs to implement new processes to adhere to SOX requirements, there is a high project risk that you don't have the necessary skill sets to implement the complex changes to your IT systems to satisfy the requirements of SOX. The business also faces a risk that not meeting the SOX requirements will subject it to regulatory scrutiny that may lead to possible fines or imprisonment.

Here is a partial checklist of elements to consider that may constitute risk factors on a project:

**Scope Risks:**
- Scope creep
- Gaps in specifications or requirements
- Dependencies that were not anticipated at the start of the project

**Schedule Risks:**
- Delay due to lack of information, slow decisions (analysis paralysis), delivery and availability of parts, learning curve
- Dependencies on other projects, project resource availability, support availability
- Estimation judgment (overoptimism)

**Resource Risks:**
- People (leaving the project permanently, leaving the project temporarily, joining the project late, working on multiple projects simultaneously)
- Outsourcing (same issues as above)
- Financial risks due to funding reallocation or cutbacks

Below are some common causes of risk that need to be evaluated on almost all projects:

- Product or process is untried and new to the organization.
- The right skill set does not exist in house to implement the project.

- The business has no formalized *basis-of-estimate* process.
- Business requires the purchase or lease of new, untried high-end hardware and/or software.
- Business opts to build and not buy software (and they are not in the software business).
- The project team is geographically dispersed.
- Uncertain whether all critical stakeholders have been brought into the project.
- Unknown whether sensitive information is properly secured and under restricted access.
- *Change management* processes are not clearly documented or followed.
- *Configuration management* processes are minimal or non-existent.
- Requirements signoff by key stakeholders is not institutionalized.
- Capital budgeting is performed by a casual top-down process instead of a bottom-up process.
- Communication among resources on a geographically dispersed team poses communication barriers.
- The manufacturing side of the business works to ISO standards—the business works to no discernable standard of project management or project execution.[1]

In your risk response planning, think of the elements that are:

- *Controllable:* If risk elements are controllable, you can deal with *causes* and either transfer (buy insurance) or avoid (change your supplier, redesign the component, etc.) the risk.
- *Uncontrollable:* If risk elements are uncontrollable, you have to deal with the *effects* of the risk and you will have to mitigate the risk, create contingency plans, or passively accept the risk potential (i.e., take it on the chin).

### Figure 14.12   SWOT Grid

|  | Strengths | Weaknesses |
|---|---|---|
| Opportunities |  |  |
| Threats |  |  |

In addition to the tools we have already reviewed, there are a few simple tools that can be used to identify and evaluate risk:

- SWOT analysis—strengths, weaknesses, opportunities, and threats
- QRAM—quantitative risk analysis matrix

The SWOT is fairly simple to set up—you need only make sure that the following elements are on the same side of the grid: *strengths* and *weaknesses* on one side; *opportunities* and *threats* on the other. The idea is to focus on areas where your *strengths* play into the *opportunity*, where the *opportunity* identifies some potential *weaknesses* you need to address, where your *strengths* can mitigate or eliminate *threats*, and finally, where your *weaknesses* may succumb to *threats*. The grid in Figure 14.12 gives you a quick picture of where you need to improve your ability to succeed.

Figure 14.13 is an example of a filled-in SWOT grid for an individual who is attempting to get into the MBA program of his or her choice.

SWOT grids can be set up to evaluate anything from new product launches to your new hotel reservation system to homeowner's insurance.

The QRAM grid gives you the opportunity to take your potential threats and assign them a *probability ranking*, an *impact ranking*, and the *potential dollar loss* that could ensue. This is usually the best way to provide the necessary data and facts that can help you obtain *management reserve* for your project (Figure 14.14). The probabilities and impacts are shown in the figure as decimals. Any risk probability over 20% will receive immediate management attention; items 1, 2,

**Figure 14.13   SWOT Grid**

|  | Strengths | Weaknesses |
|---|---|---|
| Opportunities | High GPA<br>Location<br>School ranking<br>Professors with whom<br>I want to study | No business background<br>(get some experience—<br>summer job?)<br>Math is not my strong<br>suit (look for a tutor) |
| Threats | High reading and writing<br>demands (no problem)<br>Strong analytical thinking<br>required (no problem) | Students are highly<br>competitive—others also<br>have high GPAs (how do<br>I distinguish myself?)<br>Don't like pressure<br>situations (how do<br>I prepare for this?) |

and 3 will be scrutinized by management. The chart in Figure 14.14 can be set up in Excel with little effort.

## RISK WRAPUP

There are a number of excellent books written on the subject of project risk—some are listed at the end of this chapter.

For those involved with software projects and programs, the SEI (Software Engineering Institute) at Carnegie-Mellon University has a portion of its web site exclusively devoted to *risk management, risk evaluation,* and *risk management training.* It is an excellent resource and contains publications that are helpful to the team involved in software projects (http://www.sei.cmu.edu/risk/main.html).

A final word about risk: Many people think that risk is something to be avoided at all costs. Nothing could be further from the truth. If risk is to be avoided above all else, you would never get out of bed in the morning. Everything we do in life carries some measure and component of risk. The point is, what do we do about it?

**Figure 14.14   Project Q-RAM**

| Rank | Risk | Probability (P) | Impact (I) | Dollars if Realized (D) | Overall Risk (P × I × D) |
|------|------|-----------------|------------|-------------------------|--------------------------|
| 1 | Delivery schedule threatened by strike. | 0.25 | 0.5 | $500,000 | $62,500 |
| 2 | Resource estimates may be seriously deficient. | 0.3 | 0.75 | $350,000 | $78,750 |
| 3 | Hardware requires new skill sets not in house. | 0.2 | 0.75 | $200,000 | $30,000 |
| 4 | Three disparate systems to be integrated—all dependencies may not have been identified. | 0.15 | 0.6 | $150,000 | $13,500 |

The SEI has some worthwhile words on the subject that are a fitting end to this chapter (from http://www.sei.cmu.edu/risk/overview.html):

> *Risk and opportunity go hand in hand. Many development projects strive to advance current capabilities and achieve something that hasn't been done before. The opportunity for advancement cannot be achieved without taking risk.*
> *Risk in itself is not bad; risk is essential to progress, and failure is often a key part of learning. But we must learn to balance the possible negative consequences of risk against the potential benefits of its associated opportunity.*[3]

# NOTES

1. Richard A. Brealey and Stewart C. Myers, *Principles of Corporate Finance*, Chapter 19, McGraw Hill, 2004.

2. Robert Thomsett, "The Indiana Jones School of Risk Management," *American Programmer*, vol. 5, no. 7, September 1992.
3. Roger L. Van Scoy, "Software Development Risk: Opportunity, Not Problem," Software Engineering Institute, CMU/SEI-92-TR-30, ADA 258743, September 1992.

# REFERENCES

Kendrick, Tom, *Identifying and Managing Project Risk*, Amacom, 2003.
Burlton, Roger T., *Business Process Management*, Sams Publishing, 2001.
Smith, Preston. G. and Merritt, Guy M., "Proactive Risk Management,"*Productivity*, 2002.
Lam, James, *Enterprise Risk Management*, John Wiley & Sons, 2003.
http://www.sei.cmu.edu/risk/overview.html.

# Chapter
# 15

# Design of Experiments—An Introduction

T HIS IS ONE OF the more interesting areas in the 2004 version of the *PMBOK. DOE (design of experiments)* is defined in Chapter 8, "Project Quality Management," in "Quality Planning Tools and Techniques," Section 8.1.2.3. PMI's understanding and description of the DOE process reads as follows:

> *Design of Experiments (DOE) is a statistical method that helps identify which factors may influence specific variables of a product or process under development or in production. It also plays a role in the optimization of products or processes. An example is where an organization can use DOE to reduce the sensitivity of product performance to sources of variations caused by environmental or manufacturing differences. The most important aspect of this technique is that it provides a statistical framework for systematically changing all the important factors, instead of changing the factors one at a time. The analysis of the experimental data should provide the optimal conditions for the product or process, highlighting the factors that influence the results, and revealing the presence of interactions or synergisms among the factors. . . . [1]*

Unfortunately, this definition, if not completely incomprehensible, does not further one's understanding of DOE one iota.

Depending on your experience with DOE, which with most PMs is little to none, you may find this explanation more confusing than the actual process, especially for nonstatisticians.

Try this definition on for size:

*DOE is a way of finding out what factors in your product or process have the greatest impact on the product's "critical-to-quality" (CTQ) characteristics.*

**Example:** You sell cars. Which of the following factors influence your customers to buy Brand X:

- Initial cost?
- Style?
- Safety?
- Mileage?
- Total cost of ownership?
- Resale value?
- Comfort?
- Amenities (extras like GPS, high-end stereo, etc.)?
- Image?
- Reliability? (Will it be in the shop more than I drive it?)

What if the factors that influence the buy decision are some combination of the above—how would you determine the strength of those interactions?

First, DOE makes this determination by running the fewest possible number of tests to verify the *critical-to-quality* elements and their optimal settings. Second, and very important, DOE enables the experiment designer to measure process interactions among the factors, something that you cannot accomplish with the one-factor-at-a-time (OFAT) approach.

The basic types of DOE design center on the following:

- *Fixed-effects model*: All factors are considered (e.g., if there are five coatings designed to protect wood, all five coatings are included in the experiment).
- *Random-effects model*: A sample of all possible factors is evaluated in the experiment.
- *Mixed model*: This utilizes fixed and random effects in the experiment.

The design types center on the following ideas:

- *Screening experiments*: Large number of variables → focus on finding the vital few.
- *Characterization experiments*: Find relationships among the vital few.
- *Optimization experiments*: Define the optimal settings for the vital few.

DOE utilizes something called a "randomized-block design"—experimental observations are divided into *blocks*. A schedule for allocating treatment material and for conducting treatment combinations is implemented so that the conditions in one run:

- Do not depend on the conditions of the previous run.
- Do not predict the conditions in the subsequent runs.

Randomization is necessary for conclusions drawn from the experiment to be correct, unambiguous, and defensible. One of the types of randomized block designs is called a "Latin square," in which each treatment appears in only one row and one column. (The newest game craze *Sudoku* is a puzzle based on the Latin square design.)

**Example:** An auto rental company is looking at four brands of autos for their next fleet of cars: Brands A, B, C, and D. They hire

**Figure 15.1**

| Driver\Week | Week 1 | Week 2 | Week 3 | Week 4 |
|-------------|--------|--------|--------|--------|
| Driver 1    | A      | B      | C      | D      |
| Driver 2    | B      | C      | D      | A      |
| Driver 3    | C      | D      | A      | B      |
| Driver 4    | D      | A      | B      | C      |

four drivers to test the each of the cars over a four-week period using a Latin square design (Figure 15.1).

No driver tests a car more than once in four weeks, no car is tested more than once by the same driver in four weeks, and no car is tested more than once in the same week.

## ONE-FACTOR, TWO-LEVEL DESIGN

Let's start out with a basic DOE. We have one factor in a product we need to test and we need to determine the optimal setting for that factor that yields the best result.

Let's say you are testing a ceramic-hardening process and have defined a factor that may have an impact on the process: the temperature of the oven. You want to see if a temperature of 500° will produce a different hardness than 650°. Your DOE factorial table will look like Figure 15.2.

By constructing a chart called a "main effects plot," we can see if the temperature impacts the hardness of the ceramic (CTQ). See Figure 15.3.

**Figure 15.2**

| A− (Low) | A+ (High) |
|----------|-----------|
| (500°)   | (650°)    |

**Figure 15.3**

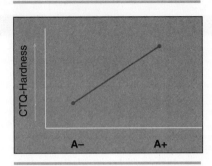

As the main effects plot shows, when the temperature increased, the hardness increased—showing a direct impact of temperature on ceramic hardness.

## TWO-FACTORIAL DESIGN

The single-factor design is very simple to follow and is fairly obvious. Let's complicate the picture slightly—we look at our initial ceramic example and decide that the *time in the oven*, in addition to the temperature, may also have an impact on the ceramic hardness.

Spinning up our factorial design, we now add another factor to the ceramic testing experiment: *time*. It can be a low of 45 minutes to a high of 90 minutes.

- The letter *A* will represent temperature:
  - □ "−" will represent low (500°).
  - □ "+" will represent high (650°).
- The letter *B* will represent time:
  - □ "−" will represent low (45 min).
  - □ "+" will represent high (90 min).

The two-factor, two-level chart now looks like Figure 15.4.

Notice each factor is paired with each other factor only once:

- A low (500°) is paired with B low (45 min).
- A low (500°) is paired with B high (90 min).

**Figure 15.4**

| Runs | A | B | $Y_1$ |
|------|---|---|-------|
| 1 | − | − | 10 |
| 2 | − | + | 20 |
| 3 | + | − | 15 |
| 4 | + | + | 25 |

- A high (650°) is paired with B low (45 min).
- A high (650°) is paired with B high (90 min).

$Y_1$ is the hardness level recorded at the end of each run. While this looks complete enough, there is another aspect that we have not considered: Is there an interaction between time and temperature? There may be a synergistic effect between the two factors that is not captured by testing one factor at a time! Based on this discovery, let's look at the factorial chart in Figure 15.5.

The sign of the *AB interaction* is created per the algebraic rules of multiplication: A negative times a negative is a positive; a positive times a negative is a negative, and so on. In this case, does the AB interaction have an impact on the hardness CTQ? Figure 15.6 shows how we figure this out.

**Figure 15.5**

| Runs | A | B | AB | $Y_1$ |
|------|---|---|----|-------|
| 1 | − | − | + | 10 |
| 2 | − | + | − | 20 |
| 3 | + | − | − | 15 |
| 4 | + | + | + | 25 |

**Figure 15.6**

| Runs | A | B | AB | $Y_1$ |
|------|-----|------|------|------|
| 1 | − | − | + | 10 |
| 2 | − | + | − | 20 |
| 3 | + | − | − | 15 |
| 4 | + | + | + | 25 |
| + | 20 | 22.5 | 17.5 | |
| − | 15 | 12.5 | 17.5 | |
| Pure effect | 5 | 10 | 0 | |

The X bar + row shows the average of all the + readings in each column. The X bar − row shows the average of all the − readings in each column. We perform a simple subtraction: X bar " + "minus X bar "−", and compute what is called the *pure effect* of each factor: A, B, and AB interaction.

Notice in this example that the AB interaction is a complete wash—the effect of A and B together nets out to zero. The pure effect of B carries the most weight by a factor of two-to-one over factor A.

The main effects plot for the AB interaction would look like Figure 15.7.

**Figure 15.7**

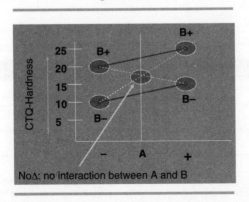

Notice something about the graph:

- The four points (the circled dots) at the end of each line in the graph correspond to the four levels in the factorial chart:
  1. When A is low (−A), there is a corresponding B low reading (−B).
  2. When A is high (+A), there is a corresponding B low reading (−B).
  3. When A is low (−A), there is a corresponding B high reading (+B).
  4. When A is high (+A), there is a corresponding B high reading (+B).
- The line connecting the B − points is parallel to the line connecting the B + points
- Since the B + line and the B − lines are parallel, it shows no process interaction between them—the delta between B high and B low is zero.

Now, let's make a change and see what happens when there *is* a process interaction and what the main effects plot looks like as a result. We run another test using different ceramic elements and the experiment yields the results seen in Figure 15.8.

Plotting our X bar averages for the pure effects of A, B, and AB, we see the results in Figure 15.9.

**Figure 15.8**

| Runs | A | B | -AB | $Y_1$ |
|------|---|---|-----|-------|
| 1 | − | − | + | 25 |
| 2 | − | + | − | 10 |
| 3 | + | − | − | 15 |
| 4 | + | + | + | 65 |

**Figure 15.9**

| Runs | A | B | AB | $Y_1$ |
|---|---|---|---|---|
| 1 | − | − | + | 25 |
| 2 | − | + | − | 10 |
| 3 | + | − | − | 15 |
| 4 | + | + | + | 65 |
| + | 40 | 37.5 | 45 | |
| − | 17.5 | 20 | 12.5 | |
| Pure effect | 22.5 | 17.5 | 32.5 | |

Drawing the main effects plot, we see graphically that there is an interaction and a synergy with the combined effects of AB that is greater than the individual contributions of A alone or B alone (Figure 15.10).

There is one additional notational type that is useful in the DOE, known as Yates Notation or the Yates Standard Order. For a two-factor model, the order is:

a. Both factors low → (1)

b. Factor a high, b low → a

**Figure 15.10**

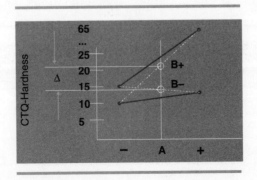

**Figure 15.11**

|      | A | B | AB |
|------|---|---|----|
| (1)  | – | – | +  |
| a    | + | – | –  |
| b    | – | + | –  |
| ab   | + | + | +  |

    c. Factor b high, a low → b

    d. Factor a and b high → ab

The Yates analysis exploits the structure of full and fractional factorials to generate least-squares estimates for all of the factor effects and factor interactions (Figure 15.11).

The usefulness of the Yates Order will become obvious as we add factors to a designed experiment, as is evidenced in the following example.

**Example:** A manufacturer of a range of equally performing floor-cleaning products wants to find the best packaging approach for the product based on design (simple or complex), price (cheap or costly), and bouquet (weak or strong). For this comparison, we create the grid seen in Figure 15.12.

By taking the one-factor-at-a-time approach, the table in Figure 15.13 shows all the possible test combinations. Think about how

**Figure 15.12**

| Factor | Name | Units | Low Level (–) | High Level (+) |
|--------|------|-------|---------------|----------------|
| A | Design |  | 1 color | 5 colors |
| B | Price | Dollars | $2 | $6 |
| C | Bouquet | Scale 1–10 | 3 (weak) | 7 (strong) |

**Figure 15.13**

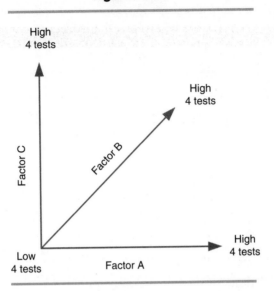

this really works: With one factor at a time you can check the multiple levels for the colors (1 for the low level but 2, 3, 4, and 5 for the high levels), multiple levels each on the dollars (2 for the low level and 3, 4, 5, and 6 at the high level), and multiple levels on the bouquet (3 at the low level and 4, 5, 6, and 7 at the high level) (a total of 16).

With the two-factorial design, we see Figure 15.14 instead.

The chart in Figure 15.15 shows how the comparisons line up in a grid.

The people who tried the cleaners rated the cleaner on a scale of 1–10, *1* being the least likely to buy and *10* being the most likely to buy (represented by $Y_1$).

The two-factorial layout shown above is called an *orthogonal array*, meaning that the factors shown in the table in Figure 15.13 do not correlate to each other in any way. (That is, a + *design* factor does not *cause* a − *price* factor or − *bouquet* factor. They are all running independently of each other.) The task is to see if the juxtaposition of the factors has any influence on the buyer and if certain combinations of factors will entice the customer to buy more than

**Figure 15.14**

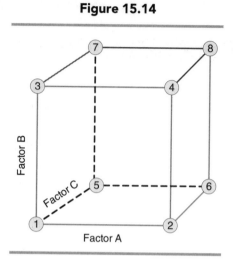

other combinations of factors. In other words, we want to determine the *effect* of each factor on the buyer.

By expanding the grid as we have in the previous examples, we will compute an X bar for all the positive effects and an X bar for all the negative effects to determine the pure effects of A, B, and C as

**Figure 15.15**

| Order | A: Design | B: Price | C: Bouquet | Y₁: Rating |
|-------|-----------|----------|------------|------------|
| 1 | (+) | (−) | (−) | 64 |
| 2 | (−) | (+) | (−) | 43 |
| 3 | (−) | (−) | (+) | 86 |
| 4 | (+) | (+) | (−) | 23 |
| 5 | (+) | (−) | (+) | 88 |
| 6 | (+) | (+) | (+) | 38 |
| 7 | (−) | (+) | (+) | 45 |
| 8 | (−) | (−) | (−) | 25 |

**Figure 15.16**

| Standard | Main Effects | | | Interaction Effects | | | | $Y_1$: Rating |
|---|---|---|---|---|---|---|---|---|
| | A | B | C | AB | AC | BC | ABC | |
| 1 | − | − | − | + | + | + | − | 25 |
| 2 | + | − | − | − | − | + | + | 64 |
| 3 | − | + | − | − | + | − | + | 43 |
| 4 | + | + | − | + | − | − | − | 23 |
| 5 | − | − | + | + | + | − | + | 66 |
| 6 | + | − | + | − | + | − | − | 88 |
| 7 | − | + | + | − | − | + | − | 45 |
| 8 | + | + | + | + | + | + | + | 38 |
| X Bar + | 53.25 | 37.25 | 59.25 | 38 | 48.5 | 43 | 52.75 | |
| X Bar− | 44.75 | 60.75 | 38.75 | 60 | 49.5 | 55 | 45.25 | |
| Effect | 8.5 | −23.5 | 20.5 | −22 | −1 | −12 | 7.5 | |

well as the process interactions of AB, AC, BC, and ABC (see Figure 15.16).

At a high level, the *effects* and the *effect interactions* point to initial differences:

- Factor B: The pure effect of price, specifically a low price (as indicated by the negative number), alone has the highest impact.

- Factor C: The pure effect of the cleaner's fragrance, in this case a stronger scent, appears to have a high impact on the customer's decision to buy that is very close to factor B, the low price.

- However, note that the effect of the combination of *packaging* and *price* (AB) shows the second-highest effect of all the groups and even exceeds the pure effect of factor C alone!

- Note that the combined effect of *packaging* and *fragrance* (AC) as well as all three combined effects (ABC) together is almost negligible.

- There is a moderate interaction between *price* and *fragrance* (BC).

- Of the three main effects individually, factor A—the packaging by itself—seems to have the most negligible impact on the customer's decision to buy.

At this point, you, the designer of the above experiment, will note the following:

- Performing the experiment one factor at a time would take twice as long and cost twice as much.

- The OFAT approach never would have revealed the AB process interaction between packaging and price. It simply never would have been considered in an OFAT (what used to be called the "Scientific Method") design at all.

Up to this point, the above example serves as an introduction to DOE—specifically a *two-level factorial design*. There is more that we can do with the example above, such as:

- Plot the half-normal probability for all the factors in the example.

- Perform the *analysis of variance (ANOVA)* to compute the accuracy of our assumptions.

- Set up predictive equations.

- Plot residuals to validate statistical assumptions.

There are also a number of other areas of study in DOE that include the following:

- Dealing with nonnormality in data
- Fractional factorials

- Minimal run designs
- General factorial designs
- Response surface methods (RSM)
- Mixture designs

## NOTE

1. *A Guide to the Project Management Body of Knowledge*, 3rd ed., Project Management Institute, 2004, 185.

## REFERENCES

Harry, Mikel, *Designed Experiments Lectures*, Arizona State University, 2001.

Del, Vecchio, R.J., *Understanding Design of Experiments: A Primer for Technologists*, Carl Hanser, 1997.

# Chapter
# 16

# Putting It All Together

$\mathbf{W}$E WILL NOW SET up a test project in which the tools we described earlier can be put to good use. For purposes of this example, we will construct a test project that utilizes *most* of the key tools described in this book. In a real working situation this might not be necessary or recommended. The toolbox is there for the user and all the tools are available—however, the practitioner's job is to use the right tool for the situation at hand. Not all the tools need to be used for every situation. Please keep this in mind as we elaborate the example. Also bear in mind that this is a high-level treatment addressing the major components of the system—the level of detail addressed here will be at a much higher level than would be addressed in an actual project or program.

## PROJECT

You have been asked to build an operations center for a large technology company that will integrate all the helpdesks in the company and provide facilities monitoring, security, 24 × 7 call emergency services, and a centralized helpdesk for all 23 physical facilities in your company across the United States, Europe, and Asia. This will require new computer hardware and software infrastructure across the enterprise. The project must be completed in 18 months at a cost not to exceed $25M.

There are six fundamental needs for the project:

1. Ability to monitor the entire company network 24 × 7. This includes wireline and wireless connectivity.
2. Ability to operate the corporate helpdesk 24 × 7.
3. Ability to remotely view and fix network problems that do not require physical presence.
4. Ability to dispatch emergency services to areas requiring a physical presence within a one-hour timeframe.
5. Ability to direct disaster-recovery operations for any location.
6. Active video monitoring and building security for internally sensitive areas and external areas.

The company has a number of projects that need to be implemented, and normally the business would perform multiple net present value (NPV) analyses to determine which project would deliver the best payback. However, there was a strong need for the new operations center based on certain failures that had occurred over the previous two years that affected sales, customer satisfaction, and the perception of the company as on the leading edge of technology. At first the company considers the build-or-buy scenario.

After sending out a request for proposal (RFP), the solutions come in from 10 companies. The business attempts to evaluate each solution using the standard weighted grid process—resulting in more confusion and disagreement. Finally, an executive who read *this book* said, "Why don't we try an analytical hierarchy process?"

## AHP

Using the six basic criteria listed above, the *Analytic Hierarchy Process (AHP)* is set up (1) to prioritize the criteria, and then (2) to measure each company against each of the criteria. Figure 16.1 gives us the sample result.

**Figure 16.1**

| Decision Criteria | Monitor 7x24 | Help desk 7x24 | Remote fix | Emergency services | Disaster recovery | Video monitoring |
|---|---|---|---|---|---|---|
| Monitor 7x24 | 1.00 | 2.00 | 3.00 | 4.00 | 5.00 | 1.00 |
| Help desk 7x24 | 0.50 | 1.00 | 2.00 | 3.00 | 5.00 | 0.50 |
| Remote fix | 0.33 | 0.50 | 1.00 | 2.00 | 1.00 | 1.00 |
| Emergency services | 0.25 | 0.33 | 0.50 | 1.00 | 1.00 | 0.50 |
| Disaster recovery | 0.20 | 0.20 | 1.00 | 1.00 | 1.00 | 0.50 |
| Video monitoring | 1.00 | 2.00 | 1.00 | 2.00 | 2.00 | 1.00 |

The weightings are shown in Figure 16.2.

A check of the consistency ratio in Figure 16.3 shows that the weighting applied was generally consistent.

As we did in Chapter 2, the 6 criteria will be individually compared against the 10 vendors to see how each vendor ranks with each criterion. We have named the companies "Company A," "Company

**Figure 16.2**

| Weights for Criteria | Monitor 7x24 | Help desk 7x24 | Remote fix | Emergency services | Disaster recovery | Video monitoring | Average |
|---|---|---|---|---|---|---|---|
| Monitor 7x24 | 0.305 | 0.331 | 0.353 | 0.308 | 0.333 | 0.222 | 0.309 |
| Help desk 7x24 | 0.152 | 0.166 | 0.235 | 0.231 | 0.333 | 0.111 | 0.205 |
| Remote fix | 0.102 | 0.083 | 0.118 | 0.154 | 0.067 | 0.222 | 0.124 |
| Emergency services | 0.076 | 0.055 | 0.059 | 0.077 | 0.067 | 0.111 | 0.074 |
| Disaster recovery | 0.061 | 0.033 | 0.118 | 0.077 | 0.067 | 0.111 | 0.078 |
| Video monitoring | 0.061 | 0.033 | 0.118 | 0.077 | 0.067 | 0.111 | 0.078 |

**Figure 16.3**

| | Monitor 7x24 | Help desk 7x24 | Remote fix | Emergency services | Disaster recovery | Video monitoring | Row Totals | Lambda Max | Consistency Index | Consistency Ratio (<0.10, OK) |
|---|---|---|---|---|---|---|---|---|---|---|
| Monitor 7x24 | 0.309 | 0.410 | 0.372 | 0.297 | 0.389 | 0.078 | 1.854 | 6.004 | 1.854 | |
| Help desk 7x24 | 0.154 | 0.205 | 0.248 | 0.222 | 0.389 | 0.039 | 1.257 | 6.141 | 1.257 | |
| Remote fix | 0.068 | 0.102 | 0.124 | 0.148 | 0.078 | 0.078 | 0.599 | 4.822 | 0.599 | |
| Emergency services | 0.031 | 0.068 | 0.062 | 0.074 | 0.078 | 0.039 | 0.352 | 4.748 | 0.352 | |
| Disaster recovery | 0.015 | 0.041 | 0.124 | 0.074 | 0.078 | 0.039 | 0.371 | 4.768 | 0.371 | |
| Video monitoring | 0.078 | 0.410 | 0.124 | 0.148 | 0.155 | 0.078 | 0.993 | 12.773 | 0.993 | |
| | | | | | | | 6.543 | 0.109 | 0.087 | Consistency OK! |

B," and so on, so that the company name will elicit no bias on the part of the reviewers.

One of the grids will be presented in Figure 16.4 so that the layout of the grid and the scoring can be seen.

The scoring for the grid went as shown in Figure 16.5.

The process was repeated five more times—once for each of the remaining criteria. Based on these comparisons, the four top-scoring companies are in the grid shown in Figure 16.6.

Each vendor proposes a unique and effective solution. Here, the process becomes more difficult, because there are features that are difficult to compare and measure in the traditional way. The business is looking for synergies between the processes as well, to help drive down the cost while providing the most effective technical and user-friendly solution. When doing this AHP in an actual decision process, also be aware that the consistency index for each selection criteria would have to be run to be confident in the selection.

## QFD

It is decided that a *quality function deployment (QFD)* would help focus on the relative strengths and weaknesses of each of the solutions and would provide an accurate scoring method that would lead the business to the best solution.

So we set up a QFD, with slightly more detail in terms of the critical requirements, needs, and wants. The high-level detail appears below:

- Monitor the entire company network 24 × 7:
  - ☐ IP telephone network
  - ☐ Wireless connectivity
  - ☐ Wireless security (WEP)
  - ☐ VPN remote network authentication by token
- Operate the corporate helpdesk 24 × 7:
  - ☐ Response time to problems for Tier I products is immediate.
  - ☐ Tier II response is within one hour.
  - ☐ Tier III response is within 4 hours.

**Figure 16.4**

| Criteria:<br>Monitor 7×24 | Company A | Company B | Company C | Company D | Company E | Company F | Company G | Company H | Company J | Company K |
|---|---|---|---|---|---|---|---|---|---|---|
| Company A | 1.00 | 0.20 | 0.33 | 0.50 | 1.00 | 3.00 | 0.14 | 5.00 | 1.00 | 0.25 |
| Company B | 5.00 | 1.00 | 2.00 | 2.00 | 5.00 | 9.00 | 0.50 | 9.00 | 5.00 | 1.00 |
| Company C | 3.00 | 0.50 | 1.00 | 1.00 | 3.00 | 7.00 | 0.50 | 7.00 | 3.00 | 1.00 |
| Company D | 2.00 | 0.50 | 1.00 | 1.00 | 2.00 | 0.33 | 0.33 | 5.00 | 0.50 | 0.50 |
| Company E | 1.00 | 0.20 | 0.33 | 3.00 | 1.00 | 3.00 | 0.14 | 5.00 | 1.00 | 0.25 |
| Company F | 0.33 | 0.11 | 0.14 | 3.00 | 0.33 | 1.00 | 0.11 | 1.00 | 0.33 | 0.11 |
| Company G | 7.00 | 2.00 | 2.00 | 3.00 | 7.00 | 9.00 | 1.00 | 9.00 | 7.00 | 2.00 |
| Company H | 0.20 | 0.11 | 0.14 | 0.20 | 0.20 | 1.00 | 0.11 | 1.00 | 0.20 | 0.11 |
| Company J | 1.00 | 0.20 | 0.33 | 0.50 | 1.00 | 3.00 | 0.14 | 5.00 | 1.00 | 0.25 |
| Company K | 4.00 | 1.00 | 1.00 | 2.00 | 4.00 | 9.00 | 0.50 | 9.00 | 4.00 | 1.00 |

**Figure 16.5**

| | Company A | Company B | Company C | Company D | Company E | Company F | Company G | Company H | Company J | Company K | Average |
|---|---|---|---|---|---|---|---|---|---|---|---|
| Company A | 0.041 | 0.034 | 0.040 | 0.036 | 0.041 | 0.066 | 0.041 | 0.089 | 0.043 | 0.039 | 0.047 |
| Company B | 0.204 | 0.172 | 0.241 | 0.146 | 0.204 | 0.199 | 0.144 | 0.161 | 0.217 | 0.155 | 0.184 |
| Company C | 0.122 | 0.086 | 0.121 | 0.073 | 0.122 | 0.154 | 0.144 | 0.125 | 0.130 | 0.155 | 0.123 |
| Company D | 0.082 | 0.086 | 0.121 | 0.073 | 0.082 | 0.007 | 0.096 | 0.089 | 0.022 | 0.077 | 0.073 |
| Company E | 0.041 | 0.034 | 0.040 | 0.036 | 0.041 | 0.066 | 0.041 | 0.089 | 0.043 | 0.039 | 0.047 |
| Company F | 0.014 | 0.019 | 0.017 | 0.219 | 0.014 | 0.022 | 0.032 | 0.018 | 0.014 | 0.017 | 0.039 |
| Company G | 0.285 | 0.344 | 0.241 | 0.219 | 0.285 | 0.199 | 0.287 | 0.161 | 0.304 | 0.309 | 0.263 |
| Company H | 0.008 | 0.019 | 0.017 | 0.015 | 0.008 | 0.022 | 0.032 | 0.018 | 0.009 | 0.017 | 0.016 |
| Company J | 0.041 | 0.034 | 0.040 | 0.036 | 0.041 | 0.066 | 0.041 | 0.089 | 0.043 | 0.039 | 0.047 |
| Company K | 0.163 | 0.172 | 0.121 | 0.146 | 0.163 | 0.199 | 0.144 | 0.161 | 0.174 | 0.155 | 0.160 |

**Figure 16.6**

| | |
|---|---|
| Company A | 0.042 |
| Company B | 0.117 |
| Company C | 0.102 |
| Company D | 0.073 |
| Company E | 0.062 |
| Company F | 0.092 |
| Company G | 0.182 |
| Company H | 0.039 |
| Company J | 0.030 |
| Company K | 0.134 |

- Remotely view and fix network problems:
  - Push software to machines.
  - Reset ID and password remotely.
  - Centrally administer all user groups.
- Dispatch emergency services:
  - Maximum 30-minute response time to all locations
- Direct disaster-recovery operations for any location:
  - Monitor and direct emergency services personnel.
  - Function as a centralized communications hub.
- Active video monitoring and building security:
  - Video chase capability—after identifying a subject, the system will automatically track the subject and keep the subject in view at all times.
  - Full pan-tilt-zoom capability.
  - Minimum of 15 frames per second.
  - Timestamped and watermarked—video clip is capable of being used as evidence in a court of law.

The QFD that appears in Figure 16.7 will show the customer wants and needs on the left-hand side of the grid, the technical response across the top of the grid, the importance rankings to the

## Figure 16.7

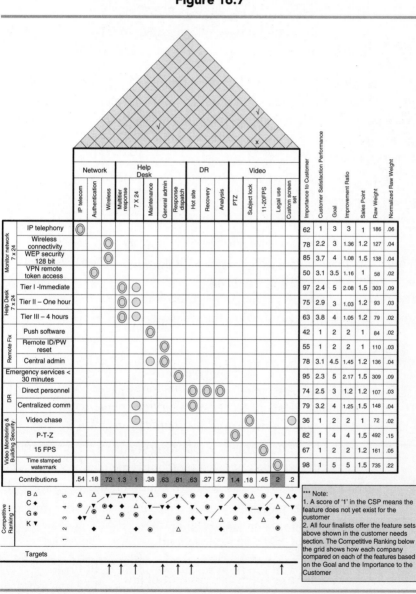

right, and the comparison of the four solutions below the grid. It is important to note a couple of points here:

1. The *competitive satisfaction performance scale* has been omitted, since there is no existing product the company makes that would compare to the products of external vendors.

2. There is no incumbent vendor against which to compare the other vendors—the comparison is a level playing field.

From the looks of the grid, it appears that Company K placed first in six of the eight critical areas and came in second in the remaining two areas. The QFD has shown us which of the elements is of greatest importance to the customer and has enabled us to compare the final four respondents in terms of customer needs.

If the customer thinks that the QFD analysis and result answers the critical needs defined for the project, they will go ahead and initiate contract negotiations with Company K.

The cost of the solution proposed by Company K is $25 million, which meets the customer budget requirements. Knowing that projects that cost over $10 million expose significant risks for the project, the company and the vendor embark on a thorough risk assessment and compile a prioritized list of the most serious risks. They are:

1. Scope risks:
   a. Addressing potential scope creep.
   b. Building the necessary change management into the process.
   c. Is the proper expectation set? The project is deadline scoped but may involve more capital. Is enough management reserve built into the plan?

2. Schedule risks:
   a. Evaluating and assessing dependencies with other projects
   b. Poor estimation on tasks completion

3. Resource risks:
   a. Availability of the right resources at the right time
   b. Critical roles backup—for people who may leave the project

# QRAM

As the company assembles the project plan with the vendor, the risks are evaluated and set up in a *quantitative risk analysis matrix (QRAM)* to give the customer some idea of the management reserve required for the project based on the critical risks. The matrix is assembled in Figure 16.8.

## Schedule, Estimation, and Resource Risks—Monte Carlo Analysis

In order to really get a glimpse of the highest-probability risks and ensure that these risks are addressed early in the project, a *Monte Carlo analysis* is created to see what the actual probabilities might be.

**Figure 16.8   Quantitative Risk Analysis Matrix**

| Risk | Probability | Impact | Potential Cost | P x I x C |
|------|-------------|--------|----------------|-----------|
| Scope Creep | 15% | 75% | 4,750,000 | $534,375 |
| Enforced change management not implemented | 10% | 85% | 1,250,000 | $106,250 |
| Expectations agreed? | 25% | 80% | 500,000 | $100,000 |
| Other project dependencies | 45% | 75% | 3,650,000 | $1,231,875 |
| Poor estimation | 20% | 50% | 1,350,000 | $135,000 |
| Resource availability | 25% | 60% | 2,475,000 | $371,250 |
| Critical roles backup | 10% | 40% | 1,275,000 | $51,000 |
| | | | Total management reserve | $2,529,750 |

The highest-risk items are (1) dependencies with other projects, (2) resource conflicts, and (3) mutually agreed project expectations, with (4) poor estimation close behind and (5) scope creep included because of the high dollar value.

The Monte Carlo is spun up as follows:

1. Derive the number of weeks' delay potentially incurred by the risk, set up as a triangular distribution (*pessimistic, most likely,* and *optimistic*—that is, a PERT estimate).

2. Estimate the dollars per week incurred by the risk.

3. Create the range of potential probabilities and associated costs in a grid.

By doing so, you will give management some hard data to ponder and open the all-important discussions on what strategies and tactics will be employed to mitigate or even eliminate the risks.

Figure 16.9 is the first grid—the *PERT analysis*. Based on this grid, and if all the risks occur simultaneously, there is a chance that the schedule will be pushed out at least 15 weeks (almost 4 months), at a cost of $9,295,000.

### Figure 16.9    Pert Analysis

| Risk (In descending dollar value) | Optimistic | Most Likely | Pessimistic | (O + 4*(ML) + P)/6 |
|---|---|---|---|---|
| Project dependencies @ $250K/week | 8 | 14 | 26 | 15 |
| Scope creep @ $200K/week | 6 | 8 | 16 | 9 |
| Resource availability @ $150K/week | 8 | 12 | 20 | 12.7 |
| Poor estimation @ $100K/Week | 6 | 13 | 21 | 13.2 |
| Agreed expectations @ $100K/week | 2 | 5 | 9 | 5.2 |

**Figure 16.10**

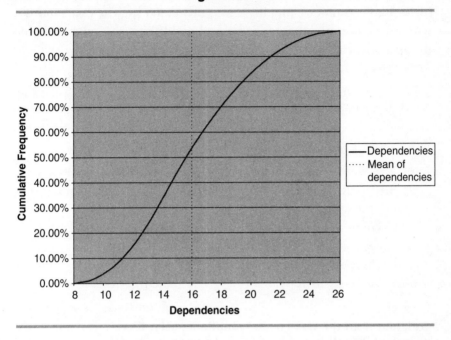

Let's see if the Monte Carlo agrees with this estimate (Figure 16.10).

To reach an 80% confidence level that *project dependencies* will be successfully addressed will take a minimum of 19 + weeks beyond the project due date, at an actual cost of $4,750,000 (19 * $250K), or almost half of the entire PERT estimation. Addressing the other four risks in the same way yields a conservative estimate for all risks in the PERT grid of approximately $11,600,000, or about $2.3M above the PERT estimate.

The weakness with using the PERT estimate is that it doesn't show you anything beyond the averages and will certainly not show you anything about how any potential dependencies across the simultaneous paths might further delay the project.

Of course, this estimate will be blown out even further if any of the risks must be addressed in *finish-to-start* sequence (i.e., if certain risks must be addressed in a specific order). We are assuming in this case that the risks can all be addressed simultaneously.

The other chart estimates appear in Figures 16.11 through 16.15—all estimates along the *x* axis are in weeks. The chart in Figure 16.15 shows the *merge bias* calculation—how the interaction of all the paths impacts the probability they will complete in the expected time frame as shown in PERT.

The chart in Figure 16.15 shows the real difference between the PERT estimates and what the Monte Carlo analysis indicates:

- PERT estimated a 15-week potential schedule overage.
- The Mote Carlo in Figure 16.10 shows that there is only a 23% probability that the overage will actually be 15 weeks. In reality, the Monte Carlo shows:
  □ There is a 50% probability that the schedule will be 17.5 weeks late.
  □ There is an 80% probability that the schedule will be almost 20 weeks late.

**Figure 16.11**

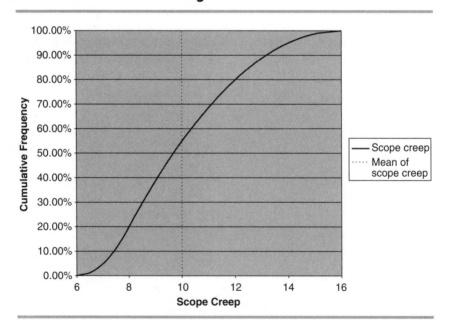

**Figure 16.12**

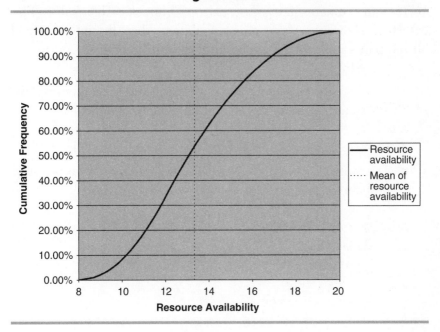

**Figure 16.13**

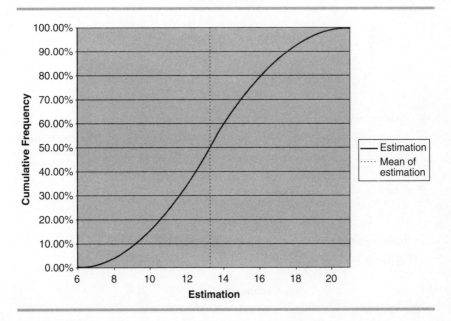

**Figure 16.14**

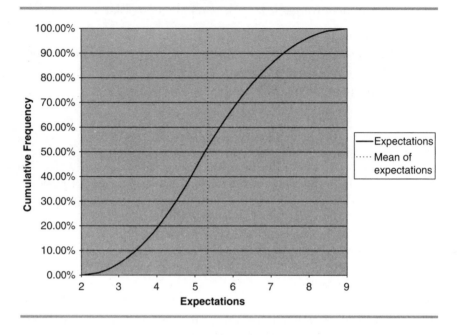

**Figure 16.15**

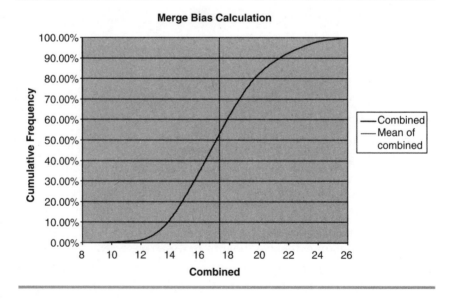

As the saying goes, when estimating project risks: When your probability of occurrence is 80% it is no longer a risk—*it's a fact*.

Based on what we have just seen, the Monte Carlo points up the critical areas that need discussion and management intervention. All-in-all, this is a much better approach than reading tealeaves and animal entrails to divine a solution to your problems.

## THE PROJECT TIMELINE

After the initial project plan and development/deployment approach are documented, the program manager (PM) sets up a high-level timeline for the entire project. We show a sample Gantt chart in Figure 16.16, done in MS Project Professional 2003.

In this representation, the project takes just under 1 year and 6 months (1 year, 4.5 months, to be exact). Given that very little substantive work is generally accomplished between Thanksgiving and the New Year—in fact, some facilities shut down completely for the last two weeks of December—the planners were wise to have the project timeline completed before Thanksgiving.

Notice from the plan that there are several major tasks that occur simultaneously, for example:

- Facility electrical and networking conduit as well as the server room hardware and software installation occur simultaneously.
- Fixed and PTZ camera installation along with the wireless infrastructure for the cameras all move on the timeline simultaneously.
- Remote site activities are also fast tracked and occur simultaneously.

These areas have strong risk potential; therefore, extra planning and care need to be taken here to address any schedule or resource dependencies. Fortunately, the QRAM assembled earlier shows that the team has given extensive thought to this risk area and has appropriately raised *project dependencies* and *resource availability* as risks—the Gantt chart shows us why.

**Figure 16.16**

| | o | Task Name | Duration | Start | Finish |
|---|---|---|---|---|---|
| 0 | | ☐ OC Implementation | 361 days | Fri 7/1/05 | Fri 11/17/06 |
| 1 | | ☐ Facility buildout | 55 days | Fri 7/1/05 | Thu 9/15/05 |
| 2 | ▦ | Electrical | 41 days | Fri 7/1/05 | Fri 8/26/05 |
| 3 | | Network conduit and cabling | 40 days | Fri 7/1/05 | Thu 8/25/05 |
| 4 | | Office furniture | 15 days | Fri 8/26/05 | Thu 9/15/05 |
| 5 | | ☐ Server Room Setup | 40 days | Fri 7/1/05 | Thu 8/25/05 |
| 6 | | OC Server hardware | 20 days | Fri 7/1/05 | Thu 7/28/05 |
| 7 | | OC software | 20 days | Fri 7/29/05 | Thu 8/25/05 |
| 8 | | ☐ Video camera installation | 55 days | Mon 9/5/05 | Fri 11/18/05 |
| 9 | ▦ | Fixed installation | 40 days | Mon 9/5/05 | Fri 10/28/05 |
| 10 | ▦ | PTZ installation | 55 days | Mon 9/5/05 | Fri 11/18/05 |
| 11 | ▦ | Wireless infrastructure | 60 days | Mon 9/5/05 | Fri 11/25/05 |
| 12 | | ☐ Remote sites | 55 days | Mon 12/5/05 | Fri 2/17/06 |
| 13 | ▦ | Remote server setup | 15 days | Mon 12/5/05 | Fri 12/23/05 |
| 14 | ▦ | BMS sensor setup | 40 days | Mon 12/5/05 | Fri 1/27/06 |
| 15 | ▦ | wireline & wireless setup | 55 days | Mon 12/5/05 | Fri 2/17/06 |
| 16 | ▦ | Integrate remote sites w/OC | 70 days | Mon 2/20/06 | Fri 5/26/06 |
| 17 | | Site Tests | 110 days | Mon 5/29/06 | Fri 10/27/06 |
| 18 | | Systems Test | 10 days | Mon 10/30/06 | Fri 11/10/06 |
| 19 | | DR Test | 5 days | Mon 11/13/06 | Fri 11/17/06 |
| 20 | | Go Live | 0 days | Fri 11/17/06 | Fri 11/17/06 |

# TOOLS FOR HANDLING SPECIFIC ISSUES

## Bayesian Analysis

In assessing the solution, one of the important areas for the customer was secured wireless access. It was thought that the best approach to securing the connection was not only through encryption and a token, but also through the use of a biometric device.

Biometric authentication poses some unique problems. There are two major issues to address in biometric authentication that are defined in security circles as *FAR (false acceptance rate)* and *FRR (false reject rate)*. FAR is the more serious of the two—you don't want to give an un-authorized person access to a secured system or a restricted area in your facility. On the other hand, you don't want to erroneously block authorized users.

Given the accuracy of the biometric testing, you can spin up a Bayesian analysis of the conditional probability that the system will deny access to an authorized person or permit access to an unauthorized person.

The Bio-Scan-O-Matic Company makes the biometric system and it has the following FAR/FRR rating:

*False Acceptance Rate*: 0.000013, or 13 in 1 million; accuracy of 99.9987%

*False Reject Rate*: 0.00025, or 25 in 100,000; accuracy of 99.975%

These numbers represent the accuracy of the biometric test.

What is the general probability that an unauthorized person will attempt to access a restricted area or system? Historical analysis shows the following:

- For a *restricted area*, it is 1 in 100,000. This number is low because there are usually several other levels of security before a user could physically get to an access point in a secured area.

- For a *restricted system*, given that you are attempting to access your company's system remotely via a wired or wireless mode over the Internet, the chance is 1 in 10 that a hacker is attempting to gain illegal access to the system.

Let's spin up the results for a restricted area first. In this case, we construct the analysis as follows:

1. The probability that you are positive—that is, attempting to access a restricted area system and are *not authorized* to do so—is 1/100,000.
2. The probability that you test positive (*unauthorized*) if you really are positive (*unauthorized*) is 99.9987%.
3. The probability that you test negative (*authorized*) but are really positive (*unauthorized*) is 0.0013% (false acceptance rate).
4. The probability that you are negative (*authorized*) but test as positive (*unauthorized*) is 0.025% (false reject rate).

The Bayesian analysis shows the following:

- 3.85%—The probability that you are unauthorized and test unauthorized
- 96.15%—The probability that you are *authorized* and test *unauthorized* (FRR)
- 99.9999999%—The probability that you are authorized and test authorized
- 0.000000013%—The probability that you are *unauthorized* but test *authorized* (FAR), or about 1.3 in 10 billion attempts

The Bayesian chart from Excel is shown in Figure 16.17.

The good news is that there is practically no chance of granting an unauthorized person access to your secured area. The bad news is that the FRR (96.15%) may prove to be frustrating to authorized

**Figure 16.17**

## Bayes' Theorem

| | Probabilities |
|---|---|
| $P_{(A)}$ = Probability of being + | 0.00001 |
| $P_{(\sim A)}$ = Probability of being − | 0.99999 |
| $P_{(B\|A)}$ = Probability you test <br> + if you are really + | 0.999987 |
| $P_{(\sim B\|A)}$ = Probability you test <br> − but are really + (the FAR) | 0.000013 |
| $P_{(B\|\sim A)}$ = Probability you test <br> + but are really − (the FER) | 0.00025 |
| $P_{(\sim B\|\sim A)}$ = Probability you test <br> − if you are really − | 0.99975 |
| $P_{(B)} = [P_{(B\|A)} \times P_{(A)}] + [P_{(B\|\sim A)} \times P_{(\sim A)}]$ | 0.0003 |
| $P_{(\sim B)} = [P_{(\sim B\|A)} \times P_{(A)}] + [P_{(\sim B\|\sim A)} \times P_{(\sim A)}]$ | 0.999740003 |
| $P_{(A\|B)} = [P_{(B\|A)} \times P_{(A)}] / P_{(B)}$ <br> (i.e., probability you are <br> + and test +) | 0.0385 |
| $P_{(\sim A\|B)} = [P_{(B\|\sim A)} \times P_{(\sim A)}] / P_{(B)}$ <br><br> FALSE POSITIVE (the FER) <br><br> (i.e., probability you are authorized <br> − but test unauthorized +) | 0.9615 |
| $P_{(\sim A\|\sim B)} = [P_{(\sim B\|\sim A)} \times P_{(\sim A)}] / P_{(\sim B)}$ <br> (i.e., probability you are − and test −) | 0.99999999987 |
| $P_{(A\|\sim B)} = [P_{(\sim B\|A)} \times P_{(A)}] / P_{(\sim B)}$ <br><br> FALSE NEGATIVE (the FAR) <br><br> (i.e., probability you are <br> unauthorized + and test authorized −) | 0.000000000130 |

users who attempt to gain legal access to your secured area. They may have to use the biometric up 15 times before they would have a 50/50 chance of being accepted by the system. Obviously, some remediation or changes in the biometric scanning pattern would be required to lower the FRR rate to an acceptable level without impacting the robustness of the FAR level.

Now let's look at the same analysis for accessing the *restricted system*:

1. The probability that you are positive—that is, attempting to access a restricted system and are *not authorized* to do so—is 1/10.

2. The probability that you test positive (*unauthorized*) if you really are positive (*unauthorized*) is 99.9987%.

3. The probability that you test negative (*authorized*) but are really positive (*unauthorized*) is 0.0013% (false acceptance rate).

4. The probability that you are negative (*authorized*) but test as positive (*unauthorized*) is 0.025% (false reject rate).

Look at the difference when the chances are 1 in 10 that the person attempting to access a restricted system via the Internet is a hacker:

- 99.78%—The probability that you are unauthorized and test unauthorized

- 0.22%—The probability that you are *authorized* and test *unauthorized* (FRR)

- 99.99985%—The probability that you are authorized and test authorized

- 0.00014%—The probability that you are *unauthorized* but test *authorized* (FAR), or about 1.4 in 1 million attempts.

This is generally good news all around: The FRR is substantially lower, so authorized users will have only occasional issues in trying to gain legal access to the system on the first attempt; the FAR is still

**Figure 16.18**

## Bayes' Theorem

|  | Probabilities |
|---|---|
| $P_{(A)}$ = Probability of being + | 0.1 |
| $P_{(\sim A)}$ = Probability of being − | 0.9 |
| $P_{(B\mid A)}$ = Probability you test<br>    + if you are really + | 0.999987 |
| $P_{(\sim B\mid A)}$ = Probability you test<br>    − but are really + (the FAR) | 0.000013 |
| $P_{(B\mid \sim A)}$ = Probability you test<br>    + but are really − (the FER) | 0.00025 |
| $P_{(\sim B\mid \sim A)}$ = Probability you test<br>    − if you are really − | 0.99975 |
| $P_{(B)} = [P_{(B\mid A)} \times P_{(A)}] + [P_{(B\mid \sim A)} \times P_{(\sim A)}]$ | 0.1002 |
| $P_{(\sim B)} = [P_{(\sim B\mid A)} \times P_{(A)}] + [P_{(\sim B\mid \sim A)} \times P_{(\sim A)}]$ | 0.8997763 |
| $P_{(A\mid B)} = [P_{(B\mid A)} \times P_{(A)}] / P_{(B)}$<br>    (i.e., probability you are<br>    + and test +) | 0.9978 |
| $P_{(\sim A\mid B)} = [P_{(B\mid \sim A)} \times P_{(\sim A)}] / P_{(B)}$ | |
| FALSE POSITIVE (the FER) | |
| (i.e., the probability you are authorized<br>(−) but test unauthorized (+)) | 0.0022 |
| $P_{(\sim A\mid \sim B)} = [P_{(\sim B\mid \sim A)} \times P_{(\sim A)}] / P_{(\sim B)}$<br>    (i.e., probability you are<br>    authorized (−) and test<br>    authorized (−)) | 0.99999855520 |
| $P_{(A\mid \sim B)} = [P_{(\sim B\mid A)} \times P_{(A)}] / P_{(\sim B)}$ | 0.000001444804 |
| FALSE NEGATIVE (the FAR) | |
| (i.e., probability that you are unauthorized<br>(+) and test authorized (−)) | |

**Figure 16.19**

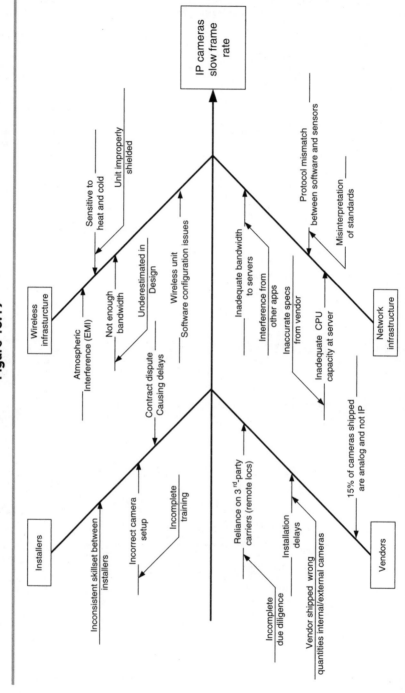

**Figure 16.20**

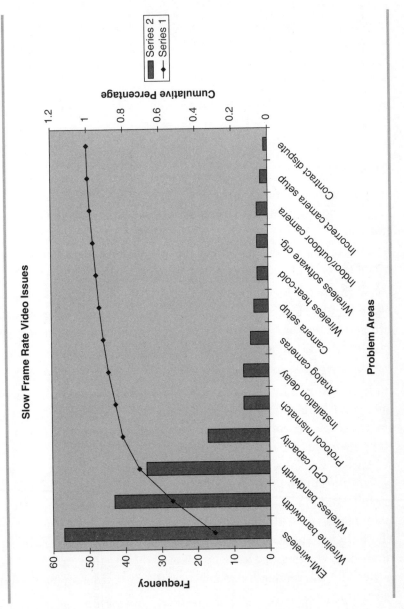

Slow Frame Rate Video Issues

high, though not quite as robust as the other process due to the fact that exposure to unauthorized persons is much higher for the Internet environment than it is for a restricted area, where there are other controls in place. Therefore, a biometric test combined with token security access (e.g., a PIN device that changes every 60 seconds) would bring the FAR rate to an even smaller number than what we achieved with the *restricted area.*

The Bayesian chart for the *restricted system* is shown in Figure 16.18.

## SPC Tools

At one point in the project, the installation of the IP video cameras hits a snag; there are myriad issues coming in from the various PMs assigned to track subproject progress in each area of the project. You decide to spin up an Ishikawa chart to identify the issues and then a Pareto chart to quantify the frequency of occurrences for each issue (Figure 16.19).

With the Ishikawa (cause-and-effect) diagram, a number of issues come to light. Using the trouble ticketing system as a reporting tool, a report of the data describing the frequency of issue occurrences is created and a Pareto analysis is graphed in Excel (Figure 16.20).

From the Pareto chart shown in the figure, it is clear that the EMI and wireless/wireline bandwidth problems are the most significant issues contributing to the slow video frame-rate. Unfortunately, these are areas that may require additional cost to remedy and if the contract for the project was signed as fixed-price, the vendor is on the hook to deliver what was specified in the contract. These elements may also represent the unidentified risk when the initial risk analysis was performed; after all, the vendor *was* chosen for its expertise. This may point out issues with the vendor's subcontractors (over which the purchaser has no direct control), or the vendor itself. At the very least, this analysis gives the customer the data and facts they need to address issues with the vendor and reach some timely and satisfying resolution.

In this chapter, we have focused on some of the less-known, less-understood tools that can be used in the project process. Please consult the reading list that follows for further information.

# FURTHER READING

Ranjit, K. Roy, *Design of Experiments Using the Taguchi Approach: 16 Steps to Product and Process Improvement*, Wiley-Interscience, 2001. (Har/Cdr edition, February 13, 2001.)

Berger, James O., *Statistical Decision Theory and Bayesian Analysis (Springer Series in Statistics)*, 2nd ed., Springer, 1985. (Corr. 3rd printing edition, March 25, 1993.)

George, Michael L., *Lean Six Sigma for Service: How to Use Lean Speed and Six Sigma Quality to Improve Services and Transactions*, McGraw-Hill, 2003. (1st edition, June 27, 2003.)

Mason, Robert L., Richard F. Gunst, and James L. Hess, *Statistical Design and Analysis of Experiments, with Applications to Engineering and Science*, Wiley-Interscience, 2003.

# Epilogue

If the material in this book was new to you, your brain must be exploding with new ideas and concepts that will help you make informed decisions on your projects. Remember, you need to practice the new concepts to make them part of your everyday process in helping you make the right decisions, understand where your real project issues exist, and bring these issues to successful resolution. The tools and supplemental reading recommendations contained herein will help you make those decisions with process, data, and facts, instead of the usual guesswork employed by management.

Good luck with your future project endeavors!

# Index